SOCIAL MEDIA
STRATEGY

SOCIAL MEDIA
STRATEGY

MARKETING AND ADVERTISING
IN THE CONSUMER REVOLUTION

Keith A. Quesenberry

ROWMAN & LITTLEFIELD
Lanham • Boulder • New York • London

Published by Rowman & Littlefield
A wholly owned subsidiary of The Rowman & Littlefield Publishing Group, Inc.
4501 Forbes Boulevard, Suite 200, Lanham, Maryland 20706
www.rowman.com

Unit A, Whitacre Mews, 26–34 Stannary Street, London SE11 4AB, United Kingdom

British Library Cataloguing in Publication Information Available

Library of Congress Cataloging-in-Publication Data

Quesenberry, Keith A., 1971–
    Social media strategy : marketing and advertising in the consumer revolution / Keith A.
Quesenberry.
        pages   cm
    Includes bibliographical references and index.
    ISBN 978-1-4422-5152-6 (cloth : alk. paper)—ISBN 978-1-4422-5153-3 (pbk. : alk. paper)—
ISBN 978-1-4422-5154-0 (electronic) 1. Internet marketing. 2. Internet advertising. 3. Social media.
4. Internet in public relations. I. Title.
    HF5415.1265.Q46   2016
    658.8'72—dc23
                                                            2015022618

∞™ The paper used in this publication meets the minimum requirements of American National
Standard for Information Sciences—Permanence of Paper for Printed Library Materials, ANSI/NISO
Z39.48-1992.

Printed in the United States of America

Brief Contents

Detailed Contents

PART II: No Hype: A Strategic Framework That Works

Part III: Choose Social Options for Target, Message, and Idea

Part IV: Integrating Social Media across Organizations

Part V: Pulling It All Together

Foreword

Are you going to read this?

Really, it's a foreword. Does anyone read forewords?

What if I write in short sentences?

What if I give you the "Top Five Really Awesome Reasons to Read My Foreword"?

What if I include a picture of a cat riding a surfboard?

Robert Dollwet of Malibu Dog Training has attracted 10.5 million views of his "HAPPY DOGS & CAT in Australia" video.

Source: Robert Dollwet, "HAPPY DOGS & CAT in Australia," CATMANTOO, May 1, 2014, https://www.youtube.com/watch?v=DePFiF-nNoE&spfreload=1. © Malibu Dog Training.

Or, what if I put myself in your shoes, as a professor, professional, or student, and create content that actually adds value to your decision about buying this book?

Good idea.

When I met Keith, I had just made the leap from the advertising agency world, where I'd happily dwelled for fifteen years, to the academic world, where I still felt a bit like a tourist. Keith had successfully made that jump years earlier, and his perspective as a professional and a professor is the core of what makes this book great.

As professors, we want theory, but we also want practice. We want real-world examples to make theory come alive to students; we want compelling questions to challenge them to think critically; we want hands-on activities to engage them in constructing their own knowledge. This book has all of that.

I think Keith wrote the book he wished he had when he was at his ad agency, trying to figure out this social media stuff. He brings the professional and academic worlds together (which is surprisingly rare), blending theory and scholarly research with practice and contemporary application, resulting in a book that's thoughtful, powerful, practical, and (bonus!) fun to read.

We live in a world of Twitter-sized attention spans, tempted by tantalizing listicles promising quick returns at every turn. But despite that "Top Five Foolproof Steps to Super Duper Fast Social Media Success" online article, social media is a long game. We've moved, as Alex Bogusky has noted, from an advertising paradigm of pay-to-play to play-to-play, where you get back what you authentically put in. And there's a lot of strategy behind those decisions about what to put in to social media. This book provides an engaging blueprint for building an effective social media framework, from helping audiences understand the context for social media, to analyzing opportunities, to developing a plan that can actually improve a brand's business (in case a picture of a surfboard-riding cat doesn't do it).

As advertising innovator Howard Gossage said, "Nobody reads ads. People read what interests them. Sometimes it's an ad." And sometimes it's a book.

—Valerie Jones, University of Nebraska–Lincoln

Acknowledgments

I would like to thank Leanne Silverman at Rowman & Littlefield for shepherding this book to publication, Bruce Bendinger who told me that I should write it, and Michael Coolsen who has helped me bridge the professional practice and academic research worlds.

Of course, there is more to life than this. I also am a proud husband and father. Thank you to my family for their love and support. Without you this book surely would not have been possible.

And all of life takes faith which comes from the one above.—John 8:32

Introduction

It is hard being a marketer or advertiser these days. Just when you think you have the game figured out, someone goes and changes the rules. You like the idea of digital media. Who doesn't like everything being measurable? But there is something unique about social media. It is much harder to figure out. The old strategies and methods just don't seem to apply. You can't simply add it to the promotional mix. Yet, you can't ignore it. Every year there is greater pressure to integrate social media and do it well. So you search. You open up Google and look for the top ten social media tips for success. We like lists because they make us feel that social media can be a simple quick fix or add-on: just follow these ten steps and you will succeed!

Yet a Google search of "social media marketing tips" returns 135 million results.[1] Start reading these lists and you find that very few tell you to do the same things. Tomorrow hundreds more social media tips will be published. Now suddenly all those simple tips are no longer so simple. In social media we don't have an information problem. We have an information overload problem.

The truth is there is no one-list-fits-all social media strategy. No matter how hard we search for that ultimate top-ten list, we will never find it. The issue with articles like "The Best Social Media Tells a Story,"[2] "Top 6 Social Media Marketing Tips,"[3] or "Social Media Marketing: How Do Top Brands Use Social Platforms,"[4] is that you can't build a social media plan out of them. The fact that 60 percent of top brands are using Pinterest does not mean it's appropriate for your organization. Even if you did use Pinterest, how would you use it? What would you post there? How would that tie into what you're doing on Facebook? Is it a good idea to tell a story in social media? Sure. But what story do you tell and where? These are answers that cannot be found in a blog post or news article about the latest social media platform, technique, tool, or case study.

What worked for Comcast Cable, Best Buy, or the Red Cross will probably not work the same for a regional bank, tech startup, or package good. Perhaps this explains why a recent American Marketing Association survey found that only 10 percent of chief marketing officers (CMOs) believe their social media is integrated into the firm's marketing strategy. Despite that finding, the same CMOs all plan to double social media spending in the next five years.[5] Social media may not be integrated, but marketers still know it is important. You would think that with the publication of new insight would come better understanding. Yet an IBM study of global CMOs reveals that the feeling of unpreparedness is actually getting worse. In 2014, 82 percent of CMOs said their organizations were underprepared to capitalize on the data explosion, up from 71 percent in 2011.[6]

What can we do? One day I was working in my home office contemplating this situation, feeling overwhelmed, when a FedEx delivery person pulled up. I noticed that on his dashboard was a box of Milk Bone dog biscuits. Seeing that he did not have a dog in the truck, I asked him about the dog treats. He said he keeps them in case of a rogue dog. I thought this was a very smart strategy that is probably not in the official FedEx employee manual. It was a back-to-basics approach that he learned from his unique experiences with customers in the field.

Like my FedEx delivery person, a successful social media strategy needs to take a step back and lay out a basic framework that is unique to the brand and its products, services, and customers. For marketers and advertisers to succeed at social media integration, they must first start in a place rooted in their distinct situation and drive a strategy of choosing social platforms and creating content based on their business objectives, marketing strategy, and target audience. Otherwise they are simply chasing 135 million different people's top social media tips that may or may not work for their organization and situation. Only when a unique plan is developed from the beginning will those tips and lists become useful because there will be a way to cut through the clutter and focus only on what advice and insight applies.[7]

This is not a textbook written from a theoretical ivory tower or a business book chronicling one person's success. It is a roll-up-your-sleeves field guide to sound social media strategy that draws from the best in academic research and professional business practice. It lays out a method that cuts through the hype and sets a strategic mindset to take advantage of the exciting opportunities of social media. Whether you are a marketing manager, advertising executive, entrepreneur, or student this text provides the context, process, and tools needed to create a comprehensive and unique social media marketing solution.

Social Media Strategy: Marketing and Advertising in the Consumer Revolution is a blueprint for the practice of marketing and advertising in a digital world where the consumer has taken control. The game has changed and you need a new plan. The consumer revolution is not about giving up or giving in; it is about adjusting methods to effect change, support traditional efforts, and leverage consumer influence for the good of the brand. Are you ready to reset your mindset about social media?

How to Use This Book

This book consists of fourteen chapters divided into five parts. Part I (chapters 1–3) provides an overview of social media. It defines the topic, looks at its scale, and covers the background and context for how we arrived at our current situation. Part I also explores the overall shift in communications and technology that have caused a rise in consumer influence and how marketers and advertisers must respond with a shift in perspective from control to engagement.

Part II (chapters 4–6) then explains a systematic process for creating a social media strategy and integrating it into traditional marketing. This part covers business objectives, target market, social media audits, big ideas, and integration.

Part III (chapters 7–10) explores eight categories of social media: social networks; blogs and forums; microblogging; media sharing; geo-location; ratings and reviews; social bookmarking; and social knowledge. Within each category the top two or three social channels are defined and explained, including users, content, and possible strategies. The objective is to select the right social media channels for plan objectives, strategy, and target audience.

Part IV (chapters 11–13) looks at how social media is affecting and influencing multiple areas of business outside of the marketing silo. It explains five strategies for the marketing and advertising function to integrate with other departments for social media success.

Part V (chapter 14) pulls every concept and process together to create and implement a complete social media plan for a business or organization. The chapter provides a sample format for writing a comprehensive social media marketing plan and explains the importance of selling the plan to key stakeholders through a presentation.

Individual chapters follow a similar format with a chapter opener "Preview" that provides context and insight for the topic, "Theoretically Speaking" sections that dig deeper into the theory behind the practice, and "Mini Cases" that show theory and strategy in practice with brand case studies. Graphs and photos throughout bring examples and research to life. Each chapter ends with questions for discussion and exercises to help explore topics further in class, on discussion boards, or as assignments.

The Social Plan (Parts 1 through 14) is a consistent overall assignment that weaves itself through the book, pulling all theories, concepts, strategies, and examples together into a unified step-by-step process to develop a social media marketing plan and presentation for a brand, product, service, or organization. Each step could serve as weekly in-class or out of class assignments or be combined into a smaller number of main reports.

Appendix A includes all fourteen social plan parts and worksheets together as a single social media plan guide coordinated with each chapter. Appendix B provides a quick social media guide in a condensed five step process, leading to a social media marketing plan and presentation. Appendix C concludes with a list of social media tools and resources to be used in the planning process and for social media implementation.

For more resources related to the book and for updates on current social media examples and channels, visit my blog at www.postcontrolmarketing.com.

Notes

1. Google search, "Top Ten Social Media Marketing Tips," accessed February 16, 2015, https://www.google.com/search?q=top+ten+social+media+marketing+tips&ie=utf-8&oe=utf-8&aq=t&rls=org.mozilla:en-US:official&client=firefox-a.

2. Tom Devaney and Tom Stein, "The Best Social Media Marketing Tells a Story," *Forbes.com,* July 23, 2013, http://www.forbes.com/sites/capitalonespark/2013/07/23/the-best-social-media-marketing-tells-a-story.

3. Chris Street, "Top 6 Social Media Marketing Tips," *Socialmediatoday.com,* July 8, 2013, http://socialmediatoday.com/chrisstreet/1577921/top-six-social-media-marketing-tips.

4. Lisa Mahapatra, "Social Media Marketing: How Do Top Brands Use Social Platforms," *IBTimes.com,* August 9, 2013, http://www.ibtimes.com/social-media-marketing-how-do-top-brands-use-social-platforms-charts-1379457.

5. Shilpa Shree, "Social Media Marketing Budgets to Double in Next Five Years!! [Report]," *Dazeinfo.com,* March 15, 2013, http://www.dazeinfo.com/2013/03/15/social-media-marketing-budgets-to-double-in-next-five-years-report/#ixzz2d5VqVqbb.

6. Dom Nicastro, "CMO: The C-Suite's Enigmatic Executive," *CMSWire.com,* March 19, 2014, http://www.cmswire.com/cms/customer-experience/cmo-the-csuites-enigmatic-executive-024570.php#null.

7. Keith Quesenberry, "There Are No Top 10 Best Rules for Social Media Marketing," *PostControlMarketing.com (blog),* August 26, 2013, http://www.postcontrolmarketing.com/?p=1270.

PART

I

An Overview of Social Media

The Scale and Scope of Social Media

The old paradigm was pay to play. Now you get back what you authentically put in. You've got to be willing to play to play.[1]

—Alex Bogusky

PREVIEW

It is appropriate to start any text on social media with mention of Wikipedia. It is both social media sourced and a social media channel. This social encyclopedia is an enormous tool for students and professionals alike, yet professor William Badke appropriately summed up the often contradicting opinions of this resource saying, "Often banned by professors, panned by traditional reference book publishers and embraced by just about everyone else, Wikipedia marches on like a great beast."[2]

Wikipedia is controversial because it somewhat replaces formal, professionally written, "for pay," encyclopedia publications. Some see it as a group of amateurs writing whatever they want, while others see it as an amazing collection of the wisdom of the crowd that is constantly fact checked and continually changing to remain current. The truth is most likely somewhere in between. Ultimately, there needs to be a balance in use of Wikipedia. A total ban ignores reality and a valuable source of information. Yet everyone, professional, professor, or student, should also be mindful about an over-reliance on any single reference source.

The American Library Association expressed concern about this over-reliance after the Wikipedia Black Out Day in 2012 when a student was quoted as saying, "If Wikipedia is gone, I don't even know how to research anymore." While some seek to ban or limit Wikipedia, others see great potential. Many publishers can now imagine the upside of Wikipedia linking to their content as an opportunity to reach greater audiences.[3] Whatever a person's opinion about Wikipedia and social media in general, one thing is certain: social media is here to stay and will only grow in scale and scope.

The Rise of Social Media

There is something uniquely different about social media. Alex Bogusky of Crispin Porter + Bogusky advertising agency described it as playing versus paying for attention and reach. What is social media? As of this writing, Wikipedia defines **social media** as computer-mediated tools that allow people to create, share, or exchange information, ideas, and pictures or videos in virtual communities and networks. As noted, Wikipedia is social media itself and can change over time as people add, subtract, correct, and generally debate over entries. Click on the "Talk" button next to "Article" in the top left of a Wikipedia entry and you will find discussion about the entry. For example, on March 6, 2012, one contributor said that the social media entry was "in a *dreadful* state. It is pretty much unreadable at the moment." There have been more than five hundred individual edits made to the social media Wikipedia entry since it first appeared on July 9, 2006. Click on the "View History" tab (at the top right of the page next to search) to view a comprehensive list of revisions and dates.[4]

As the definition states, social media is all about creating and sharing information and ideas, whether it's Wikipedia entries or Facebook updates about favorite football teams, fabulous cheesecakes, and what famous people wore to an awards show. As more and more people created their own personal and professional content online it began to grow in amount and importance comparable to corporate- or organization-produced content. As views of amateur content have increased over time, a transfer of power has occurred. Social media has risen in both amount and attention, shifting content from a conventional publisher-centric model to a more user-centric one.[5] **User-centric** simply means having more control, choices, or flexibility where the needs, wants, and limitations of the end user are taken into consideration.[6] This is a term that can apply to many industries and disciplines from media to marketing.

This shift in power is especially evident in journalism. In the past, the main form of communication with a journalistic publication from consumer to publisher occurred through letters to the editor. Of those submitted letters, only a few would have been published. Now many publications enable blog-style commenting on their articles and enlist many more contributors to their publications through blog articles and commentary. In addition, many personal blogs have risen to professional publication status.

Yet, it is important to note that the rise in new technology didn't create a rise in our desire for social interaction. Social interactions have always occurred. In the past, humans did not need social networks to be social. We always found ways to socialize in community without technology. What makes social media different are the software applications that have built communities and networks so that social interactions can now occur virtually.[7] The big rise in social commentary online did not occur with the invention of the Internet or even the first version of the World Wide Web. It happened specifically with the advancement in features and capabilities called Web 2.0.

Early Internet communication was limited to passive viewing of content on static pages. Companies and organizations created web pages, but they were more like digital brochures. Marketers and advertisers wrote and designed corporate websites that they planned to remain the same for the next several years. Interactivity was limited to email on a contact page. However, a shift in capability happened in the first few years of the twenty-first century that changed everything. This shift was so dramatic it was called Web 2.0, a term popularized in 2004 by open-source software advocate Tim O'Reilly and implying a comprehensive new software release of the World Wide Web, taking it from version 1.0 to version 2.0.

Yet the web's inventor, Tim Berners-Lee, says there was no technical update to the web. He argues that he always envisioned the web as "a collaborative media, a place where we could all meet and read and write." What did change was the development of web browser technologies such as Ajax and JavaScript that enabled live two-way communication, plus Flash, which brought audio and video content to websites. Whether a person sides with O'Reilly or Berners-Lee, **Web 2.0** is the common term used to designate the collective technology changes in the way web pages were made and used that took them beyond the static pages of earlier websites.[8]

Web 2.0 takes on many forms such as social networking sites, blogs, wikis, forums, photo and video sharing sites, collaborative tagging, social bookmarking, ratings, and reviews. For Tim O'Reilly's early list of Web 1.0 versus Web 2.0 examples see table 1.1.[9]

Table 1.1. Tim O'Reilly's List of Web 1.0 vs. Web 2.0 Examples

Web 1.0		Web 2.0
DoubleClick	vs.	Google AdSense
Ofoto	vs.	Flickr
Akamai	vs.	BitTorrent
mp3.com	vs.	Napster
Britannica Online	vs.	Wikipedia
personal websites	vs.	blogging
Evite	vs.	Upcoming.org and EVDB
domain name speculation	vs.	search engine optimization
page views	vs.	cost per click
screen scraping	vs.	web services
publishing	vs.	participation
content management systems	vs.	wikis
directories (taxonomy)	vs.	tagging ("folksonomy")
stickiness	vs.	syndication

Source: James Governor, Duane Nickull Duane, and Dion Hinchcliffe, "Chapter 3—Web 2.0 Architectures," *Web 2.0 Architectures* (Sebastopol: O'Reilly Media, 2009), accessed February 16, 2015, http://oreilly.com/web2/excerpts/web2-architectures/chapter-3.html#tim_apostrophy_s_list_of_web_1.0_vs._web.

Please note that his list today has been revised and can be viewed on the O'Reilly Media website.

Social media depends on web-based technologies and now mobile technology to create highly interactive platforms for co-creating, sharing, discussing, and modifying user-generated content. These universal changes have significantly affected the way individuals, communities, and organizations communicate.[10] The old model of larger organizations communicating to a mass number of individuals started to break down with Web 2.0. Suddenly individuals had a way to communicate directly to other individuals. They also had the potential to skip traditional gatekeepers to reach a mass audience. For businesses and organizations this change was very significant. As Web 2.0 expanded consumer influence, the communication power of enterprise and traditional publications diminished. Thus, as Alex Bogusky indicates in his quote at the beginning of the chapter, marketers and advertisers can not buy attention in a social media channel as they can for a traditional advertising channel.

The Size of Social Influence

As people's attention and time has shifted to online activity, marketers have been able to monitor their actions and decisions. The increase in digital activity has increased a marketer's ability to collect consumer data. **Big data** refers to massive amounts of data so large or complex they are difficult to process using traditional data processing applications. It includes data such as transactions, email, messages, activity logs, and social media text.[11] Big data has become a buzzword in recent years for good reason. According to industry reports by 2013, 90 percent of all the world's data was created within the last two years and of that, 80 percent was content created from sources like Instagram, YouTube, and social media posts.[12]

Not only has the amount of information collected been dramatic, but this data has also dramatically impacted business. In 2015, *Forbes* released a report titled, "Data Driven and Digitally Savvy: The Rise of the New Marketing Organization." This global survey found organizations that are leaders in data-driven marketing are almost three times more likely to have increased revenues (55 percent versus 20 percent) than their laggard counterparts. The authors of the study argue that increased data and analysis is creating a growing advantage gap between data-driven and traditional marketing approaches.[13]

The amount of digital data is growing fast, and so are the social media channels that are creating much of it. One illustration of the pace of growth is to compare how long different media took to reach 50 million users. For example, it took radio thirty-eight years to reach 50 million users. The pace quickened with television. After TV was introduced in the 1950s it took thirteen years to reach 50 million users. Yet today, the pace of adoption in social media is tremendous. After Facebook's introduction, it only took the social network three and a half years for 50 million users to open accounts.[14] Now Facebook has more than one billion monthly active users. But this amazing growth is not limited to Facebook alone. Twitter now has more than 500 million users, and more than one billion unique users visit YouTube each month. LinkedIn users are active in more than two million groups, and even one of the newer social channels, Pinterest, has nearly 50 million users.[15] These numbers are sure to be significantly higher within the coming year.

The enormous size of social media and the data it generates present an immense opportunity. Yet many marketers today are slow to take advantage of it. Columbia Business School reports US marketers are still concentrating most of their research efforts on traditional data collection (see figure 1.1). Even though digital research is generally more robust, just 35 percent of marketers monitor social media content, only 33 percent track social network influencers, and a mere 19 percent collect customer mobile data. It seems that big data buzz may not be translating into big business practice.[16] As indicated in the *Forbes* report, the companies who are taking advantage of social media research are gaining a competitive advantage for their early actions.

Obviously social media is not a fad. From 2012 to 2013 Facebook grew 202 percent while Google+ grew by 788 percent.[17] New social media networks such as Snapchat have grown even faster. Social media is becoming ubiquitous. For many marketers and advertisers, this is a very scary thought because social media strategy is so very different from traditional marketing. Social media cannot simply be added as an additional advertising outlet. Integrating social media requires an entire shift in mindset. Yet advertising and marketing practitioners can and should be excited about increased capabilities and untapped opportunities. The shift to a user-centric model represents a huge opportunity for organizations that have struggled to buy awareness in the old expensive publisher-centric mass media model.

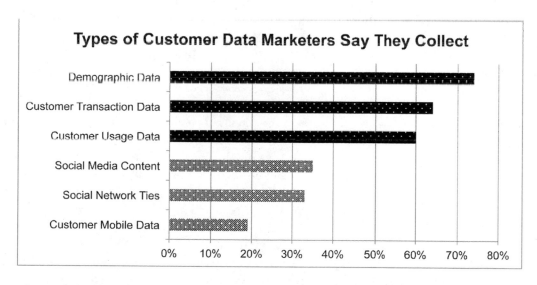

Figure 1.1. Types of Data Collected by Marketers

(Dark bars indicate traditional data and light bars indicate digital data.)

Source: David Rogers and Don Sexton, "Marketing ROI in the Era of Big Data: The 2012 BRITE/NYAMA Marketing in Transition Study," March 4, 2012, http://www8.gsb.columbia.edu/rtfiles/global%20brands/2012 -BRITE-NYAMA-Marketing-ROI-Study.pdf.

In the past, budgets have been an overwhelming deciding factor in a brand's share of voice. A large advertising budget bought increased brand awareness. Today, big brands with small budgets, small businesses, startups, and nonprofits can use social media to help level the awareness playing field. Social media strategy can be effective at almost any budget level. The potential earned media opportunities are what make a difference in driving visibility through buzz and viral spread to reach mass audiences.[18] Social media can also help make traditional marketing and advertising efforts more effective. Integration is key and running a marketing or advertising plan with social media can pay off in real business results. A study published in the *Journal of Marketing Research* found that electronic word-of-mouth by customers delivers nearly twice as much customer acquisition compared to traditional marketing.[19]

How do marketers or advertisers take advantage of social media's powerful benefits? All organizations, big brands, small startups, or nonprofits must learn to play a new game with new rules. Alex Bogusky reminds us that social media doesn't allow brands to buy their way in. Everyone must play the social media game by following a very different set of marketing rules. What are those rules? That is what this book will lay out—a systematic process for ensuring strategic action in social media.

While there are no "Top 10 Best Social Media Marketing Rules," there is a shift in mindset and a strategic framework that can be followed to integrate social media into organizations to supercharge marketing and advertising efforts and meet organizational goals. Success takes more than opening a lot of social media accounts. It is very tempting for marketers to jump into social media by opening accounts in every new social network and app, but even the largest enterprises don't have enough time and resources to win at every social channel. Like all marketing, strategy is needed to focus limited resources. Researching and developing a solid game plan is the only way to win. Take the time now to take a step back and see the strategic forest for the social media trees. Build a solid framework with a well-researched and thought-out social media plan. Don't head into this new marketing game without a new playbook. Play the right way and the rewards can be immense.

Research into electronic word-of-mouth (eWOM) suggests that it is seen as a reliable source of information, significantly affects the perceived value of a firm's offering, and has a direct relationship with loyalty intentions.[20] In other words, social media supercharges the potential of word-of-mouth and word-of-mouth is one of the most effective business tools. Marketers have always known this, but up until the creation of social media, word-of-mouth simply did not scale. Today we have seen consumer-produced YouTube videos garner views once only obtainable through a TV media buy, and some consumer-created blogs have monthly subscriptions larger than top publications such as *Time* magazine and the *New York Times*. Word-of-mouth on Web 2.0 scales.

This is an exciting time to be a marketer, advertiser, and entrepreneur. Best-selling business-book author Seth Godin captured this excitement well when he said, "If you can make it clear to consumers that you have a better offer, it's infinitely easier to acquire a million customers than ever before."[21] Big data is a big opportunity. The scale and scope of social media are enormous, and it will only continue to grow. If marketers and advertisers learn to think differently and utilize social media correctly, they can exploit this scale and scope for the benefit of their organizations.

MINI CASE

KONY 2012

Perhaps no other case study demonstrates both the enormous potential and possible pitfalls of social media success better than what happened to the organization Invisible Children upon releasing their video KONY 2012 on YouTube. In only six days it reached 100 million views and more than fifty thousand comments to become the most viral video in history.[a]

The thirty-minute documentary told the story of Joseph Kony, an African warlord who has been kidnapping and killing citizens in his country for more than two decades. The film urged people to support the nonprofit and help the cause. A big response would seem like a blessing; however, the response was so enormous that the organization's email system broke and the computer system crashed, locking its sales force out of the online store. Also, due to the tremendous rise in buzz, Invisible Children cofounder Jason Russell flew nonstop between media appearances, managing only two hours of sleep in four days.

The organization did benefit with more than triple its previous year's revenue, but the instantaneous fame and pressure ended up being too much to bear for Russell.[b] The same buzz that can spread a message so quickly can also draw harsh and very public criticism. In less than two weeks, Russell had a highly publicized mental breakdown that took a toll on him and his family personally as well as the professional image of the entire organization. In the short term, the nonprofit greatly increased its efforts in Africa, but by 2014 the charity found itself in debt and struggling to survive.[c] The challenge of having an enormous viral hit is surviving the mass attention and then following up to keep the momentum going.

---

[a] Todd Wasserman, "'KONY 2012' Tops 100 Million Views, Becomes the Most Viral Video in History [STUDY]," Mashable.com, March 12, 2012, http://mashable.com/2012/03/12/kony-most-viral.

[b] Claire Suddath, "'Kony 2012': Guerrilla Marketing," BusinessWeek.com, August 30, 2012, http://www.businessweek.com/articles/2012-08-30/kony-2012-guerrilla-marketing.

[c] Sam Sanders, "The 'Kony 2012' Effect: Recovering From A Viral Sensation," NPR.com, June 14, 2014, http://www.npr.org/2014/06/14/321853244/the-kony-2012-effect-recovering-from-a-viral-sensation.

Theoretically Speaking: Interactivity and Two-Way Communication

Professor John Deighton of Harvard Business School defines **interactive marketing** as the ability to address the customer, remember what the customer said, and then address the customer in a way that illustrates the organization remembers what the customer told them.[22] Deighton's definition comes from the marketer's perspective, but what do consumers view as interactive? Researchers Sally McMillian and Jang-Sun Hwang tell us that study into interactivity has been defined by using multiple processes, but three elements tend to appear as the basis of a consumer's perceived interactivity of marketing and advertising communication: direction of communication, user control, and time.[23]

First interactivity must enable two-way communication that provides mutual conversation and the ability to offer feedback. Other researchers, Brian Massey and Mark Levy, take this notion further, stating that interactivity provides interpersonal communication and friendly interface that leads to positive word-of-mouth for companies.[24] Second, user control is also seen as a key characteristic of interactivity. In general, the web has given users this control through more content and navigation options than traditional media. Third, the perception of interactivity is important to consider. This perception is impacted by the time or the speed at which messages can be delivered. The longer a consumer waits for a response the less interactive the communication is perceived to be. In *The Art of Human-Computer Interface Design*, Chris Crawford captures this thought, stating that interactivity means the computer does not inhibit the user by slowing communication.[25] Today this also means that the marketer is not slow to respond to the consumer.

As marketers integrate social media channels and strategy into traditional marketing, these three elements of interactivity should be considered. When comparing and analyzing marketing or advertising strategies and options, consider how the decision will increase or decrease consumer perception in: multi-direction of communication, user control, and response time.

SOCIAL PLAN PART 1

Discover and Explore

The first part of the social media plan is to become familiar with the types of social media and various social media features. Based on the definition of social media given in this chapter, search and identify various social media channels. Go beyond the well-known networks such as Facebook, YouTube, and Twitter. After identifying several digital social channels, explore the features unique to each and use those features to determine social media categories. In other words, what is the main activity on the channel? Why does it exist? Finally, provide examples of how marketers could take advantage of each channel. The best way to learn the most about a social media channel is to open an account and become a user. After exploration report the following:

1. Based on the definition of social media, list five different websites or apps that you feel are social media channels. Explain why each one was chosen.
2. Explore each channel and explain the features and capabilities of each.
3. Look at each channel's features, determine the main differences between each, and place the channels into categories such as photo sharing or news aggregation.
4. Explain three ways a marketer could use each channel for promotion.

QUESTIONS FOR DISCUSSION

1. Going back to the *KONY 2012* case study, what do you think Jason Russell and Invisible Children could have done differently to avoid the problems they had? What can they do now to ensure future success?

2. Find a startup that has achieved enormous success. What role did social media play in the organization's rise?
3. Research a company that has gone out of business or is struggling. How did the organization's lack of social media integration or adaptation to changing technology contribute to their demise?
4. Write your own definition of social media. What is missing from the Wikipedia version? If you feel your definition is better go onto Wikipedia and change it.

ADDITIONAL EXERCISES

1. Visit the Wikipedia page "List of Social Networking Websites" (http://en.wikipedia.org/wiki/List_of_social_networking_websites). Scroll down the list. How many have you heard of? Start to think about which of these social networks would attract the potential customers of a specific brand, and where those potential customers may be most active. Are there social sites where customers are active, yet the brand is not?
2. How big is social media? Research the number of subscribers or viewers of traditional media such as top newspapers, magazines, and TV shows. Now look up the number of monthly active users of the top social networking sites. How do the numbers compare? To take this analysis one step further, look up the cost of an advertisement to reach those viewers or readers in traditional media advertising. Compare that to the cost of social media to reach a similar number of viewers or users.

Notes

1. Amelia Burke, "Planning and Evaluating Digital Media Campaigns for the Public Sector," *Social Marketing Quarterly*, May 22, 2011, http://www.socialmarketingquarterly.com/planning-and-evaluating-digital-media-campaigns-public-sector.

2. William Badke, "What to Do with Wikipedia," *Online* 32, no. 3 (2008): 48–50.

3. Henrietta Thornton-Verma, "Reaching the Wikipedia Generation," *Library Journal* 137, no. 7 (2012): 32–40.

4. "Social Media," Wikipedia, last modified on February 13, 2015, http://en.wikipedia.org/wiki/Social_media.

5. Terry Daugherty, Matthew S. Eastin, and Laura Bright, "Exploring Consumer Motivations for Creating User-Generated Content," *Journal of Interactive Advertising* 8, no. 2 (2008): 16–25.

6. "Definition of User-centric," *PC Magazine*, accessed February 16, 2015, http://www.pcmag.com/encyclopedia/term/59259/user-centric.

7. "Social Media," Wikipedia, last modified on February 13, 2015, http://en.wikipedia.org/wiki/Social_media.

8. "Web 2.0," Wikipedia, last modified on February 13, 2015, http://en.wikipedia.org/wiki/Web_2.0.

9. James Governor, Duane Nickull Duane, and Dion Hinchcliffe, "Chapter 3—Web 2.0 Architectures," *Web 2.0 Architectures*. Sebastopol: O'Reilly Media (2009), accessed February 16, 2015, http://oreilly.com/web2/excerpts/web2-architectures/chapter-3.html#tim_apostrophy_s_list_of_web_1.0_vs._web.

10. Lowell D'Souza, "What Does 'Interactive Marketing' Mean?" MarketingBones.com, April 2, 2010, http://marketingbones.com/what-does-interactive-marketing-mean.

11. "Definition of: Big Data," *PC Magazine*, accessed February 16, 2015, http://www.pcmag.com/encyclopedia/term/62849/big-data.

12. Michele Nemschoff, "Social Media Marketing: How Big Data Is Changing Everything," CMSWire.com, September 16, 2013, http://www.cmswire.com/cms/customer-experience/social-media-marketing-how-big-data-is-changing-everything-022488.php.

13. "New Report Shows Data-Driven Marketing Drives Customer Engagement & Market Growth," Forbes.com, January 8, 2015, http://www.forbes.com/sites/forbespr/2015/01/08/new-report-shows-data-driven-marketing-drives-customer-engagement-market-growth.

14. "Reaching 50 Million Users," Visual.ly, accessed February 16, 2015, http://visual.ly/reaching-50-million-users.

15. Steve Olenski, "Is the Social Media Slumber Finally Over for Big Brands?" Forbes.com, July 22, 2013, http://www.forbes.com/sites/steveolenski/2013/07/22/is-the-social-media-slumber-finally-over-for-big-brands.

16. David Rogers and Don Sexton, "Marketing ROI in the Era of Big Data: The 2012 BRITE/NYAMA Marketing in Transition Study," March 4, 2012, http://www8.gsb.columbia.edu/rtfiles/global%20brands/2012-BRITE-NYAMA-Marketing-ROI-Study.pdf.

17. Marcus Tober, "Social Media Growth Forecast: Google+ to Overtake Facebook?" Searchmetrics SEO (blog), June 20, 2013, http://blog.searchmetrics.com/us/2013/06/20/social-media-growth-forecast-google-to-overtake-facebook.

18. Amelia Burke, "Planning and Evaluating Digital Media Campaigns for the Public Sector," *Social Marketing Quarterly,* May 22, 2011, http://www.socialmarketingquarterly.com/planning-and-evaluating-digital-media-campaigns-public-sector.

19. Julian Villanueva, Shijin Yoo, and Dominique M. Hanssens, "The Impact of Marketing-Induced versus Word-of-Mouth Customer Acquisition on Customer Equity Growth," *Journal of Marketing Research* 45, no. 1 (2008): 48–59.

20. Thomas W. Gruen, Talai Osmonbekov, and Andrew J. Czaplewski, "eWOM: The impact of customer-to-customer online know-how exchange on customer value and loyalty," *Journal of Business Research* 59, no. 4 (2006): 449–456.

21. Jeff Howe, "How Hashtags and Social Media Can Bring Megacorporations to Their Knees," TheAtlantic.com, June 8, 2012, http://www.theatlantic.com/business/archive/2012/06/the-rise-of-the-consumerate/258290.

22. John A. Deighton, "The Future of Interactive Marketing," *Harvard Business Review* 74, no. 6 (1996): 151–160.

23. Sally J. McMillan and Jang-Sun Hwang, "Measures of Perceived Interactivity: An Exploration of the Role of Direction of Communication, User Control, and Time in Shaping Perceptions of Interactivity," *Journal of Advertising* 31, no. 3 (2008): 29–42.

24. Brian L. Massey and Mark R. Levy, "Interactivity, Online Journalism, and English-Language Web Newspapers in Asia," *Journalism & Mass Communication Quarterly* 76, no. 1 (1999): 138–151.

25. Chris Crawford, "Lessons from Computer Game Design," *The Art of Human-Computer Interface Design*, edited by B. Laurel (Reading, MA: Addison-Wesley, Inc., 1990), 103–111.

Shifting Influences and the Decline of Push Marketing

The buying of time or space is not the taking out of a hunting license on someone else's private preserve, but is the renting of a stage on which we may perform.[1]

—Howard Gossage

PREVIEW

Social interaction is a process of reciprocal stimulation or response between two people.[2] Interaction or being social is central to human beings. Even our knowledge of objects or the "physical world" is almost always in reference to human matters. And when human concerns, objects, and social interaction are placed together you almost always have a story. Psychology researchers Stephen Read and Lynn Miller remind us of this insight in "Stories Are Fundamental to Meaning and Memory: For Social Creatures Could It Be Otherwise?"[3] Story is a powerful device for marketing and advertising that many in business overlook.

Researchers have argued that stories are central to human interaction because they provide useful memory structures.[4] Yet Read and Miller take this thought further, saying that stories serve as important social goals that help enable successful social interaction. British anthropologist and evolutionary psychologist Robin Dunbar found that stories are powerful enablers for group identity and social cohesiveness.[5] Researchers John Tooby and Leda Cosmides have established that stories help with conformity to group norms and values, which in turn enables greater cooperation.[6] In other words, humans are social, just all want to get along, and stories help us feel like part of the crowd.

Social media is a great platform to tell stories and provides an ideal space to fulfill the human need for interaction. It is a powerful tool that serves to bring groups of people together for conformity, cooperation, memory, and meaning. Over time social media posts and comments end up telling group and individual stories. A marketer who understands this can bring people together for conversation within their brand story. Thus, brand participation in social media can provide a powerful tool for marketing and advertising. The rise of social media is the story of the rise of a powerful new persuasive and pervasive communications medium.

When Push Comes to Shove

Howard Gossage was an innovative copywriter active during the Creative Age of advertising in the 1950s and 1960s and is credited with many innovations in industry practice. He was honored by trade publication *Advertising Age* as the twenty-third most influential advertising person of the twentieth century behind Dan Wieden and David Kennedy of Nike "Just Do It" fame. Gossage understood the human need for interaction and story. He was said to have started his advertising agency to create riveting conversations with consumers.[7]

Conversation is defined as an informal talk involving two people or a small group of people. Yet a conversational style can also be written with writing that is similar to an oral discussion.[8] In his day, Gossage was talking about creating a conversation with customers in print and television advertising with perhaps radio, outdoor, and direct mail. Gossage and other great copywriters knew that good advertising copy was written like a spoken conversation.

The problem today with the Gossage quote that opens this chapter is that it has become harder and harder to buy people's time and space. No matter how much a marketer or advertiser talks, it is not much of a conversation if no one reads or hears the message. Marketers and advertisers may still rent the stage to present their messages, but when they look out into the crowd, there are a lot fewer people in the audience. The advertising stage has traditionally been mass media print publications and television shows, but the number of readers and viewers has been dropping.

Pew's Project for Excellence in Journalism reports that single-copy sales of magazines fell for four consecutive years starting in 2007 and dropped a staggering 9 percent in 2011. Paid subscriptions also dropped 2.5 percent during that same period. Newspapers have not fared much better. The number of newspapers in the US fell 16 percent from 1,611 in 1990 to 1,350 in 2012. Daily and Sunday circulation dropped 30 percent from 1990 to 2010.[9]

TV media is losing advertising audience at an even more alarming rate. Research by Morgan Stanley reports there has been a 50 percent collapse in average broadcast network TV audience ratings since 2002. The story gets worse when advertisers realize that they have actually paid over 50 percent more in terms of network average cost per million (CPM) during the same period.[10] Not only are marketers losing audience, but they are also paying more for fewer viewers. Some may call this insanity—doing the same thing over and over yet expecting different results.

The story in cable doesn't get much better for traditional advertisers. Increased bandwidth in cable has led to further segmentation of mass audiences. Specialized channels have increased dramatically. Just looking at the "C's" on the a typical cable channel listing illustrates the depth and specialization of this expansion with genres such as the Cartoon Network, Church Channel, Comedy Central, Cooking Channel, and Crime & Investigation Network.[11] In 2014, the average US TV home received 189 channels and tuned in to 17 of those channels per week.[12] Outside of the Super Bowl, mass audience rarely exists in television anymore.

As if these trends were not challenging enough for marketers and advertisers, another development has further deteriorated audience attention. When marketers look out at these diminished audiences, they see a third screen distracting them. Illuminated smartphones and tablets are constantly spewing news updates, posts, tweets, check-ins, or simply funny cat videos to divide attention. By definition, **attention** is the selective narrowing or focusing of consciousness and observance on something.[13] Attention is becoming a rare commodity today. Divided attention has become a normal state of mind for most people.

Overall, people's attention is shifting from traditional to digital media. For the first time in 2013, time spent per day with online and mobile media surpassed time spent with traditional media such as television, radio, and print (see table 2.1).[14] Even if marketers manage to find a small portion of their target audience through traditional media, messages are not guaranteed to reach them because their heads are turned down toward their mobile devices.

Table 2.1. Time Spent per Day with Major Media by US Adults from 2010 to 2013

	2010	2011	2012	2013
Digital	*3:11*	*3:49*	*4:33*	*5:16*
–Online	2:22	2:33	2:27	2:19
–Mobile	0:24	0:48	1:35	2:21
–Other	0:26	0:28	0:31	0:36
TV	*4:24*	*4:34*	*4:38*	*4:31*
Radio	*1:36*	*1:34*	*1:32*	*1:26*
Print	*0:50*	*0:44*	*0:38*	*0:32*
–Newspapers	0:30	0:26	0:22	0:18
–Magazines	0:20	0:18	0:16	0:14
Other	*0:45*	*0:37*	*0:28*	*0:20*
Total	**10:46**	**11:18**	**11:49**	**12:05**

Source: "Digital Set to Surpass TV in Time Spent with U.S. Media," eMarketer.com, August 1, 2013, http://www.emarketer.com/Article/Digital-Set-Surpass-TV-Time-Spent-with-US-Media/1010096.

Note: Hours and minutes spent with each medium regardless of multitasking.

Digital media started with desktop and laptop computers, but more and more activity is shifting to mobile. What defines mobile? **Mobile media** is a personal, interactive, Internet-enabled and user-controlled portable platform for the exchange of information.[15] As technology continues to change, scholars will most likely debate what constitutes mobile media. However, all agree that mobile has helped contribute to the end of traditional mass communication.

Traditional one-way "push marketing" channels are disappearing or dividing, audiences are dwindling, and consumers are tuning out with ever-increasing digital distraction. Yet marketers continue with more effort to push more messages through. The increased growth and segmentation of media combined with the increase of new forms of advertising has created an enormous amount of media clutter.

In the 1970s, the average person saw roughly five hundred advertising messages a day.[16] Some forty years later, this has increased ten times to the mind-numbing average of up to five thousand ads a day.[17] When push comes to shove, perhaps it is time that marketers need to stop shoving so much.

Howard Gossage was said to be ahead of his time. Eerily, he may have been further ahead than people thought. It is hard to believe that this 1960s advertising copywriter could have seen the future of social media. Yet, there is something to learn from his desire to have conversations with consumers. Perhaps he knew that at the heart of us all, we are social creatures prone to distraction, and were like this even before the current glut of

---

 Push versus Pull

What are push and pull marketing? The American Marketing Association describes the traditional **push strategy** as a manufacturer enticing other channel members to carry a product, versus a **pull strategy** that aims marketing efforts at the end consumer to persuade the consumer to request the products from retail channels.[a] In this sense the difference is really between trade (business to business) or consumer (business to consumer) communication.

However, a push strategy is not to be confused with **push marketing**, which is focused on interrupting potential customers, usually through the purchase of ads. In contrast, **pull marketing** attempts to attract the customer to brand communication by providing valuable content, which is usually delivered via social media.[b] In social media, pull marketing can be used for both consumer (business to consumer) and trade (business to business) communication.

---

[a] American Marketing Association, "Dictionary," accessed February 16, 2015, https://www.ama.org/resources/Pages/Dictionary.aspx?dLetter=P.

[b] Gary Garth, "Pull Marketing vs Push Marketing: Definition, Explanation & Benefits," WhiteSharkMedia.com (blog), July 27, 2012, http://blog.whitesharkmedia.com/why-every-small-mid-sized-business-focus-pull-marketing.

clutter. Gossage is also the one who said, "Nobody reads ads. People read what interests them. Sometimes it's an ad." For those who want to master social media marketing, this sentiment is truer now than ever.

Mass Media to Consumer Communication

Seth Godin, marketer, entrepreneur, and author of *Idea Virus* and other influential marketing books, said, "Conversations among the members of your marketplace happen whether you like it or not."[18] Here he captures a key truth about consumers—they like to talk. **Word-of-mouth** communication is when people share information about products or promotions with friends and is one of the oldest forms of marketing.[19] Deliver a good product or service, and the customer talks to his or her friends and family, generating awareness for the brand and delivering increased sales for free. Of course, this same personal communication system also works in reverse. If the customer had a bad experience, they are likely to tell friends and family not to buy. In the past, this was not a huge problem because the delivery system was small. People only had so many friends and they had to make an effort to visit or call them to pass on the information one or a few at a time.

Today, the definition of "friend" has changed and the delivery system has enlarged. Of the more than one billion people on Facebook, each has an average of 224 "friends," and they can communicate with those friends quickly and easily from most anywhere in the world.[20] The rise of social media networks, mass adoption by the general public, and portability of access through expanding Wi-Fi and cellular broadband have dramatically increased the influence of consumer word-of-mouth.

The dramatic growth of social media has been fueled through mobile devices. A full 40 percent of cell phone owners use a social networking site on their phone, and 28 percent do so on a typical day.[21] The power of consumer voice has grown so dramatically through social media that in 2004, a new trade group, the Word-of-Mouth Marketing Association (WOMMA), was launched to establish standards and best practices. WOMMA research reports that 81 percent of consumers are influenced by a friend's social media posts.[22]

This spread of consumer influence is shifting power from institutions to individuals. One example is twenty-three-year-old Molly Katchpole. In 2011, she led a consumer revolt against Bank of America's new five-dollar monthly debit card fee. From links posted on Facebook and Twitter she garnered more than ten thousand signatures for her Change. org online petition. *ABC News* and other media outlets picked up the story and pushed signatures up to thirty thousand. After weeks of bad publicity, Bank of America gave in and revoked the fee. Verizon also bowed to social media–empowered consumers when it decided to revoke its new two-dollar convenience charge for debit card payments.[23] In fact, 33 percent of consumers say they have used social media as an outlet to rant or rave about a company, brand, or product with 40 percent claiming their aim was to influence others when expressing a preference online.[24]

How big is this consumer voice? As of 2013, 72 percent of online adults used social network sites, and these users are not just young adults. People older than sixty-five have tripled their presence on social networks from 13 percent in 2009 to 43 percent in 2013.

Plus, this increased social activity spreads beyond Facebook to multiple social networks and apps. Nearly 20 percent of adults online now also use Twitter.[25]

What are these socially active consumers talking about? On social networking sites 25 percent are revealing their dissatisfaction with companies, brands, or products; 23 percent are talking about companies, brands, or products they like; and 19 percent are giving product reviews and recommendations (see figure 2.1).[26]

WOMMA reports that the average American mentions a brand some sixty times a week in online and offline conversation.[27] Forrester Research further reports that these consumers create 500 billion social media product and service influence impressions on one another annually.[28] Through social media posts, comments, ratings and reviews consumers command a powerful voice in brand communication.

This increased consumer voice through social networks is very influential. A Nielsen study reveals that 90 percent of online consumers trust recommendations from people they know and a full 70 percent trust unknown users, compared to only 14 percent who trust traditional advertising.[29] This social media word-of-mouth has also been linked to sales. A study in the *Journal of Marketing Research* found that purchase decisions can be influenced by others' opinions and that increased positive online word-of-mouth volume produces increased sales impact.[30] Yet most marketing plans and budgets still devote the majority of their time and money to traditional advertising. Perhaps that is why 70 percent of brand marketers surveyed by the CMO Council (Chief Marketing Officer) said that they planned to increase spending on social media marketing from 2012 to 2013.[31]

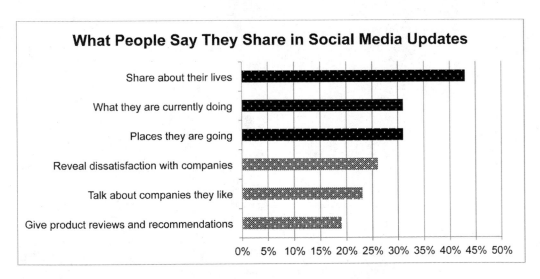

Figure 2.1. Types of Information People in US Share via Social Media Updates

(Dark bars indicate personal information and light bars indicated brand-related.)

Source: Whitney Heckathorne, "Speak Now or Forever Hold Your Tweets," HarrisInteractive.com, June 3, 2010, http://www.harrisinteractive.com/NewsRoom/HarrisPolls/tabid/447/mid/1508/articleId/403/ctl/ReadCustom%20Default/Default.aspx.

MINI CASE

Sony Europe

As a demonstration of how opposite social media thinking can be from traditional marketing, this case shows how Sony Europe succeeded by leveraging an online community through social media instead of simply pushing advertising content through the new channel. As more and more consumers were asking customer-service questions via social media, Sony faced an enormous challenge, considering they have thousands of different products.

In response, Sony Europe created an online community of Sony users and began to identify and reward the most valuable super-fans. **Super-fans** are a company's most active online consumers who answer forum questions, write in-depth blog posts, and provide valuable feedback without collecting a fee. Sony's fifty super-fans were invited to product launches, offered new products, and given all-expenses-paid trips to biannual super-fan conferences. The result has been thousands of customer questions answered every year with an 85 percent solve rate that saves the company millions in support costs.[a]

Why do super-fans provide all this free product support and marketing buzz even before they are found and rewarded by companies such as Sony? Self-presentation theory explains motivations behind human behavior to project an image of oneself to other people. These behaviors are activated by the presence of other people observing behavior such as in an online community. Many people want to be perceived as knowledgeable, helpful, and friendly—especially in front of an audience. This audience-pleasing motivates the behavior of helping others learn about a brand and solve problems around a product for the reward of feeling better about one's self image.[b] Online brand communities provide an audience that super-fans want to please. Instead of trying to control unofficial brand or product communication, smart marketers encourage fan communities and reward the most active users to help them grow.

[a] Jeremy Taylor, "Social CRM Cast Study: Sony Europe Creates a Community of Super-fans," OurSocialTimes. com, May 14, 2014, http://oursocialtimes.com/social-crm-case-study-sony-europe-creates-a-community-of -super-fans.

[b] Erving Goffman, *The Presentation of Self in Everyday Life.* New York: Doubleday Anchor Books (1959).

All this growth in social media presents an enormous opportunity. Yet many marketers view it as a threat. Empowered consumers generating and sharing their brand comments and content do not fit neatly into current models of marketing.[32] Most marketing principles and strategies today still operate on a marketer- or advertiser–control model. Social media breaks marketer and advertiser control and thus breaks the traditional model that most have learned and practiced. However, going back to Seth Godin's quote, whether marketers like it or not the control model has to change. Marketers can no longer keep their heads in the sand pretending they still have control. Simply ignoring social conversation will not work.

The good news is that if marketers choose to enter the social conversation through engagement, it can be very effective. **Engagement** is involvement, interaction, intimacy, and influence between an individual and a brand.[33] Engagement is effective. WOMMA reports that 78 percent of consumers indicate being influenced by a brand's social media posts.[34] Compare this to the Nielsen report of only 14 percent of consumers trusting traditional advertising. Marketers and advertisers need to learn to talk and interact with consumers in a very different way if their brands are to have a chance in this highly transparent, consumer-empowered environment.[35]

Theoretically Speaking: Social Presence and Media Richness

What are the theories behind this phenomenon of social media? Researchers Andreas Kaplan and Michael Haenlein propose that social presence theory and media richness theory are key elements of social media.[36] **Social presence theory** states that media differ in the degree of social presence (acoustic, visual, and physical contact) they allow between two communication partners. Social presence is influenced by the intimacy (interpersonal versus mediated) and immediacy (asynchronous versus synchronous) of the medium. Social presence is thought to be higher for interpersonal (face-to-face discussion) than mediated (television) and for synchronous (live chat) than asynchronous (email) communications. The higher the social presence, the larger the social influence that the partners have on each other's behavior.[37] It is not hard to see how this theory predicts social media to be more influential than traditional media whether for personal or marketing and advertising communication.

Closely related is **media richness theory,** which states that media differ in the degree of richness they possess—the amount of information they allow to be transmitted in a given time. If a medium is richer (it can transmit more information) it will be more effective in communication. Social media is rich in its ability to transmit text, sound, video, and images and it can transmit this information instantaneously in both directions to or from anyone around the world. Marketers who apply these theories to social media versus traditional media such as print, radio, and television will quickly see how advanced this communication medium is in terms of its potential for effectiveness.[38]

 SOCIAL PLAN PART 2

Adding to the Noise

Is an organization adding to the clutter? In the earliest stages of a social media plan, the goal is to start getting a sense of the brand's image in the marketplace. Take an inventory of all marketing and advertising activities and messages. Then determine how "pushy" the brand's marketing communication has become: Is the brand heavily reliant on push marketing through traditional media? In social media, is the brand intrusive with one-way sales-focused posts, or are posts helpful and responsive? Make a list or spreadsheet of all consumer touch points in traditional, digital, and social media. Analyze the type of messages the company is promoting in each, and report the answers to the following questions:

1. Is the communication company-focused or consumer-focused?
2. Is the information useful, newsworthy, entertaining, or valuable?
3. Do consumers perceive the message as an unwanted interruption or a welcome message?
4. Take an inventory of all brand marketing and advertising activities and rate the "pushiness" of brand communication. Is the brand over-reliant on traditional media? Are they using social media as more of a one-way communication channel? On a scale of 1 to 10, how much is the brand contributing to media clutter?

QUESTIONS FOR DISCUSSION

1. How powerful and influential is social media word-of-mouth? Find an example of where social word-of-mouth has made or broken an organization and an example where it has changed a government or culture.
2. How much do you think consumer conversations actually influence purchasing decisions? Can you quantify this influence or find research that proves it?
3. Howard Gossage said we should not try to hunt our target audience, but instead entertain. Describe three of your favorite TV commercials and describe three of your least favorite. List characteristics of each category. What makes one group of ads more favorable than the other? Do your observations apply to online videos as well?
4. This chapter discusses evidence of media clutter such as the number of cable channels available in the average household (189). In what ways are marketers of traditional TV channels and TV shows using social media to grab and hold viewers' attention?

ADDITIONAL EXERCISES

1. Type in the Google search box a brand name and "+ complaints." Then hit return. How many customers are talking about the company? What are they saying—is it positive or negative? And where are they saying it? Now narrow the search to news, video, and blogs. Repeat the same search on Twitter. Read reviews of the company on retail or review sites. Remember that the Internet is one of the first places people turn when seeking information about a brand, product, or service. With this in mind, what is the overall image of the brand when you take into account official brand communication and social media content?
2. Take a day and log your activity on your devices (desktop, laptop, smartphone, tablet). How many times a day do you check your devices, by device? Categorize each interaction by purpose, such as reading email, texting, reading news, checking social media, and posting or commenting on social media. Note the time of day and time in minutes. Then add up the total for the day in each category. What percent of your time is spent on your devices and what percent of your time is spent on social media? How does this compare to your traditional media usage? Do the results surprise you? What do they say for marketers? What do they say to you personally?

Notes

1. Howard Gossage, *The Book of Gossage.* Chicago, IL: The Copy Workshop (2006), p. 20.

2. "What Is Social Interaction?" *Psychology Dictionary,* accessed February 16, 2015, http://psychologydictionary.org/social-interaction.

3. Stephen J. Read and Lynn C. Miller, "Stories Are Fundamental to Meaning and Memory: For Social Creatures Could It Be Otherwise?" In R. S. Wyer Jr. (Ed.), *Knowledge and Memory: The Real Story: Advances in Social Cognition, Volume VII.* New York: Psychology Press (2014).

4. Robert C. Schank and R. P. Abelson, *Scripts, Plans, Goals, and Understanding.* Hillsdale, NJ: Lawrence Erlbaum Associates (1977).

5. Robin Dunbar, "Co-evolution of Neocortex Size, Group Size and Language in humans," *Behavioral and Brain Sciences* 16, no. 4 (1993): 681–735.

6. John Tooby and Leda Cosmides, "The Psychological Foundations of Culture," In Jerome H. Barkow, Leda Cosmides, and John Tooby (Eds.), *The Adapted Mind: Evolutionary Psychology and the Generation of Culture.* New York: Oxford University Press (1992).

7. David Klein, "Special Report: The Advertising Century." *Advertising Age,* March 29, 1999, http://adage.com/article/special-report-the-advertising-century/howard-luck-gossage/140202.

8. "Conversation," Merriam-Webster.com, accessed February 16, 2015, http://www.merriam-webster.com/dictionary/conversation.

9. Rick Edmonds, Emily Guskin, Tom Rosenstiel, and Amy Mitchell, "The State of the New Media 2012." Stateofthemedia.org, accessed February 16, 2015, http://stateofthemedia.org/2012/newspapers-building-digital-revenues-proves-painfully-slow/newspapers-by-the-numbers.

10. Jim Edwards, "BRUTAL: 50% Decline in TV Viewership Shows Why Your Cable Bill Is So High." BusinessInsider.com, January 31, 2013, http://www.businessinsider.com/brutal-50-decline-in-tv-viewership-shows-why-your-cable-bill-is-so-high-2013-1#ixzz2f5VViddn.

11. "Verizon FiOs Channel Lineup," Verizon.com, accessed February 16, 2015, Retrieved from http://www.verizon.com/home/fiostv/digital-tv-channels/?CMP=DMC-CVZ_ZZ_FT_Z_ZZ_N_X004#channels.

12. "Changing Channels: Americans View Just 17 Channels Despite Record Number to Choose From," Nielsen.com, last modified May 6, 2014, http://www.nielsen.com/us/en/insights/news/2014/changing-channels-americans-view-just-17-channels-despite-record-number-to-choose-from.html.

13. "Attention," Merriam-Webster.com, accessed February 16, 2015, http://www.merriam-webster.com/dictionary/attention.

14. "Digital Set to Surpass TV in Time Spent with U.S. Media," eMarketer.com, August 1, 2013, http://www.emarketer.com/Article/Digital-Set-Surpass-TV-Time-Spent-with-US-Media/1010096.

15. Ran Wei, "Social Media: Coming of Age with a Big Splash," *Mobile Media & Communication* 1, no.1 (2013): 50–56.

16. Steuart Henderson Britt, Stephen C. Adams, and Allan S. Miller, "How Many Advertising Exposures Per Day?" *Journal of Advertising Research* 12, December (1972), 3–9.

17. Louise Story, "Anywhere the Eye Can See, It's Likely to See an Ad," NYTimes.com, January 15, 2007, http://www.nytimes.com/2007/01/15/business/media/15everywhere.html.

18. Seth Godin, "What Every Good Marketer Knows," SethGodin.com (blog), May 9, 2005, http://sethgodin.typepad.com/seths_blog/2005/05/what_every_good.html.

19. American Marketing Association, "Dictionary," accessed February 16, 2015, https://www.ama.org/resources/Pages/Dictionary.aspx?dLetter=W.

20. Sara Goo, "Facebook: A Profile of its 'Friends,'" Pewresearch.org, May 16, 2012 from http://pewresearch.org/pubs/2262/facebook-ipo-friends-profile-social-networking-habits-privacy-online-behavior.

21. Joanna Brenner and Aaron Smith, "72% of Online Adults Are Social Networking Users," Pewinternet.org, August 5, 2013, http://pewinternet.org/Reports/2013/social-networking-sites .aspx.

22. "WOMMAPEDIA," Wommapedia.org, accessed February 16, 2015, http://www.womma pedia.org.

23. Jeff Howe, "How Hashtags and Social Media Can Bring Megacorporations to Their Knees," TheAtlantic.com, June 8, 2012, http://www.theatlantic.com/business/archive/2012/06/ the-rise-of-the-consumerate/258290.

24. Whitney Heckathorne, "Speak Now or Forever Hold Your Tweets," HarrisInteractive .com, June 3, 2010, http://www.harrisinteractive.com/NewsRoom/HarrisPolls/tabid/447/mid/ 1508/articleId/403/ctl/ReadCustom%20Default/Default.aspx.

25. Brenner and Smith, "72% of Online Adults are Social Networking Users."

26. Heckathorne, "Speak Now or Forever Hold Your Tweets."

27. "WOMMAPEDIA," Wommapedia.org.

28. Josh Bernoff, "Spotting the Creators of Peer Influence," AdAge.com, April 20, 2010, http://adage.com/article/digitalnext/marketing-spotting-creators-peer-influence/143372.

29. "Global Advertising: Consumers Trust Real Friends and Virtual Strangers the Most," Nielsenwire (blog), July, 2010, http://blog.nielsen.com/nielsenwire/consumer/global-advertising -consumers-trust-real-friends-and-virtual-strangers-the-most.

30. Yubo Chen, Wang Qi, and Jinhong Xie, "Online Social Interactions: A Natural Experiment on Word-of-Mouth Versus Observational Learning," *Journal of Marketing Research* 68, April (2009): 238–254.

31. Shea Bennett, "70% of Marketers Plan to Spend More on Social Media This Year [STUDY]," *MediaBistro.com*, August 19, 2013, http://www.mediabistro.com/alltwitter/social-marketing-spend _b48102.

32. Sean Corcoran, "Revisiting the Meaning of Engagement," Forrester.com (blog), April 12, 2011, http://blogs.forrester.com/sean_corcoran/11-04-12-revisiting_the_meaning of engagement

33. Andreas M. Kaplan and Michael Haenlein, "Users of the World, Unite! The Challenges and Opportunities of Social Media," *Business Horizons* 53, no. 1 (January–February 2010): 59–68.

34. "WOMMAPEDIA," *Wommapedia.org.*

35. Mandy Ewing, "Integrated Marketing Communications Measurements and Evaluation," *Journal of Marketing Communications* 15, no. 2–3 (2009): 103–117.

36. Kaplan and Haenlein, "Users of the World, Unite!"

37. John Short, Ederyn Williams, and Bruce Christie, *The Social Psychology of Telecommunications.* Hoboken, NJ: John Wiley & Sons (1976).

38. Richard L. Daft and Robert H. Lengel, "Organizational Information Requirements, Media Richness, and Structural Design," *Management Science* 32, no. 5 (1986): 554–571.

A Marketer's Point of View

Moving from Control to Engagement

As the distracted consumer flits back and forth between watching TV, texting their friends, looking up information on actors, or just aimlessly surfing while the TV's on in the background, getting through to them with marketing messages on any device becomes harder and harder.[1]

—Sean Carton

PREVIEW

At the beginning of the twentieth century, John Wanamaker opened what would become the first department store. Seen as a pioneer in marketing and integral to the establishment of the profession of advertising, Wanamaker started his stores in Philadelphia and later expanded to cities such as New York, London, and Paris. Known as "The Grand Depot," the twelve-story Wanamaker's in Philadelphia famously took up an entire city block. The store pioneered the now-standard retail practices of fixed prices and money-back guarantees, expressed then as a revolutionary principle: "One price and goods returnable." A devout Christian, Wanamaker believed that if everyone was equal before God, then they should all be equal before price. This retail pioneer also started the practice of advertising and hired the first full-time advertising copywriter, John E. Powers.

Despite John Wanamaker's marketing philosophy and strong belief in the power of advertising, he is also well known for a phrase that is still talked about today: "Half the money I spend on advertising is wasted. The trouble is, I don't know which half."[2] As more and more marketing and advertising moves online, more and more consumer actions are becoming traceable. Perhaps all the advancements in measurable digital marketing and big data have made this statement less applicable today. If John Wanamaker were alive, would he still say it?

The Advertising Age Is Over

From the Super Bowl to *Mad Men,* advertising has become more visible in popular culture, but with the advancement of digital media the practice of advertising has undergone nothing short of a revolution. **Advertising** is defined as the placement of announcements and persuasive messages in time or space purchased in mass media.[3] The basis of the advertising profession was to craft persuasive messages and then purchase space in mass media to reach a large audience. Following this formula, advertising became a very effective marketing tactic for well over a hundred years.

Yet the advertising industry and the marketing professionals who hire advertising executives have gone through dramatic changes in the past few decades. The changes occurred in bits and pieces, but came to a more noticeable head in 2009 when the eighty-year-old leading trade publication *Advertising Age* boldly announced, "The Ad Age Is Over." The article "Cannes Swept by PR, Integrated, Internet Winners" explained that for the first time in history the top prize in the most prestigious advertising-industry award show went to an advertisement made for the Internet rather than television. The film jury handed its sole Grand Prix to an Internet film for Philips electronics.

In that same year, a tourism campaign for Queensland, Australia, took the first Public Relations Grand Prix along with new Direct and Cyber Cannes award categories. David Lubars, then chief creative officer of BBDO North America and president of the Cannes film and press juries, predicted, "The way the world is heading is voluntary engagement."[4] These were signs that the future of marketing was here. Mass marketing was moving into a new digital environment where the consumer had more involvement and integrated communication efforts were needed to reach a fragmented target audience. Mass media was diminishing and the method of persuasion transforming. Marketers and advertisers have entered a new age of engagement where they have less influence over all the messages consumers read, hear, and watch about their brands. Marketing departments and the advertising agencies they hire have moved from controlled push marketing to a more interactive engagement marketing.

If the ad age is over and new media is getting so much attention, should marketers simply drop traditional advertising efforts and move to all interactive digital and social media engagement marketing? Research says no. A study published in the *International Journal of Integrated Marketing Communications* analyzed integrated marketing communications touch points used in 421 Effie Award–winning campaigns from 1998–2010. Effie Awards are another prestigious award show for advertising and marketing professionals, except that winners are determined based on proven results. Effie campaigns are advertising success stories that are awarded for effectiveness. Each entrant submits verifiable data that demonstrates the campaign has met its marketing and advertising objectives.

C MINI CASE

Queensland Tourism

In 2009 Tourism Queensland challenged its advertising agency to deliver a global campaign that would raise awareness of the Islands of the Great Barrier Reef across cultures and backgrounds. With a relatively small budget, the effort tapped into a universal desire and wrote an employment ad for "The Best Job in the World."[a] The recruitment ads were placed in fifteen countries and described a six-month contract paying $150,000 (£75,000) to live in a rent-free luxury home on Hamilton Island and blog about the experience. Candidates had to upload an application video to islandreefjob.com. The public voted for the final sixteen, who were interviewed in person.

The campaign garnered worldwide media attention through traditional advertising and public relations and benefited from the power of word-of-mouth and social media engagement with the consumer. Results included more than 8 million website visitors, 34,000 video applications from 197 countries, a 67 percent increase in Facebook fans, and a 93 percent increase in Twitter followers. The PR value was estimated to be nearly $400 million, and more than 9,000 passengers booked trips to Queensland following the campaign.[b]

[a] "The Best Job in the World," iab.net, accessed February 17, 2015, http://www.iab.net/media/file/Sample_Case_Study.pdf.

[b] "Tourism Queensland 'Best Job in the World' Social Media campaign," UTalkMarketing.com, April 12, 2010, http://www.utalkmarketing.com/pages/article.aspx?articleid=17349&title=tourism-queensland-%E2%80%98best-job-in-the-world%E2%80%99-social-media-campaign.

The research found that in twelve years of Effie Award–winning campaigns there was an overall increase in the number of marketing or consumer touch points from an average of two (such as TV and print) to six (such as TV, print, radio, PR, interactive, consumer involvement). Additionally, it was found that old traditional media such as TV has not been replaced by the new digital media. Instead emerging media has been added to traditional advertising media to ensure success.[5] As mass media has fragmented, advertising has had to spread its persuasive messages over more and more places to reach the same audience and achieve successful results. See table 3.1 for a list of example Effie Award–winning marketing campaigns and their increased touch-point usage over the twelve-year study period.

How should marketers respond to this new multi-touch-point, engagement reality? Marketers and advertisers need to adjust their perspective from a strict, top-down control strategy to a more participative and interactive one.[6] As Jeff Howe said in *The Atlantic,* "Now, a brand's success has everything to do with the global, real-time, 24/7, electronic conversation taking place around it. As consumers gain leverage, corporations are learning to obey."[7] Yet practicing marketing and advertising in this post-control world doesn't mean all brands and organizations are simply at the mercy of the consumer. There is room for strategy and influence and possibly even greater opportunity for success.

Table 3.1. Effie Award Winners by Touch Point from 1998 to 2010

Year	Sponsor and Title	Touch Points	Touch Point Categories
1998	Maytag, "Keeping Your Cool"	1	TV
1999	YoCrunch, "Smooth & Crunchy"	2	Radio, Retail
2000	Volkswagen, "New Jetta Launch"	3	TV, Radio, Interactive
2001	Maybelline, "Maybe She's Born With It"	4	TV, Print, Sponsorship, Retail
2002	LA Times, "Connecting Us"	5	TV, Radio, Print, OOH, Retail
2003	Bud Light, "Great Lengths"	6	TV, Radio, Print, Interactive, OOH
2004	Yahoo Search, "The New Yahoo"	7	TV, Radio, PR, Interactive, OOH, Guerrilla
2005	Breathe Right, "Back in the Sack"	8	TV, Radio, Print, Direct Mail, PR, Interactive, Guerrilla
2006	Infinity Broadcasting, "How Far Will You Go?"	9	TV, Radio, Print, PR, Interactive, OOH, Retail, Consumer
2007	Saab, "Born From Jets"	10	TV, Radio, Print, Direct Mail, PR, Interactive, OOH, Retail
2008	Mayfield Dairy, "Nurture Milk Launch"	11	TV, Print, Direct Mail, OOH, PR, Direct Email, Design, Interactive, Retail, Guerrilla, Consumer
2009	Dos Equis, "The Most Interesting Man In The World"	12	TV, Radio, Print, Direct Email, PR, Design, Cinema, Interactive, Sponsorship, Retail, Guerrilla, Consumer Involvement
2010	Clear Wireless, "Welcome to the Future"	13	TV, Radio, Print, Direct Mail, Direct Email, PR, Cinema, Interactive, OOH, Trade, Sponsorship, Retail, Guerrilla

Source: Keith A. Quesenberry, Michael K. Coolsen, and Kristen Wilkerson, "IMC and The Effies: Use of Integrated Marketing Communications Touchpoints Among Effie Award Winners," *International Journal of Integrated Marketing Communications* 4, no. 2 (2012): 60–72.

Note: OOH is out-of-home advertising sources such as billboards and transit ads.

Whether marketers view this shift in perspective as obeying the consumer or choosing to change, organizations must let go of the traditional message-control model. Empowered consumers generating and sharing their own brand content do not fit neatly into current models of marketing.[8] Some estimate that consumers are now generating at least a quarter of all messages about a brand on the web. This shift is much bigger than simply purchasing more consumer touch points to continue to reach an audience with advertiser-crafted sell messages. Social media is a different medium where users have very different expectations. Traditional advertising is built upon purchasing consumer attention through interruption while social media must build interest and engagement with those consumers to be effective.

Thus social media is not a quick add-on, like picking up another advertising channel such as TV, radio, or billboards. Social media must be approached in a separate way, but still integrated into traditional marketing promotion. When marketers open a social engagement channel, they will also find questions and interactions with consumers that have more to do with other business units such as operations, customer service, and human resources. A social media strategy affects the entire business organization and must be built from the ground up, integrating all business units.

Marketing must be careful not to underestimate the extent of this change from control to engagement. This seemingly simple adjustment in mindset can make a vast difference in practice. A shift of this magnitude occurred with the rise of a new discipline: integrated marketing communications (IMC). IMC arose out of a desire and need for marketers and advertisers to integrate messages for consistency across traditional media channels and marketing communication disciplines. This was a change in the way managers thought about marketing to improve efficiency of promotional communication. Later it also became an effective tool to combat the proliferation of media clutter and build awareness in light of decreasing mass media audience.[9] Marketers could no longer rely on reaching their target markets by buying mass audience attention in one or two places.

With IMC, communications touch points are managed together for consistency and greater impact. Yet even this system and strategy are now breaking down. Integrated marketing communication is no longer enough because social media is not just another organization-controlled touch point. The consumer has a more powerful voice and therefore has a say in brand communication (see figure 3.1). Today consumers create communications about businesses and organizations, good, bad, and indifferent that marketers cannot directly control. Consumers have their own mass media channels that marketers cannot buy and traditional marketing practices don't account adequately for this social media–empowered consumer.[10] Thus even an integrated marketing communications approach must evolve into a more engagement model centered on a more powerful and influential consumer.

Therefore, marketers must now do more than create consistent marketing messages pushed out to consumers. Both company-generated messages and consumer-generated communications should be integrated through engagement to create one cohesive marketing strategy. Social media creates conversations with consumers rather than one-sided strictly persuasive or sales-oriented brand messages.[11] Because the marketer cannot predict what the customer will say, the strategies must also be more flexible and nimble, accounting for more immediate adjustment, response, and inclusion of other business units like customer service.

This shift does not mean social media marketing is not persuasive. The business objectives to sell a product or service remain the same, but the method to achieve those results needs to change. Interrupting sell messages should be balanced with content of value that attracts the audiences. Push sell messages should be supplemented with two-way consumer communication that involves them in the brand. Again, this shift in mindset and strategy is not about completely giving up all control of a brand; it is about changing methods to maintain control and influence in a new consumer-controlled social media reality.

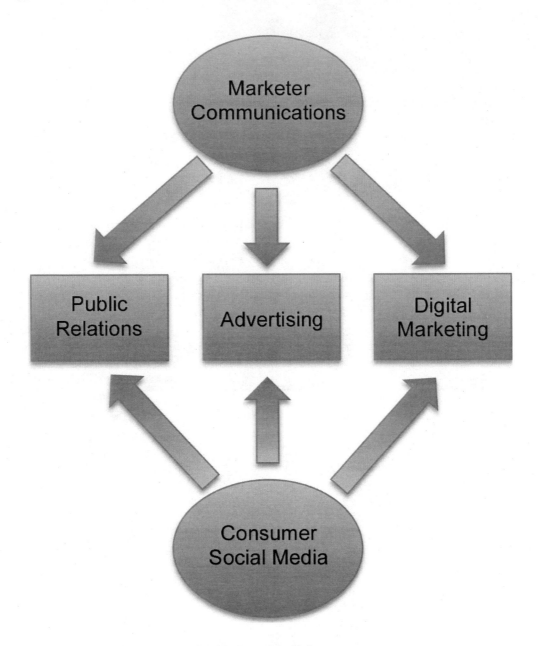

Figure 3.1. Control marketing is breaking down.

From Interruption to Engagement

What would a marketer or advertiser do if they could not interrupt their audience? How would that change their marketing-communication strategy and tactics? The answer to these questions requires a new model of marketing. This new model requires both interaction and integration of all information between the company and consumer.[12] Moving beyond traditional integrated marketing communications, marketers must now take a step back to include all sources of brand messages. The big difference now is that this not only includes brand communication produced by other business units or marketing partners, but also all consumer-generated brand content. Think of this new role as less of an integrated communications creator or controller and more of an integrated communications manager. In this new role, marketers and advertisers must also move from an overall emphasis on interruption to more of an engagement perspective. When thinking about reaching a target audience with brand messages, traditional interruptive advertising still plays a role, but engagement should be a key consideration.

With the rise of the third screen and simultaneous digital and social media usage, it can be hard to tell if anyone is really paying attention to traditional media channels. As author Sean Carton says in a *ClickZ* article on the distracted consumer, "In a media marketplace that's increasingly fragmented and deficient in consumer attention, social media is one place where people tend to spend lots of time engaged with content and opinions."[13] To succeed today, marketers must draw interest from the consumer where their attention is shifting, and must do it in way to which they will respond.

If mass media is losing consumer attention and that attention is shifting to social media, then marketers and advertisers must follow to maintain brand attention. In this sense, social media is not a development taking away control from a marketer or advertiser. If brands learn to play by the new engagement rules, social media actually represents an opportunity to maintain control. Social media integration just may be the glue that can hold the professional practice of marketing, advertising, and public relations together in this new age of interactive media. Web 2.0 was not developed to kill advertising or traditional marketing. Marketers and advertisers must simply evolve with these developments into matching practices of Advertising 2.0, and Marketing 2.0.

Professor John Deighton of Harvard Business School argues that the digital interactive transformation of marketing has become one of consumer collaboration. This new marketing model now includes a consumer's use of digital media or user-generated content that lies beyond the control of marketers. Deighton states, "The shift from broadcasting to interaction within digital communities is moving the locus of control over meanings from marketer to consumer and rewarding more participatory, more sincere and less directive marketing styles."[14] Thus learning to give up control and engage with the consumer sooner than competitors could reward a marketer and their organization with a competitive advantage.

To gain this advantage, the new marketing and advertising professional should manage and integrate all brand related communication, whether organization-created or consumer-generated, through more of a two-way conversation. Part IV of this book will explain in more detail how this engagement goes beyond marketing to other organizational areas. To be the most effective social media management and strategy must include other business units or disciplines such as research, product development, and customer service.

When a marketer or advertiser opens a two-way communication channel with a customer, the customer does not distinguish between brand and customer-service messaging, but rather views the brand as one whole. In the new consumer collaboration model, companies become a hub for the constant flow of brand discussion as they monitor, respond, facilitate consumer buzz, and integrate consumer social feedback into other organizational activities. Perhaps IMC should evolve from integrated marketing communications to integrated communication management where marketer and consumer both contribute to the brand and its products and services. Marketing 2.0 and Advertising 2.0 recognize the power of the consumer social media voice to create and spread brand messages, improve operations and customer service, and provide valuable product, service, and marketing insight to supplement traditional research.

Adjusting to this transformation is challenging. It requires changes in strategy, tools, and organization, but there is reward for the organizations that embrace the shift in mindset and implement a social media strategy correctly. Research into electronic word-of-mouth communication (eWOM) suggests that it is seen as a reliable source of information, significantly affects the perceived value of a firm's offering, and has a direct relationship with loyalty intentions.[15] The consumer voice generates brand awareness, increases brand value, and builds loyalty. In social media, loyalty is contagious. Marketers have always known word-of-mouth is the best form of advertising. Now through social media it has finally reached the scale and scope to be a significant business objective-reaching strategy.

Theoretically Speaking: The Four Ps to the Four Cs

A basic principle in marketing is the **Four Ps**, which divides the marketing mix or function into four interconnected parts: product, price, promotion, and place (distribution).[16] The Four Ps concept was first introduced by Jerome E. McCarthy and then popularized by Philip Kotler, the Father of Modern Marketing.[17] This traditional Four Ps view of marketing has been taught since the 1960s. However, in the 1980s Gordon Bruner and other scholars started to argue that the Four Ps were no longer adequate to describe the new breadth of marketing applications. Bruner proposed a new marketing mix termed the **Four Cs** of concept, channels, costs, and communication.[18] The Four Cs were said to address changes in marketing tools and consumer perspectives.

Around the same time, the concept of integrated marketing communications (IMC) was introduced by Don E. Schultz and other scholars. The practice of IMC argues for the integration of what were previously seen as separate methodologies: advertising, sales promotion, direct marketing, and public relations. Thus, **integrated marketing communications** seeks to align and coordinate all marketing communications delivered to consumers to present a cohesive whole that persuades consumers to purchase.[19] IMC is also said to focus more on consumer-centric communication to meet the needs and desires of the customer.

More recently, Robert Lauterborn has further refined the Four Cs concept, emphasizing the value of customers and the importance of convenience and relationships. The Four Cs can be explained as customer not product, cost not price, convenience not place, and communicate not promote. In this shift in perspective from marketer to consumer, value defines the product in the marketplace instead of product features. In this perspective, consideration is paid to the customer's needs, limited money, and shopping experience, and communication becomes more interactive and relational.[20] Whether you believe that the Four Ps are relevant or not, it is clear that the marketing mix has changed and marketers' strategies must change along with it.

S SOCIAL PLAN PART 3

Quantifying Engagement

Ask and answer these questions: Is the brand integrating the consumer's voice into the organization? In what areas are consumers being integrated and engaged, and how much? In this part of the social media plan, visit all the active social media accounts for the brand, product, or service. Visit each account and scroll down the posts. Who is talking? Is it only the brand or are consumers responding? When consumers do respond, does the brand respond back? Is the brand fixing customer-support problems via social media? Has the brand ever considered or used consumer product or service ideas given in social media feedback? Conduct this research and then report findings in these areas:

1. List all brand social media channels with account names and active brand participants.
2. Gauge the interaction by quantifying brand versus consumer posts.
3. Provide example responses in each category: customer support, product/service ideas, promotions, and appreciation.
4. Explain any evidence that the brand has acted on customer social media contributions such as improving the product or service or using brand content.
5. List possible social media channels where the brand's consumers are active but the brand is not.

QUESTIONS FOR DISCUSSION

1. The distracted consumer is a marketing problem, but also a human one. In the book *The Shallows: What the Internet Is Doing to Our Brains*, Nicholas Carr presents research arguing that the Internet is physically changing our brains and reducing attention spans.[21] How distracted are you? Do you find your attention span waning?
2. Is the advertising age over? Find your own evidence to prove or disprove this statement.
3. What are your thoughts on integrated marketing communication? Is it always necessary, or do you believe a campaign could still be a success by using only one touch point, such as TV or just social media?
4. What makes a marketing message worthy of your engagement? Brainstorm and list the main factors or categories of content that grab and keep your attention.

ADDITIONAL EXERCISES

1. Go back to the John Wanamaker quote: "Half the money I spend on advertising is wasted. The trouble is, I don't know which half." Do you believe this statement is still true today? Find evidence, tools, and research that prove John Wanamaker wrong. How do you know advertising works today? Is 100 percent of advertising spending not wasted, or has the percentage changed, and to what?

2. Take an evening during prime-time television and perform a content analysis of all the TV commercials you see in one hour. Which commercials mention social media and what social media channels are included? Be sure to capture all the ways social media is integrated into the commercial messages. Do the social media icons simply appear at the end of the commercial or do the advertisers ask the viewer to do something?

Notes

1. Sean Carton, "Marketing to the Distracted Consumer," ClickZ.com, October 24, 2011, http://m.clickz.com/clickz/column/2119225/marketing-distracted-consumer.

2. "John Wanamaker (1838–1922) Retailer, Philadelphia," AdAge.com, accessed February 16, 2015, http://adage.com/article/special-report-the-advertising-century/john-wanamaker/140185.

3. American Marketing Association, "Dictionary," accessed February 16, 2015, https://www.ama.org/resources/pages/dictionary.aspx?dLetter=A.

4. Laurel Wentz, "Cannes Swept by PR, Integrated, Internet Winners," AdAge.com, June 29, 2009, http://adage.com/print?article_id=137630.

5. Keith A. Quesenberry, Michael K. Coolsen, and Kristen Wilkerson, "IMC and the Effies: Use of Integrated Marketing Communications Touchpoints Among Effie Award Winners," *International Journal of Integrated Marketing Communications* 4, no. 2 (2012): 60–72.

6. Keith A. Quesenberry and Michael K. Coolsen, "How to Integrate Social Media into Your Marketing Strategy: Best Practices for Social Media Management," *Advertising Age Research Reports*, May 20, 2013, from http://adage.com/trend-reports/report.php?id=74.

7. Jeff Howe, "How Hashtags and Social Media Can Bring Megacorporations to Their Knees," TheAtlantic.com, June 8, 2012, http://www.theatlantic.com/business/archive/2012/06/the-rise-of-the-consumerate/258290.

8. Gordon C. Bruner II, "The Marketing Mix: Time for Reconceptualization," *Journal of Marketing Education* 11, no. 2 (1989): 72.

9. Michael Ewing, "Integrated Marketing Communications Measurements and Evaluation," *Journal of Marketing Communications* 15, No. 2–3 (2009): 103–117.

10. Quesenberry and Coolsen, "How to Integrate Social Media into Your Marketing Strategy."

11. Thorsten Hennig-Thurau, Edward C. Malthouse, Christian Friege, Sonja Gensler, Lara Lobschat, Arvind Rangaswamy, and Bernd Skiera, "The Impact of New Media on Customer Relationships," *Journal of Service Research* 13, no. 3 (2009): 311–330.

12. Quesenberry and Coolsen, "How to Integrate Social Media into Your Marketing Strategy."

13. Carton, "Marketing to the Distracted Consumer."

14. John Deighton and Leora Kornfeld, "Digital Interactivity: Unanticipated Consequences for Markets, Marketing, and Consumers," *Harvard Business School,* September 26, 2007, http://www.hbs.edu/faculty/Publication%20Files/08-017_1903b556-786c-49fb-8e95-ab9976da8b4b.pdf.

15. Thomas W. Gruen, Talai Osmonbekov, and Andrew J. Czaplewski, "eWOM: The Impact of Customer-to-Customer Online Know-how Exchange on Customer Value and Loyalty," *Journal of Business Research* 59, no. 4 (2006): 449–456.

16. American Marketing Association, "Dictionary," accessed February 17, 2015, https://www.ama.org/resources/pages/dictionary.aspx?dLetter=T.

17. Teo Graca, "The Evolution of Advertising—Social Media Has Taken Charge," Advertising Advocates.com, accessed February 17, 2015, http://articleadvocates.com/articleadvocates/display.cfm/6623.

18. Neelima Mahajan, "The Thinker Interview with Philip Kotler, the Father of Marketing," *CKGSB Knowledge*, October 8, 2013, http://knowledge.ckgsb.edu.cn/2013/10/08/marketing/philip-kotler-four-ps-model-marketing-still-king.

19. Don Schultz, Charles H. Patti, and Philip J. Kitchen, *The Evolution of Integrated Marketing Communications*. Abingdon, Oxon: Routledge (2013).

20. Lucian J. Lombardi, "The 4Cs of Marketing," *LIMRA's Marketfacts Quarterly* 29, no. 4 (2010): 71–90.

21. Nicholas Carr, *The Shallows: What the Internet Is Doing to Our Brains*. New York: W. W. Norton (2010).

PART

II

No Hype:
A Strategic
Framework That
Works

Lay a Foundation,
Frame the Conversation

You should never go to battle before you've won the war on paper.[1]

—Philip Kotler

PREVIEW

For years, consultants have been telling a story about Yale's graduating class of 1953. Researchers reportedly surveyed the seniors and found that only 3 percent had specific, written goals for the future. Twenty years later, researchers polled the surviving members of the class and found that the 3 percent with goals had accumulated more wealth than the other 97 percent of the class combined! This is a fascinating story, but in 1996 Lawrence Tabak reported in *Fast Company* that it was completely untrue.[2] In fact, Yale University Library received so many requests for the study that they report on their website that they have determined no "goals study" ever occurred.[3]

However, the nonexistence of the Yale study motivated Gail Matthews of Dominican University to conduct her own. In a survey of 149 participants Matthews found that those who wrote goals actually accomplished significantly more than those who did not.[4] Despite the true or untrue status of the Yale story, having specific written goals is important.

Goals, Analysis, and Targets

So far, this book has looked at the history and definition of social media and noted the changes in mass media, marketing, and advertising. This has provided valuable background and context to establish how persuasive and influential social media has become. There is a strong argument for why organizations should be active in social media. Of course, most businesses have heard this message and many have in fact responded. As of 2014, 80 percent of Fortune 500 corporations were on Facebook and 83 percent had Twitter accounts.[5] Yet as Philip Kotler points out, going into the social media battle and having a plan are very different actions.

Knowing an organization should be active in social media and even having social media accounts is not difficult. Many sources have published articles and videos on how to set up social accounts quickly and easily. For example, *Social Media Examiner* published a blog post on how to set up a Facebook business page in minutes.[6] However, learning to use that page effectively is an entirely different game. It is a game marketers cannot win unless they take the time to plan an effective strategy.

In a survey of global chief marketing officers, 82 percent felt they were not prepared to deal with the data explosion, and two-thirds of chief marketing officers reported that they were not ready to cope with social media.[7] Why? Having a Twitter page and updating it with corporate press releases or promotions is not a winning social media strategy. This is treating social media as simply another traditional media channel to push out marketing control messages. Used the wrong way, a Facebook or Twitter page simply becomes another outlet to add to advertising clutter like digital billboards or bathroom-stall advertising.

How should marketers communicate in these new social media outlets? They must go back to the very beginning of marketing. A **market** is defined as a place where products are bought and sold.[8] The best-selling book *The Cluetrain Manifesto* reminded marketers that marketing originated in traditional physical markets. In those open squares, "Markets are conversations, talk is cheap, silence is fatal."[9] Old-time markets began as a place where people talked about what they cared about and the goods on the table between them. As the distance between producer and consumer grew, a gap between our business voice and our authentic voice appeared.

Marketing became an applied science to engineer responses through calibrated stimuli—control marketing. Social media bridges that gap, and brings the consumer and merchant back to the table in a personal conversation. Consequently, for social media success marketers need to start with a customer-centric marketing strategy.

One of the most basic strategic processes in marketing is a situation analysis, and one of the most powerful tools in situation analysis is the **SWOT** (strengths, weaknesses, opportunities, threats) analysis. Although credited to various people, no one knows the true origin of this concept. It may be that SWOT originated in a number of places, or became commonplace in the training rooms of corporate America in the 1950s and 1960s.[10] Either way, a structured planning method for marketing strategy starts by setting a goal and then collecting primary and secondary research data.

A **goal** is simply something that a person or group is trying to achieve.[11] Goals expressed in specific terms are objectives. Goals and objectives should be organization-driven, but can vary wildly. A goal could be a straight increase in sales of a product or service, or an increase in donations or volunteers for a nonprofit. Perhaps a brand is suffering from a negative image and goals would be about changing consumer perception. A startup may want to increase general awareness or an established company may need to increase awareness of social responsibility efforts or a new product.

Whether performing a SWOT analysis on a brand, product, service, individual, for-profit, or nonprofit, goals should always be expressed specifically as objectives that are SMART. **SMART objectives** are specific, measurable, achievable, relevant, and timely.[12] Expressing goals as quantified SMART objectives ensures that they are measurable and thus success can be proven and effort can be justified.

After specific and measurable objectives have been set, begin gathering internal and external data to identify the main categories of a SWOT analysis: strengths, weaknesses, opportunities, and threats. Many organizations have existing primary research that is very useful for this analysis. This information can usually be found within the organization or on corporate websites and in industry trade association reports. There is a wealth of secondary research available as well. Start with Google, but also consider company profile databases such as Standard & Poors, International Directory of Company Histories, and Hoover's. Annual reports can be obtained from corporate websites or the SEC. If accessible, use Mintel Oxygen, Marketline, and SRDS for valuable reports and research insight. PrivCo is also a good resource for private company data.

Marketers should always start with existing or secondary research, but may find a need for new or primary research to make informed strategic decisions or to ensure objectives

---

 Objectives Should Meet SMART Guidelines

- **Specific:** If objectives are to increase sales, express this in terms of an exact percentage or dollar increase. If objectives are to increase awareness, state it in concrete terms such as a percent of awareness among a target market.
- **Measurable:** A specific objective is useless unless it can be measured. If the objective is to increase awareness by 40 percent, current awareness levels must be known and there must be a plan to collect awareness levels later.
- **Achievable:** A sales increase of 400 percent is exciting, but is it feasible? Perhaps there isn't even the production capacity to meet that objective. If objectives are too big, they are setting the plan up for failure. Are the necessary resources and support available?
- **Relevant:** Objectives must match organization vision and mission. A specific, measurable, and attainable objective may still not be important to leadership or make a direct contribution to the organization's purpose.
- **Timely:** Any goal may be attainable given enough time, yet waiting ten years to increase sales 10 percent may be too little, too late. Set a due date to give a sense of urgency, ensure the objective is measurable, and then judge whether efforts have been a success.

are measurable. **Secondary research** discovers information previously researched for other purposes that is publicly available. **Primary research** is new research to answer specific questions, and can include questionnaires, surveys, or interviews.[13]

Smart research is an investment to help avoid costly mistakes down the road. Too many times marketers skimp on research up front only to succumb to the old adage, "There's never enough money to do it right the first time, but always enough to do it twice." These days, it does not take a lot of effort to write and field an online survey. Consider fielding independent research via tools such as SurveyMonkey or Google Docs. What type of data could and should be captured?

Gather Primary and Secondary Data About:

- History of the organization
- Product and/or service description
- Current marketing campaign/efforts
- Recent sales/performance history
- Industry overview/trends
- Key competitor actions

Don't forget the business trade press, which can share valuable developments and insights. Many research companies such as Gartner, Nielsen, and Forrester issue press releases that highlight key findings. Sometimes the trade press will obtain research reports and write articles about key research highlights. Product industry trade organizations will occasionally conduct research and issue reports for their members. Other organizations such as the Pew Research Center and US Census Bureau issue data and reports for free. For information specific to social media, look to outlets such as *Social Media Examiner, Mashable,* and *MediaPost,* or try marketing and advertising trade groups such as WOMMA, the American Marketing Association (AMA), the American Association of Advertising Agencies (AAAA), or American Advertising Federation (AAF). Also check with university and public libraries for access to valuable databases.

It is also important to gather all information about current marketing activity. Is there an existing advertising campaign that is currently running? Does the brand have a tagline, certain imagery, or a spokesperson that appears in all promotional material? What is the idea or theme behind their current ads, whether traditional or digital media? It is important to collect and analyze marketing effort to ensure integration with any new social media strategy. For example, you probably cannot imagine any new social media strategy for Progressive Insurance that doesn't include their brand spokesperson, Flo.

Once data is gathered, organize the information into meaningful categories. Start with a blank SWOT template such as the one shown in figure 4.1. Identify internal strengths and weaknesses and external opportunities and threats. **Internal factors** are the factors that occur within an organization and impact the approach and success of operations. **External factors** consist of a variety of factors outside the organization that marketers typically don't have direct control over.[14] Summarize the facts that may be helpful or harmful to attaining your goals as bullet points in each quadrant. Marketers should use

	Helpful	Harmful
Internal	**S** Strengths	**W** Weaknesses
External	**O** Opportunities	**T** Threats

Figure 4.1. SWOT Analysis Graphic Template

Source: "SWOT Analysis," Wikipedia, last modified January 15, 2015, http://en.wikipedia.org/wiki/SWOT _analysis.

their best judgment in listing only the most relevant and important factors. The objective of a SWOT graphic is to see the big picture, not list all the details.

From this big picture of the current environment try to identify internal factors that match external factors. For example, match internal strengths with external opportunities. Try many combinations. There is no one right answer, but several promising strategies should start to emerge. There will be varying degrees to which an organization's resources and capabilities match external factors to form a strategic fit.

It is also important to keep in mind that specific objectives may have to be modified once research has been evaluated. If a more promising opportunity is discovered, go back and modify the original objective, as long as it still fits SMART guidelines and is in line with organizational vision and mission.[15]

Don't underestimate the importance of vision. Take time to evaluate the organization's vision or reason for existence. The vision of Ben & Jerry's is most likely different from that of Häagen-Dazs, and that should make a difference in objectives and strategy. Vision is often expressed as a mission statement, which can usually be found on corporate websites. A **mission statement** is a written declaration of an organization's core purpose and focus that tends to remain unchanged over time.[16]

Finally, identify a target audience for the social media communications effort. Note that a target audience may be different from a target market. A **target market** is identified in business and marketing plan objectives and represents a group of people who share common wants or needs that an organization serves. On the other hand, a **target audience** is a group of people identified as the intended recipient of a communications message.[17]

For example, a nonprofit may have a target market of people in need to provide services and have a target audience of people who provide support through donation of time or money.[18] There may also be important target audiences who are not in the target market, but influence end users to make conversion decisions. This is an especially important consideration in social media, where a quarter of consumers may influence the purchases of the rest.[19] The important decision here is to identify the group that is most likely to respond positively to the effort and directly or indirectly contribute to helping meet organization goals and objectives.

In defining a target for a social media effort, narrow the selection by more closely defining who is most likely to respond to the brand, product, service, or organization. See table 4.1 for possible variables and bases of segmentation.

A famous example of a target market not matching target audience is Old Spice (see Mini Case: Old Spice New Target). Here the marketer and their advertising agency selected women as the target audience for a campaign where the target market, the main users of the product, were men.[20] This strategy was a more customer-centric marketing effort rooted in consumer insight.

As with SMART objectives, be sure the target audience designation is specific. Define the target in terms of both demographic and psychographic information. **Demographic variables** can include information such as age range, gender, geographic location, ethnic background, marital status, income, and education. When possible always quantify these designations with specific numbers, such as women age twenty-five to thirty-four. Not only does this ensure one person's interpretation of middle age is the same as someone else's, but it will also match advertiser and publisher standards for buying media. Most agree that eighteen- to twenty-four-year-olds have more in common with each other in terms of interests, needs, and desires than they do with forty-five- to fifty-four-year-olds.

Another factor to consider is **generational targeting,** where broader age groups such as baby boomers or millennials may have similar desires compared to previous generations. **Psychographic variables** consist of more internal factors such as values, attitudes, interests, lifestyle, and behavior. For example, not all eighteen to twenty-four-year-old male millennials are interested in rugby, robotics, or running equally. Define the target audience utilizing both these types of information. Then create a complete customer profile or buyer persona with an in-depth description of the target, not only to define who may respond, but also why.[21] A **buyer persona** is a semi-fictional portrayal of the ideal customer based on real data.[22] Think of a buyer persona as the historical fiction story of a single person in the target audience that fills in a real life around the data.

In *The Art of War,* Sun Tzu taught that true strategy was not planning by working through an established list, but rather responding to changing conditions.[23] The same thought applies when developing a social media strategy. Marketers and advertisers may need to adjust this process to the situation. In some organizations, the target audience may be fixed. Start there and work back toward setting objectives and performing the SWOT

Table 4.1. Variables and Basis of Segmentation

Geographic	Demographic	Psychographic	Behavioral
Basis such as region, climate, population density, and growth rate	Basis such as age, gender, ethnicity, education, occupation, income, and family	Basis such as values, attitudes, and lifestyle	Variables such as usage rate, price sensitivity, brand loyalty, and benefits sought

C   MINI CASE

Old Spice New Target

In 2010 the men's body wash category was growing, but Old Spice's sales were slipping. Procter & Gamble's research found that 60 percent of men's body washes were purchased by women. For the first time, Old Spice marketing was targeted to women with its "The Man Your Man Could Smell Like" campaign.[a] It received a lot of attention, but did it deliver business results?

In the first three months, Old Spice captured 76 percent of all online conversations about male body-wash brands, with more than half of that coming from women. This resulted in Old Spice becoming the #1 all-time most viewed and #2 most-subscribed branded channel on YouTube. The six-month campaign generated 1.7 billion total impressions, and sales more than doubled versus the prior year, with an increase of 125 percent.[b]

---

[a] "Old Spice Campaign Is Not Only Great, It Sells—Now #1 in U.S. in Both Dollar and Volume Share," CampaignBrief.com, July 16, 2010, http://www.campaignbrief.com/2010/07/old-spices-campaign-is-not -onl.html.

[b] "Old Spice Case," Effie Awards, accessed February 17, 2015, http://www.apaceffie.com/docs/default -source/resource-library/oldspice_case_pdf.pdf?sfvrsn=2.

---

analysis. Or the target audience may change in the midst of the process as new information and insight is discovered.

Listening to what people are saying in a social media audit may change the target audience completely. Remain flexible and respond to changing conditions, yet stay rooted in a solid foundation that meets the organization's goals, leverages research insight, and maintains communications focus. Take Philip Kotler's advice in formulating the plan to win the battle on paper, but follow Sun Tzu's foresight in keeping it flexible and be willing to use an eraser.

Listen with a Social Media Audit

Ernest Hemingway said that he learned a great deal from listening carefully, yet most people he knew never listened.[24] A shortcoming of many marketing and advertising people is that they like to hear themselves talk. Maybe this is a characteristic that drew them into the field. Being able to talk serves them well in convincing people to bet millions on marketing and advertising ideas. Yet listening is also a key to success.

Marketers may not be seeking a Nobel Prize in Literature like Hemingway, but getting the crowds to like and share brand content is surprisingly similar to developing a best-selling novel. In 2010 Edward Moran and Francois Gossieaux performed a study of more than five hundred companies and found that marketers developing a social media strategy must first listen to what online communities are saying about their products and where they are saying it.[25]

Furthermore, not listening can get organizations into big trouble. In 2006, Dave Carroll composed a song about United Airlines' mishandling of his $3,500 guitar and their refusal to compensate him (see figure 4.2). Within one week, the video received 3 million views, 14.5 million by 2015, and coverage in media such as CNN, the *Wall Street Journal*, BBC, and the *CBS Morning Show*.[26]

The magazine *Fast Company* reported that Carroll contacted United for nine months with calls and emails, but only after the video's success, and United Airlines' stock price drop of 10 percent, did the company try to make things right.[27] Today, Carroll has written a book about the experience called *United Breaks Guitars: The Power of One Voice in the Age of Social Media*.

The initial step in listening is a social media audit. A **social media audit** is a systematic examination of social media data. In this phase of social media planning, think of the

Figure 4.2. "United Breaks Guitars" is still gaining views.

Source: "United Breaks Guitars," Sons of Maxwell, accessed January 18, 2015, https://www.youtube.com/watch?v=5YGc4zOqozo. © Dave Carroll Music

social media audit as taking a snapshot of all social media activity in and around a brand and then evaluating the information gathered. It is a social situational analysis that includes both internal company social media actions and external consumer social media activity.

First, listen to what consumers are saying about the brand, product, service, organization, and key personnel. Also listen to what is being said by and about its main competitors. Listen with an outside perspective to what the organization and its employees are currently saying on official corporate social media accounts and unofficial or personal accounts. A combination of internal and external social talk data will help identify challenges or problem areas within the current social media environment. The audit will also identify possible opportunities that may become significant parts of a strategic plan.

Second, organize the collected data and make it accessible for meaningful analysis. To accomplish this, use a **social media audit template** (see table 4.2). The template provided is divided into three key areas of talk for listening and analysis: company, consumer, and competitor. In each area, gather information and record what is found into "W" categories. These categories come from the principle of the **Five Ws**, by which journalists are directed to find out the who, where, what, when, and why of a story.[28]

Data collection and analysis should occur in these key categories: who—company, consumers, competitors; where—social media channel (YouTube, Facebook, Pinterest, etc.) and environment (describe the look and feel); what—type of content (articles, photos, videos, questions, etc.) and sentiment (positive, negative, neutral); when—frequency of activity (number of posts, comments, views, shares, etc. per day, week, or month); why—purpose (awareness, promotion, complaint, praise, etc.).

To be effective, the audit need not track down and collect each digital conversation. The objective of the social media audit is not to capture every mention, but to gather a snapshot of the social talk—enough to get an accurate picture of what is currently happening in the social space.

For current company social media efforts, it is important to determine purpose and note key performance indicators (KPIs), if any. A **KPI** is simply a key indicator that is used as a type of performance measurement.[29] Try to determine the purpose of each social channel. For example, why does the organization have a Pinterest page and how is success being measured? For some this may be easy to answer and for others it could be a wake-up call. "Because everyone else is using it" is not an acceptable answer. Larger organizations may have to divide the "Company" category further into departments, offices, or employees. Perhaps several departments or local offices are each operating their own company social media account. Or numerous high profile employees are active in talking about the organization on their personal accounts. It is important to capture what each is communicating and discern whether they are presenting a unified brand image.

When determining the "Why" or purpose of a communication channel, dig deep and find a strategic reason that directly supports organizational objectives or mission. If a strategic purpose cannot be found for being in a specific social media channel, then it needs to be reevaluated. Is maintaining the social media account worth the organization's time and effort? Finally, score each observation as either a problem or an opportunity. Use a five-point scale with 1 being a problem and 5 indicating an opportunity. This will help sort out areas for offensive and defensive social strategy.

Table 4.2. Social Media Audit Template

Who	Where (Channel/Environment)	What (Type of Content/ Sentiment)	When (Date/Frequency)	Why (Purpose/KPI*)	Problem Opportunity 1 2 3 4 5
Company					
1.					
2.					
3.					
Consumer					
1.					
2.					
3.					
Competitor					
1.					
2.					
3.					

* KPI is key performance indicators.

Listening to what customers, competitors, critics, and supporters are saying is key to getting results from social media campaigns. How does someone listen? In Charlene Li and Josh Bernoff's book *Groundswell,* they describe two listening strategies: homegrown monitoring and professional monitoring. **Homegrown monitoring** includes simply typing into the Google search box the brand or product name with the word "complaint" or "love," or performing a Google blog search and searching names and hashtags in social media networks. Discover what people are saying who have tweeted a company, product, or CEO's name. Find public support forums, fan clubs, and sites such as Yelp or TripAdvisor and check the ratings and reviews on Amazon.com. Do the same search for competitors as well.[30]

Professional monitoring includes brand monitoring or setting up a private community. Professional monitoring doesn't always mean paid. There are numerous free social media monitoring tools such as SocialMention.com, BoardReader.com, and IceRocket.com. There is also Twitter Search (search.twitter.com), Facebook Search (facebook.com), Talkwalker search (talkwalker.com), and Google Alerts (google.com/alerts). Hootsuite (hootsuite.com/plans) offers a free basic account that will monitor up to three social profiles.

The homegrown method and free monitoring tools should suffice at first. Marketers and advertisers can find enough information for the social media audit and to formulate a solid social media strategy. This is especially suitable for students, small businesses, and startups. Yet homegrown monitoring efforts don't scale. If a marketer is serious about social media and has a budget for it, now is the time to invest in a paid social media monitoring service and content management system or pay a research company to start a brand community. Partnering with a vendor will save time in collecting data, delivering new content, and issuing reports.

Costs for paid social media monitoring vary widely from $20 a month to $10,000 a month or more, based on needs, time, and long-term strategy for listening, content publishing, analytics, and reports.[31] This expense could also be divided among departments. For example, chapter 13 details how real-time social media monitoring can turn into a real asset for customer service.

There are numerous paid and free tools offering many ways to analyze, measure, display, and create reports to gain insight from listening. Author Pam Dyer published a comprehensive list of "50 Top Tools for Social Media Monitoring, Analytics and Management" in *Social Media Today.* Take a look at table 4.3 for a highlight of resources available with both paid and free social media listening options.[32]

Many paid services also offer limited free versions or free trials. Hootsuite offers a free version that allows up to three social profiles with basic analytics, scheduling, and app integrations. Professionals are eligible for a free thirty-day trial of Hootsuite Pro, which includes up to fifty social profiles, one free enhanced analytics report, and one free team member. Students may also be eligible for free ninety-day access to Hootsuite Pro as part of a higher education program. The student version also allows access to free training and the opportunity to earn Hootsuite Certification. Inquire about the program through your university or professor.

Many marketers today are also investing in a social media command center. A **social media command center** is a branded social media monitoring room acting as a central,

Table 4.3. Tools for Social Media Monitoring

Paid Tools	Free Tools
Alterian	Mention
Bottlenose	Klout
Sysomos	TweetDeck
Collective Intellect	BackTweets
Sprout Social	Buffer
Talkwalker	Facebook Insights
Vocus	Hootsuite
Hootsuite	IceRocket
NetBase	Pinterest Web Analytics
Twitalyzer	Social Mention
Buzz Equity	TweetBeep
Synthesio	Netvibes
Trackur	Google Alerts

Source: Pam Dyer, "50 Top Tools for Social Media Monitoring Analytics, and Management," Socialmediatoday. com, May 13, 2013, http://www.socialmediatoday.com/content/50-top-tools-social-media-monitoring-analytics -and-management.

visual hub for social data. These centers tend to be set up in high-profile locations within company offices. In 2010 Gatorade built their mission-control center in the middle of the marketing department at their Chicago headquarters. Radian6 and IBM partnered with the sports beverage brand to build a custom war room that monitors the brand in real time across social media.[33]

After social conversation data has been collected and categorized into company communication, consumer communication, and competitor communication, it must be analyzed. Like any audit, data needs to be examined to formulate a judgment. What is the data saying? Does it point to any opportunities? Are there any trouble spots? How is the existing social media activity performing in terms of helping to meet organizational goals and objectives?

If serious or not-so-serious negative issues have been found, they need to be addressed before starting any additional social media effort. If company social media channels are not integrated with the same brand, look, feel, and voice, this needs to be corrected as well. Drawing additional attention to existing social channels that are not unified is a waste of new efforts. Is there a discernible pattern in consumer negative chat? If significant numbers of customers are complaining about a similar customer-service or product issue, it needs to be corrected now, before a new social strategy is set into place. Sending more people to a flawed issue will only increase the negative talk.

Don't skip the beginning of the next chapter about making repairs. If marketers don't fix complaints, it will only send a loud message to existing customers that the organization doesn't listen. Remember that individual consumer complaints are now heard by many. Don't be like most people Ernest Hemingway observed who never listen. Make a bold move to fix problem areas and take a first step toward social media marketing success.

Theoretically Speaking: Market Segmentation

Market segmentation is defined as "grouping potential customers into sets that are homogeneous in response to elements of the marketing mix."[34] Wendell Smith introduced the concept in 1956,[35] and then Russell Haley in 1968[36] expanded segmentation bases to include psychographic variables. Market segmentation is a valuable strategic tool to help organizations focus marketing activities on target segments. This activity helps concentrate limited resources to make them more impactful.

Traditionally, market segmentation has fallen into two approaches. **Common-sense market segmentation** is when managers use a single segmentation criterion, such as age, to split consumers into homogeneous groups. On the contrary, **data-driven market segmentation** is when managers analyze more complex sets of variables. Common-sense segmentation is simple and easy, but a business basing its strategy on more data-driven approaches with more psychographic and demographic bases for segmentation will perform better.[37]

Many have heard the saying, "Birds of a feather flock together." This holds true in most people's personal experiences. They tend to gravitate towards likeminded individuals. It also holds true in marketing and advertising. The more research-driven segmentation bases marketers and advertisers uncover, the tighter the target audience and social media efforts will be.

 SOCIAL PLAN PART 4

Objectives, Target, Situation Analysis, and Audit

In this part of the social media plan, first identify quantified and time-bound business objectives and specifically define the target audience for listening and communication. Then gather a snapshot of the organization's industry, recent performance of the brand, existing marketing campaign, and all current social media talk and traditional marketing promotion for the product or service and its competitors. This part of the plan is about identifying where the business or organization wants to go and where it is currently. Cover these four areas in this report, following the process and tools outlined in this chapter:

1. Identify overall SMART business objectives.
2. Perform a situation analysis and develop a complete SWOT table.
3. Explain the current marketing campaign and identify key themes, images, and taglines.
4. Define a target audience with multiple bases of segmentation.
5. Perform a social media audit, report results, and describe insights gained.

QUESTIONS FOR DISCUSSION

1. Why must marketers select target markets? Wouldn't targeting a broader audience, or everyone, result in more sales?

2. Is increasing the number of organizational social media accounts a good objective? Why or why not?
3. After the first social media audit, can brands then stop listening? Why or why not?
4. How should brands respond to negative comments on social media? Should the brand ignore comments, dispute them, or try to censor them?

ADDITIONAL EXERCISES

1. Find an organization's business plan, marketing plan, or corporate "About Us" web page. Look at the mission, objectives, and/or target market. Are they accurate and relevant? Now look at their social media efforts. Do they match? Everything done in social media should be checked to ensure it is in line with organizational vision and mission. Every social effort should help meet business objectives and be focused on talking to and with the right target audience. If there is a disconnect between the stated mission and current social media activity, which should be updated?
2. Log onto Twitter and look at the streams of several large businesses in a specific industry, such as cellular service providers. Look at companies like Verizon, AT&T, T-Mobile, Sprint, and Boost. Are most of the tweets from the marketer? Do they respond to customers, and how? Are there a lot of complaints? What are most about? Is the channel active? How many followers does each have? Quantify and compare engagement. In just a couple of minutes you should form a quick assessment of efforts and gain some key insights. Which of the competitors is doing the best job?

Notes

1. Philip Kotler, "Kotler's Quotes," accessed February 17, 2015, http://www.pkotler.org/kotlers-quotes.

2. Lawrence Tabak, "If Your Goal Is Success, Don't Consult These Gurus," FastCompany.com, December 31, 1996, http://www.fastcompany.com/27953/if-your-goal-success-dont-consult-these-gurus.

3. "Yale Business Answers Now," Library.yale.edu, accessed February 17, 2015, http://faq.library.yale.edu/recordDetail?id=7508&action=&library=yale_business&institution=Yale.

4. Gail Matthews, "Summary of Goals Research," Dominican.edu, accessed February 17, 2015, http://www.dominican.edu/academics/ahss/undergraduate-programs-1/psych/faculty/fulltime/gailmatthews/researchsummary2.pdf.

5. Nora Barnes and Ava Lescault, "The 2014 Fortune 500 and Social Media: LinkedIn Dominates as Use of Newer Tools Explodes," Umassd.edu, accessed February 17, 2015, http://www.umassd.edu/cmr/socialmediaresearch/2014fortune500andsocialmedia.

6. Andrea Vahl, "How to Set Up a Facebook Page for Business," SocialMediaExaminer.com, March 26, 2013, http://www.socialmediaexaminer.com/how-to-set-up-a-facebook-page-for-business.

7. "Stepping Up to the Challenge: CMO Insights from the Global C-suite Study," IBM Institute for Business Value, March 2014, http://public.dhe.ibm.com/common/ssi/ecm/gb/en/gbe03593usen/GBE03593USEN.PDF.

8. "Market," Merriam-Webster.com, accessed February 17, 2015, http://www.merriam-webster.com/dictionary/market.

9. Rick Levine, Christopher Locke, Doc Searls, and David Weinberger, *The Cluetrain Manifesto*. Cambridge, MA: Perseus Publishing (2000).

10. Tim Friesner, "History of SWOT Analysis," MarketingTeacher.com, accessed February 17, 2015, http://www.marketingteacher.com/swot/history-of-swot.html.

11. "Goal," Merriam-Webster.com, accessed February 17, 2015, http://www.merriam-webster.com/dictionary/goal.

12. George T. Doran, "There's a S.M.A.R.T. way to write management's goals and objectives," *Management Review* 70, no. 11 (1981): 35–36.

13. "Business Case Studies," Businesscasestudies.co.uk, accessed February 17, 2015, http://businesscasestudies.co.uk/food-standards-agency/market-research-and-consumer-protection/primary-and-secondary-research.html#ixzz3IgNvWPPI.

14. Neil Kokemuller, "What Are Internal & External Environmental Factors That Affect Business?" SmallBusiness.Chron.com, accessed February 17, 2015, http://smallbusiness.chron.com/internal-external-environmental-factors-affect-business-69474.html.

15. "SWOT analysis," Wikipedia, last modified January 15, 2015, http://en.wikipedia.org/wiki/SWOT_analysis.

16. "Mission Statement," BusinessDictionary.com, accessed February 17, 2015, http://www.businessdictionary.com/definition/mission-statement.html.

17. "Target Audience," BusinessDictionary.com, accessed February 17, 2015, http://www.businessdictionary.com/definition/target-audience.html.

18. Eria Tambien, "The Difference Between a Target Market & Target Audience," *eHow.com*, November 15, 2012, http://www.ehow.com/about_6747097_difference-target-market-target-audience.html.

19. "WOMMAPEDIA," wommapedia.org, accessed February 17, 2015, http://www.wommapedia.org.

20. "Old Spice Campaign Is Not Only Great, It Sells—Now #1 in U.S. in Both Dollar and Volume Share," CampaignBrief.com, July 16, 2010, http://www.campaignbrief.com/2010/07/old-spices-campaign-is-not-onl.html.

21. Adrianne Glowski, "5 Critical Tips for Identifying Your Target Audience," Technori.com, accessed February 17, 2015, http://technori.com/2013/02/3122-5-critical-tips-for-identifying-your-target-audience.

22. Sam Kusinitz, "The Definition of a Buyer Persona [in Under 100 Words]," HubSpot (blog), March 8, 2014, http://blog.hubspot.com/marketing/buyer-persona-definition-under-100-sr.

23. Sun Tzu, *The Art of War*, accessed February 17, 2015, http://www.gutenberg.org/ebooks/132.

24. "Ernest Hemingway Quotes," Brainy Quotes, accessed February 17, 2015, http://www.brainyquote.com/quotes/authors/e/ernest_hemingway.html.

25. Edward Moran and Francois Gossieaux, "Marketing in a Hyper-social World: The Tribalization of Business Study and Characteristics of Successful Online Communities," *Journal of Advertising Research* 50, no. 3 (2010): 232–239.

26. John Deighton and Leora Kornfeld, "United Breaks Guitars Case," *Harvard Business Review*, June 2010, http://http://hbr.org/product/united-breaks-guitars/an/510057-PDF-ENG.

27. Ravi Sawhney, "Broken Guitar Has United Playing the Blues to the Tune of $180 Million," FastCompany.com, July 7, 2009, http://www.fastcompany.com/blog/ravi-sawhney/design-reach/youtube-serves-180-million-heartbreak.

28. John Kroll, "Digging Deeper into the 5 W's of Journalism," *International Journalist Network*, November 21, 2013, http://ijnet.org/en/blog/digging-deeper-5-ws-journalism.

29. Todd Wasserman, "What Is a Key Performance Indicator?" Mashable.com, March 11, 2013, http://mashable.com/2013/05/11/kpi-definition.

30. Charlene Li and Josh Bernoff, *Groundswell, Expanded and Revised Edition: Winning in a World Transformed by Social Technologies*. Boston, MA: Harvard Business Review Press (2011).

31. Jay Baer and Amber Naslund, *The Now Revolution: 7 Shifts to Make Your Business Faster, Smarter, and More Social*. Hoboken, N.J.: Wiley (2011).

32. Pam Dyer, "50 Top Tools for Social Media Monitoring, Analytics, and Management," SocialMediaToday.com, May 13, 2013, http://www.socialmediatoday.com/content/50-top-tools -social-media-monitoring-analytics-and-management.

33. Adam Ostrow, "Inside Gatorade's Social Media Command Center," Mashable.com, June 15, 2010, http://mashable.com/2010/06/15/gatorade-social-media-mission-control.

34. J. M. Choffrey and G. L. Lilien, "Industrial Market Segmentation," in J. M. Choffrey and G. L Lilien (Eds.), *Marketing Planning for New Industrial Products*. New York: John Wiley and Sons (1980), 74–91.

35. Wendell R. Smith, "Product Differentiation and Market Segmentation as Alternative Marketing Strategies," *Journal of Marketing* 21, no. 1 (1956), 3–9.

36. Russell I. Haley, "Benefit Segmentation: A Decision Oriented Research Tool," *Journal of Marketing* 32, no. 30 (1968): 30–35.

37. Sara Dolnicar and Friedrich Leisch, "Using Graphical Statistics to Better Understand Market Segmentation Solutions," *International Journal of Market Research* 56, no. 2 (2014): 207–230.

Make Repairs and Jumpstart the Conversation

We think our job is to take responsibility for the complete user experience. And if it's not up to par, it's our fault, plain and simply.[1]

—Steve Jobs

PREVIEW

Social networks began with the intention to be a private conversation between "friends." Yet today any complaint or random thought that used to be shared personally between friends is now published in mostly a public and searchable forum. Facebook Graph Search allows any user to search any Facebook post or comment appearing under a public setting. It is also just as easy for a Facebook friend to repost to their network or take a screen grab and post anywhere.[2]

Researchers from Cornell University and Facebook discovered how influential these posts could be. On average, twice as many Facebook posts contain positive words (47 percent) as negative words (22 percent). However, this study found that people who had positive words removed from their news feeds made fewer positive posts and more negative ones and people who had negative words removed made fewer negative posts and more positive.

The research was based on the concept of emotional cognition.[3] **Emotional cognition** is a psychological phenomenon in which a person or group influences the emotions and behavior of another through conscious or even unconscious emotions.[4] This study emphasizes the importance of fixing problems that may be creating negative social talk.

Fix Operations, Product, and Service Issues

Let's say that through social media monitoring or listening research, an organization discovers a serious customer service issue that is causing a lot of negative social media comments from customers. Or perhaps there is a substantial quality issue in product delivery that continues to show up in customer ratings and reviews. Many marketers would easily say that this is a customer-service department or operations responsibility. In the new social media landscape, these issues become marketing and advertising concerns even if these business functions don't have direct control over them. Steve Jobs may have been talking about user interfaces or operating systems, but the same thought applies to marketers who must now take responsibility for the entire user experience with a brand.

Customer service is the process of ensuring customer satisfaction, often while performing a transaction, taking a sale, providing post-purchase support, or returning a product or service.[5] Customer service can take the form of personal interaction, phone call, or Internet chat, usually provided by customer-service representatives. **Operations** is tasked with converting inputs such as materials, labor, and information into outputs such as goods, services, and value-added products that can be sold for a profit.[6] In general, operations makes what consumers buy, marketing gets the customers, and customer service keeps those customers happy.

Why should marketing get involved in an operations or customer-service issue? As Steve Jobs probably would have said, marketing is to blame. Marketing and advertising make product and service claims or promises to consumers. When the product, service, or experience doesn't live up to that promise, the wrong communication has been delivered. If the message, product, or service is not adjusted, then any new efforts to increase social media talk will only increase negative communications. If marketing or advertising does not address the root cause, it is merely setting itself up for failure in meeting its own objectives and goals.

Advertising creative director Jerry Della Famina once said, "Nothing kills a bad product faster than good advertising. Everyone tries the thing and never buys it again."[7] Today, this happens even faster, because every bad customer experience can be instantly told to hundreds of people through social media channels. Plus, once social media posts or comments are published, they do not disappear like a negative newspaper print article, TV report, or personal interaction by the water cooler. Social media is forever and is only a Google search away. For a marketing department to reach its ultimate objectives, they must involve themselves in other departments of the organization. Prevention is the best medicine.

For years organizations have been set up with dedicated business functions in departments such as accounting, marketing, and human resources. These units or "silos" often have separate goals, leadership, and resources. This can lead to a silo mentality where each department rarely interacts with other business units. In many ways the power and influence of social media is forcing down these disciplinary or business-unit silos.

Consumers don't see organizations as separate operating units with independent budgets, management, goals, and objectives. Consumer conversations in social media impact all business units (see figure 5.1). This is the main message in part 4 of this book, "Integrating Social Media across Organizations." Marketing simply cannot be only about

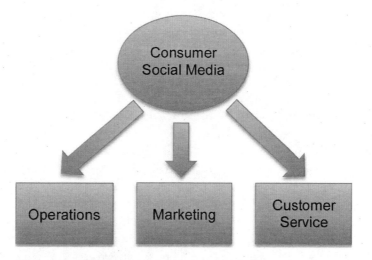

Figure 5.1. Social media impact all business units.

marketing anymore and must work across strategic business units. A **strategic business unit** (SBU) is a fully functional and distinct unit that develops its own strategic vision and direction.[8] Today, marketers and advertisers need to worry about other business functions. The good news is that if marketing becomes the social media expert in an organization, it becomes more valuable to all business units and will earn a larger role in the entire organization. This means a seat or more prominent seat in the corporate suite.

If there is a discrepancy between product or service promise and delivery, a change must be made. In some instances the marketing and advertising message needs to be adjusted to lower expectations and promise a less-ambitious customer experience. No matter what improvements are made, perhaps the organization simply can't meet overzealous communication expectations. Other times, social media listening will uncover a customer service, product, or operations issue that needs to be fixed no matter what the communications message. The key is to stop further social media promotion until adjustments are made.

From 2001 to 2011 Altimeter Research studies found that the number one cause of social media crises was exposure to a poor customer experience.[9] Every organization most likely has numerous competitors ready to take advantage of any weakness. Consider negative social media talk as an early-warning system to get any product or service issues right before they cause real damage.

As the collector of this information, marketing must sometimes be the bearer of bad news. Communicate to and engage with other organizational departments to try to resolve the issues as soon as possible. Fix them before more consumers find out. Fix them and go out of the way to make it right with current customers. In turn, they will most likely reward the organization with positive talk. **Silo syndrome** is when a department or function, like marketing, develops its own culture and has trouble working with other functions such as operations, customer service, or sales.[10] Marketers and advertisers should avoid silo syndrome and start collaboration and coordination with other strategic business units from the very beginning of the social media strategy process.

Steven Cody, CEO of Peppercorn public relations, talks of company-crushing, social-media-driven uprisings, saying, "People are pissed because they feel no one's listening to them. And often, no one is listening to them." If people are mad, listen to them and fix it. No matter the root of the problem. If the CEO said something dumb in a comment, encourage the CEO to apologize or correct it. If people are upset about ingredients in a product, change them or explain them better.

Changing the problem is what happened with lean finely textured beef. "Pink slime" was a filler made from meat scraps that used to comprise many beef products such as fast-food hamburgers. The industry considered this an acceptable ingredient until *ABC News* ran a series that triggered a social media backlash, protest, and boycott targeted toward elementary schools, supermarkets, and restaurants. Those companies listened, contacted operations, and then manufacturing adjusted its process and dropped producers of pink slime from the supply chain. The negative social talk died down.[11]

In *Social Media Marketing an Hour a Day*, Dave Evans calls this consumer-influence process the social feedback cycle. A central concept of marketing is the purchase funnel, by which companies move prospective consumers from awareness to consideration and finally purchase through marketer-generated activity. In each step, the number of consumers gets smaller. Evans adds user-generated activity after purchase, when consumers use the product or service and then talk about it on social media, where the funnel gets larger again and then cycles back to the consideration phase where prospective customers read posts, comments, ratings, and reviews. Social media conversation is so powerful because it has a unique ability to influence the consideration phase of this traditional marketing purchase funnel through the social media consumer feedback.

The **social feedback cycle** is social media connecting post-purchase social media conversation back to the purchase process, where social media is the product of operations based on the expectation given in marketing.[12] A television advertisement is good at generating awareness, but when consumers are really contemplating a purchase, they go to the Internet to see what other consumers think. This is where they see post-purchase consumers talking on social media about their experience with the brand, product, or service. The talk can be positive or negative and it carries more influence than marketing's traditional consideration phase point-of-purchase materials such as in-store posters.

Big Ideas and Being Interesting

In *Four Quartets*, T. S. Eliot wrote, "Distracted from distraction by distraction." This poetic reflection on the nature of time and order of the universe was written nearly fifty years before the Internet existed and nearly seventy years before Web 2.0.[13] Yet the quote provides an astonishing observation on the current state of humans living in a continuously connected digital world. Todd Gitlin's review of *The Shallows: What the Internet Is Doing to Our Brains* adds another characterization. He appropriately sums up Nicholas Carr's book, saying that our information society has turned into the interruption society.[14]

The Pew Research Center has found that people see this distraction as a negative aspect of mobile connectivity. A quarter of US survey respondents said cell phones make it harder to give people attention and focus on single tasks.[15] Perhaps people are still operating under the myth that they are great multitaskers. However, there has been growing evidence that the ability to multitask is a myth. It can take up to 40 percent more time than single-tasking—especially for complex undertakings.[16]

As early as 2004, researchers in the *Journal of Advertising* sought to discover why people avoid advertising on the Internet. What they found was that prior negative experience, ad clutter, and goal impediment were the most significant explanations. The authors note, "The unexpected appearance of advertising messages on the Internet disrupts user tasks or goals and causes consumers to extensively avoid the noise."[17] Remember Howard Gossage from chapter 2: "Nobody reads ads. People read what interests them."

How do marketing messages not become the noise people want to avoid? Forget brand, product, and service for a moment and delve into the mind of the consumer. Become an account planner, and dig deep for consumer insights that can turn into actionable strategy. Account planning is a discipline imported from the UK to US advertising agencies in the 1990s that has since expanded to marketing departments, PR firms, and design agencies as an important method and discipline. The account planner basically finds consumer insight through research and ensures the customer's perspective is represented in the marketing communications and advertising process.

 What Is Account Planning?

Account planning is designed to bring the consumer's perspective into the process of developing creative advertising messages and executions. While others worry about sales, clients, media placement, and creative awards, an account planner's job is to seek consumer truth and insight through primary and secondary research so advertising is relevant, entertaining, memorable, and effective.[a]

One of the most famous and successful examples of an account-planner-driven big idea in advertising strategy was the California Milk Processor Board's "Got Milk?" campaign. By now this campaign is so ubiquitous that every business from bath remodeling to used-car dealers has commandeered the slogan. But this great campaign started with an account planner's consumer research, which led to a "milk deprivation insight." This is the feeling people get when they run out of milk for something that really needs milk.

How powerful was this consumer insight? It led to an advertising campaign that stopped a twenty-year sales decline. The advertising agency on the campaign, Goodby, Silverstein & Partners, used surveys and focus groups, but also collected research by placing video cameras in refrigerators and removed the milk to see how people genuinely reacted.[b]

---

[a] "What Is Planning?" Apg.org.uk, accessed February 17, 2015, http://www.apg.org.uk/#!co-howto becomeaplanner/ctyy.

[b] Jeff Manning and Kevin Keller, "Making Advertising Work: How GOT MILK? Marketing Stopped a 20 Year Sales Decline," *Marketing Management*, January/February (2003).

Working on a project with a good account planner can be a hundred times easier and can help produce some of the most effective campaigns. If an organization doesn't have an official account planner, take on the mindset of one. Scour existing organizational research and research others have performed, and seek employees' knowledge of the target audience. What kind of information should marketers and advertisers be searching for? Actionable insight. *Merriam-Webster* defines insight as "the ability to understand people and situations in a very clear way" or "the understanding of the true nature of something."[18] The word actionable has its root in the law, but simply means, "able to be used as a basis or reason for doing something."[19] In other words, find **actionable insight,** or a true understanding of people or a situation that can be used to meet objectives of a marketing effort.

Insight can be found anywhere. Renowned advertising copywriter David Ogilvy found it reading technical articles to pen one of the most famous and successful advertising headlines: "At 60 miles an hour the loudest noise in this new Rolls Royce comes from the ticking of its electric clock."[20] This line takes insight from the obsessive luxury mindset of the Rolls Royce target audience, brilliantly combines it with a product feature, and turns a mechanical detail into an emotional pull. In a similar way, Goodby, Silverstein & Partners found insight with video cameras in refrigerators. "Got Milk?" took that insight about people's reaction to a specific situation and made it a reason to keep refrigerators always stocked with milk. Marketers and advertisers should search for that actionable insight that will lead to a big business-objective-exceeding idea.

In a campaign for a regional airport, the insight came from an informal trip to the airport terminal. The advertising-agency people noticed the short trip, close parking, and small lines compared to the big city airports they normally drove hours to fly out of on business trips. The consumer insight became actionable when it was linked to the marketing strategy and service benefits. The idea was a scavenger-hunt challenge in which two local radio celebrities raced each other to Chicago and back—one flying out of the regional airport and the other driving to the closest big-city airport. The result was a campaign that not only announced the airport's new direct flight but also delivered the busiest month in the airport's history. Many times an insight is a common problem or solution to a problem. Sometimes it is simply a way of looking at a situation with empathy that acknowledges how the consumer feels.

In another successful campaign for a company that sold health insurance plans to businesses, the insight was found in the fact that the target audience, human resource (HR) managers, had gone through a lot emotionally. HR managers had nothing but bad news to deliver to their employees year after year for several years. The thought of holding yet another company meeting to inform employees that premiums were going up by double digits was downright depressing. Empathy, something the large competitor insurance company lacked, was the insight. It became actionable when linked to the smaller company's more flexible plans, and account representatives who were empowered to deliver customized solutions that helped soften premium hikes. The campaign featured crying HR managers in print and HR managers singing the blues on the radio.[21]

A highly successful smoking-cessation campaign was inspired by research reported in an academic journal that linked quitting smoking with the same feeling people have in bad romantic relationships. The resulting campaign featured a woman trying to break up with a jerk boyfriend dressed as a cigarette.[22] Finding the right insight can make it easy to translate into media communication built around social interaction. Both the insurance and smoking-cessation campaigns would integrate nicely into social media content.

Actionable insights can lead to big ideas. British brand-consulting firm Millward Brown defines a **big idea** as a driving, unifying force behind brand marketing efforts.[23] How does one know when they have a big idea? In three decades of working with companies, Chris Wirthwein, CEO of 5MetaCom, has found ten qualities that differentiate big ideas from "not so big ideas." See table 5.1 for an excerpt from his *Entrepreneur* article, "What's the Big Idea?"[24]

When selecting a big idea or big insight a main consideration should be making sure it is social. Social media is about personal interaction, and placing that at the heart of a marketing or advertising campaign is an excellent jumpstart. Think about the difference between traditional ads and the successful social media campaigns. A big idea in traditional advertising is not always a big idea in social media. Standard advertising practice places a corporate logo in the bottom right of a print ad. Yet in social media, it is hard to be personal with a corporate logo. Big ideas in social media should have personal interaction built in.

In the previous smoking-cessation example it is fairly easy to see how an abusive cigarette boyfriend could play well in social media. Do not assume that this means a big idea must have a character. Without a character, social media big ideas can emphasize consumer-generated content or even employee-generated content. Imagine the "Got Milk?" campaign interacting with consumers by inviting them to share their own milk-deprivation stories. Consumers would become content generators for the effort. Zappos .com has built its brand on the insight that consumers love excellent customer service. So their big idea is having more than five hundred employees posting on social media as themselves, providing that exceptional customer-service experience.[25]

Perhaps what is needed is simply spending time watching the target audience. The academic term for this is observational ethnographic research. Informally this can be accomplished by activities such as working the lunch hour at a convenience store, observing an operation at a hospital, informally asking questions of customers in a department store,

Table 5.1. Ten Qualities That Set Big Ideas Apart

1. **Transformation:** Can it change attitudes, beliefs, and behaviors?
2. **Ownability:** How closely can it be connected to your brand only?
3. **Simplicity:** Do people get it without explanation?
4. **Originality:** Is it unique enough to grab attention?
5. **Surprise:** Will people see it as unexpected in a good way?
6. **Magnetism:** Does it have a special allure or attraction?
7. **Infectiousness:** How memorable is the idea?
8. **Contagiousness:** Will it compel people to tell others?
9. **Egocentricity:** Is it about people's self-interest?
10. **Likability:** How much will people like it? Don't underestimate this one.

Source: Chris Wirthwein, "What's the Big Idea? 10 Qualities That Set Big Ideas Apart," Entrepreneur.com, October 20, 2014, http://www.entrepreneur.com/article/238441.

or touring factories and talking to workers. Even observing personal experiences with products, friends, family, and life in general can provide valuable insight. Never underestimate the power of instinct and don't hesitate to seek out the data and research to justify a gut feeling. The subconscious mind is often right.

To jumpstart the social media conversation, the big idea needs to be based on actionable consumer insight. This will make the marketing interesting, driving key factors needed to make a social media campaign successful. When marketers know the audience well, they deliver what the audience wants. A great social media strategy can be brilliant on paper, but a flop in the social world, like a job candidate who has an exceptional resume but falls short in person.

Also, an idea is not big if it is not interesting. Ads can buy attention, but social media must earn attention. In a world where we are constantly being "distracted from distraction by distraction," interruption is becoming less and less effective. Social media big ideas must be unifying but also interesting and engaging. Social media strategy is about creating relationships with consumers, not creating ads.

Big ideas must also have legs. **Having legs** means a campaign theme can be executed in many ways, in many different media, for a long period of time.[26] Having legs also refers to ideas big enough to take advantage of current events. How fast is the idea? Timing is another key to being interesting. Standup comics know this. So did the marketers at Oreo when they took advantage of the Super Bowl blackout years ago by sending out a quick tweet: "Power Out? No problem," with an image of an Oreo cookie and the line, "You can still dunk in the dark." It was retweeted ten thousand times in one hour. The image

MINI CASE

Chipotle Scarecrow

Chipotle Mexican Grill has prevented negative social media by improving their product and then talking about issues consumers care about in entertaining ways. Chipotle has changed their product and operations to support sustainable farming, which is expressed in their Food with Integrity marketing campaign. In 2013 they created a mobile game and animated short film, "The Scarecrow," telling the story of a scarecrow's fight against corporate food production.

The film reached 6.6 million YouTube views in less than two weeks.[a] Supported by a small online and mobile ad campaign, plus PR outreach, the campaign generated more than a half-billion media impressions and the game was downloaded more than five hundred thousand times in six weeks. The free iOS game delivered a sustainability message in a fun way, but also let players earn buy-one-get-one-free deals on Chipotle menu items, which drove traffic to the store.[b]

[a] Jason Ankeny, "How These 10 Marketing Campaigns Became Viral Hits," Entrepreneur.com, April 23, 2014, http://www.entrepreneur.com/article/233207.

[b] Karlene Lukovitz, "Client of the Year: Chipotle Mexican Grill—The Content Marketing Master," MediaPost .com, January 8, 2014, http://www.mediapost.com/publications/article/216937/client-of-the-year-chipotle -mexican-grill-the-c.html.

released during the thirty-four-minute blackout was designed, captioned, and approved within minutes. What was the ROI on this tweet compared to a multimillion-dollar thirty-second Super Bowl TV spot?[27]

Theoretically Speaking: Ethnographic Observational Research

Ethnographic research has its roots in anthropology or the social sciences, but now marketing has found this method to be useful in studying the culture of consumers. **Ethnography** is investigation of a group or culture based on immersion and/or participation to gain comprehensive understanding.[28] This type of investigation is often conducted via observational research. **Observation** is a form of qualitative research that involves the systematic collection of data where researchers use all of their senses to examine people in natural settings and situations.[29] Some researchers emphasize a distinction between observation and participant observation. As early as 1958, Raymond Gold described the roles a participant observer could play.[30] The following methods of observation could prove useful in various situations:

1. Direct or participant observation via handwritten or electronic field notes.
2. Self-reports via written and photographic journals kept by study participants.
3. Secondhand reports by people directly involved in the situation being studied.
4. Electronic observation via video or audio recorder, Internet, or GPS.[31]

SOCIAL PLAN PART 5

Repair Plan and Big Idea

In this part of the social media plan, go back to the social media audit to quantify and analyze negative versus positive social media content. In addition, the tool Socialmention .com may help in quantifying overall social media sentiment toward the brand. If negative commentary is significant, specifically identify customer-service, product, operations, HR, or marketing-message problems that may be causing negative social media talk. Create an interdepartmental plan to fix the root cause of negative comments. Even if negative talk isn't significant, identify a plan to reduce the negative comments that are there. Next gather and conduct consumer research through various primary and secondary methods to discover a key actionable consumer insight that leads to a campaign big idea that is interesting and has legs. Report all research, findings, plans, and ideas in these areas:

1. Identify top brand social complaints and the root business-unit cause.
2. Devise an interdepartmental plan to fix issues and reduce negative talk.
3. Gather all research and uncover a key actionable consumer insight.
4. Create an interesting big idea that has legs across traditional and social media.

QUESTIONS FOR DISCUSSION

1. If a company is used to planning out an advertising campaign with three print ads, two radio spots, and a TV commercial six months in advance, what challenges must they overcome in implementing a successful social media campaign?
2. Is anxiety and concern about unapproved social media messages warranted? What could go wrong? Can you think of any specific examples?
3. If you are a marketer used to approving every brand message before it goes out, what best practices should be put in place to minimize concern?
4. Why is ethnographic observational research valuable? What are the potential differences in results or insight in observation versus traditional market-research surveys and focus groups?

ADDITIONAL EXERCISES

1. Do some silo smashing. Visit a customer-service department and ask what the number one complaint is and how they deal with it. Visit operations and ask questions and listen. If the brand manufactures products, go on a factory tour. Talk to the managers and the employees on the front lines. Ask questions about their goals, accomplishments, and challenges. Don't forget to visit human resources and get their perspective. Do they have an employee social media policy in place? Students can perform this exercise by contacting the company they are working on, finding secondary research, or simply thinking from each perspective.
2. Get out of advertising-campaign thinking. Look at the social media stream of a brand that is currently excelling in social media. What do you notice about their messages? Are they contrived, fine tuned, and overly clever? Or are they natural, in the moment, and more personal or human? Can you imagine your brand communicating like this? Devise a strategy that plans messages on a social media calendar, but also allows for live, unscripted interactions. What guidelines are needed to allow social media that happens in the moment?

Notes

1. "Steve Jobs Quotes," BrainyQuote.com, accessed February 17, 2015, http://www.brainy quote.com/quotes/keywords/fault.html.

2. "Facebook Graph Search Makes Old Posts and Comments Searchable," SexySocialMedia .com, accessed February 17, 2015, http://www.sexysocialmedia.com/facebook-graph-search -makes-old-posts-and-comments-searchable.

3. Sherrie Bourg, "High Octane Women," PsychologyToday.com, October 20, 2012, http:// www.psychologytoday.com/blog/high-octane-women/201210/the-emotional-contagion-scale.

4. Tanya Lewis, "Emotions Can Be Contagious on Online Social Networks," Scientific American.com, July 1, 2014, http://www.scientificamerican.com/article/facebook-emotions -are-contagious.

5. "Customer Service," Investopedia Dictionary, accessed February 17, 2015, http://www .investopedia.com/terms/c/customer-service.asp.

6. "Operations Management," Investopedia Dictionary, accessed February 17, 2015, http:// www.investopedia.com/terms/o/operations-management.asp.

7. "Famous Quotes on Advertising & Copywriting," ZagStudios.com, accessed February 17, 2015, http://www.zagstudios.com/ZagStudios/famous_quotes_on_advertising.html.

8. James Carnrite, "Strategic Business Units: Examples, Definition & Quiz," Education -Portal.com, accessed February 17, 2015, http://education-portal.com/academy/lesson/strategic -business-units-examples-definition-quiz.html#lesson.

9. Priit Kallas, "(Report) Social Media Crises on Rise: The Social Business Hierarchy of Needs," September 28, 2011, from http://www.dreamgrow.com/report-social-media-crises -on-the-social-business-hierarchy-of-needs.

10. Evan Rosen, "Smashing Silos," Businessweek.com, February 5, 2010, http://www.business week.com/managing/content/feb2010/ca2010025_358633.htm.

11. Jeff Howe, "How Hashtags and Social Media Can Bring Megacorporations to Their Knees," TheAtlantic.com, June 8, 2012, http://www.theatlantic.com/business/archive/2012/06/ the-rise-of-the-consumerate/258290.

12. Dave Evans, *Social Media Marketing an Hour a Day, 2nd Ed.* Indianapolis, IN: John Wiley & Sons (2012).

13. T. S. Eliot, "Four Quartets 1: Burnt Norton," *Poetry X*, edited by Jough Dempsey, July 13, 2003, http://poetry.poetryx.com/poems/755.

14. Todd Gitlin, "The Uses of Half-True Alarms," NewRepublic.com, June 7, 2010, http:// www.newrepublic.com/book/review/the-uses-half-true-alarms.

15. Aaron Smith, "The Best (and Worst) of Mobile Connectivity," PewInternet.org, November 30, 2012, http://pewinternet.org/Reports/2012/Best-Worst-Mobile/Key-Findings/Overview .aspx.

16. Jim Taylor, "Technology: Myth of Multitasking," PsychologyToday.com, March 30, 2011, http://www.psychologytoday.com/blog/the-power-prime/201103/technology-myth-multitasking.

17. Chang-Hoan Cho and John Hongsik Cheon, "Why Do People Avoid Advertising on the Internet?" *Journal of Advertising* 33, no. 4 (2004): 89–97.

18. "Insight," Merriam Webster.com, accessed February 17, 2015, http://www.merriam -webster.com/dictionary/insight.

19. "Actionable," Merriam-Webster.com, accessed February 17, 2015, http://www.merriam -webster.com/dictionary/actionable?show=0&t=1380381609.

20. David Ogilvy, *Ogilvy on Advertising*. New York: Random House (1983).

21. "HealthAmerica: Get Relief from the Insurance Renewal Blues," Dawhoise.com, accessed February 17, 2015, http://dawhois.com/www/healthamericachoice.com.html.

22. Kathleen Sampey, "Neiman Debuts Anti-Smoking Ads," *Adweek* 43, no. 46 (2002): 6.

23. Rob Hernandez, "Big Ideas: Research Can Make a Big Difference," MillwardBrown .com, accessed February 17, 2015, http://www.millwardbrown.com/docs/default-source/insight -documents/points-of-view/Millward_Brown_POV_Big_Ideas.pdf.

24. Chris Wirthwein, "What's the Big Idea? 10 Qualities That Set Big Ideas Apart," Entrepreneur.com, October 20, 2014, http://www.entrepreneur.com/article/238441.

25. Nicole Kelly, "What Zappos Insights Can Teach Us About Social Media Values," Social-MediaExplorer.com, November 17, 2011, http://www.socialmediaexplorer.com/social-media -marketing/what-zappos-insights-can-teach-us-about-social-media-values.

26. "Have Legs," *Cambridge Dictionaries*, accessed February 17, 2015, http://dictionary.cambridge .org/us/dictionary/british/have-legs.

27. Katherine Fung, "Oreo's Super Bowl Tweet: 'You Can Still Dunk in the Dark,'" Huffington Post.com, February 4, 2013, http://www.huffingtonpost.com/2013/02/04/oreos-super-bowl -tweet-dunk-dark_n_2615333.html.

28. "Ethnography," Writing@CSU, accessed February 17, 2015, http://writing.colostate .edu/guides/page.cfm?pageid=1345&guideid=63.

29. "Observation," Robert Wood Johnson Foundation, accessed February 17, 2015, http://www.qualres.org/HomeObse-3594.html.

30. Raymond L. Gold, "Roles in Sociological Field Observation," *Social Forces* 36 (1958): 217–213.

31. University of Kansas, "Section 3. Data Collection: Designing an Observational System," Community Tool Box, accessed February 17, 2015, http://ctb.ku.edu/en/table-of-contents/evaluate/evaluate-community-interventions/design-observational-system/main.

The Magic Number 3: Integrating Social, Marketing, and PR

> Welcome to convergence culture, where old and new media collide, where grassroots and corporate media intersect, where the power of the media producer and the power of the media consumer interact in unpredictable ways.[1]
>
> —Henry Jenkins

PREVIEW

What happened to the "information superhighway"? First appearing in 1983, the phrase **information superhighway** describes a telecommunications infrastructure used for widespread, rapid access to information.[2] It was a way for people to talk about the possibilities of new connections brought about with the development of the Internet. In the mid-1990s enthusiasm for the Internet as an amazing source of knowledge exploded as the term "information superhighway" appeared in more than 4,500 major newspapers around the world. Yet a year later the term died down to half that number and by 1999 the news media played down information-superhighway imagery to fewer than nine hundred mentions. Instead the term "e-commerce" rose in popularity as people began to talk more about the possibilities of electronic commerce. By 1999 major newspapers mentioned the term "e-commerce" more than 20,641 times.[3]

    E-commerce describes activities related to the buying and selling of goods and services over the Internet.[4] Why did the conversation shift so dramatically from information superhighway to e-commerce? People realized they could make money on the superhighway and then the

71

emphasis became more on commerce than knowledge. Information was still shared, but the emphasis began to focus on building business in the new connected electronic marketplace. Today society may be turning back to the original vision as marketers must now share valuable knowledge in social media to gain an audience to maintain and grow commerce.

The Real Convergence

Academic researchers and industry practitioners have predicted convergence of media and technology for a long time, yet as Henry Jenkins, renowned media scholar points out, the actual convergence has happened in unpredictable ways. Within the concept of convergence there are two types or possibilities. One is convergence by the concentration of media. The other is convergence through the advance of technology. At first it was predicted that all devices would converge into one central machine that did everything for consumers.

What scholars are actually noticing is that the technological hardware is diverging and it is the content that is converging.[5] The main vehicle for that converging content is the Internet. Thus a new term has emerged called **IP convergence,** which means using the Internet Protocol (IP) as the standard transport for transmitting all information such as video, data, music, and TV teleconferencing.[6]

What are some examples of converging content? Newspapers and magazines have struggled in the transition to a more digital economy and many have gone out of business. The newspapers and magazines still in business are printing, but now they are also online and have added video and blogs and Twitter content to their stories. In addition, newspapers and magazines are creating mobile-optimized websites and developing apps for tablets and smartphones. Some newspapers like the *New York Times* or the *Wall Street Journal* have ventured into audio and video podcasts.

Television shows are now multimedia spectacles as they scroll tweets across live programming and create rich interactive websites that encourage the use of multiple media to enhance the content of the program. News, TV shows, music, and movies stream via the Internet and many customers are switching their phone service to the Internet. Many people's phones are actually used more for texting, social media, Internet access, video, radio, search, and apps than calling.

These trends have great implications for marketers and advertisers. Organizations can no longer buy the attention of mass audiences as they could via traditional advertising. Instead, successful marketers are investing in multiple media buys filled with "converged content." As discussed in chapter 3, integrated marketing communication has developed into a primary strategy for marketers. This holistic approach leverages consistency of message and emphasizes complementary use of online and offline media for greater impact. Now it is evolving further to include the consumer conversation generated in social media.

As early as 2005, the *Wall Street Journal* reported that integrated marketing was the focus of most job searches for advertising agency executives.[7] Integration has been an important topic for marketers and advertisers who need to adjust strategies to fit with the new reality of converged media. When putting together a social media plan, marketers must not ignore the other communication activities in the organization. Whether social media is the lead or will support more traditional efforts, it must be completely integrated.

Traditional efforts have not gone away, but they must be supplemented with cross-discipline efforts.

Today fewer people are talking about the coming media convergence because it is already here. Instead all communications professionals are focusing on **converged media,** which is the combining or blurring of paid (advertising), owned (brand sites and accounts), and earned media (social and PR). Altimeter Group released a report in 2012 laying out a converged media strategy that uses all these channels through a consistent storyline, look, and feel. In order to accomplish this strategy, Altimeter emphasizes that execution requires silo smashing for cross–channel integration.[8] The consumer does not see a difference in disciplines and is simply interacting in the new reality of media. Thus, social media integration is an essential strategy as people consume more and more converged media.

 The Attention Economy

The Internet started with the promise of an information superhighway delivering all the wisdom of the world. Yet within a decade the discussion quickly shifted to the promise of sales through e-commerce. Nearly fifteen years later, an ever-increasing number of technology companies are now battling for consumer attention. Once they get attention and build an audience, they resell that attention back to marketers. In "The Distraction Economy: How Technology Downgraded Attention," Tomas Chamorro-Premuzic of *The Guardian* points out that when information has no limits, attention becomes rare and precious.[a] What is rare and precious becomes very valuable to those who obtain it.

As early as 1997 Michael H. Goldhaber wrote of this in *WIRED* magazine. He proposed that we are not living in an information economy. On the contrary, he argues that the purpose of economics is to study how society uses scarce resources, and today information is not the resource that is scarce. Information is overflowing and available everywhere. Because of this, attention has become the scarce and desirable resource and thus society is now living in an attention economy.[b]

In relation to marketing, **attention economics** deals with the problem of getting consumers to consume advertising. Since the cost to transmit advertising to consumers is now sufficiently low, more ads can be delivered to a consumer than the consumer can pay attention to and process. Thus, the consumer's attention becomes the scarce resource to be allocated.[c] As the entire economy shifts more toward attention, marketing and advertising should grow in importance and play more of a central role in business.

[a] Thomas Chamorro-Premuzic, "The Distraction Economy: How Technology Downgraded Attention," TheGuardian.com, December 15, 2014, http://www.theguardian.com/media-network/media-network-blog/2014/dec/15/distraction-economy-technology-downgraded-attention-facebook-tinder.

[b] Michael H. Goldhaber, "Attention Shoppers!" Wired.com, December 1997, http://archive.wired.com/wired/archive/5.12/es_attention.html.

[c] "Attention Economics," Wikipedia, accessed February 17, 2015, http://en.wikipedia.org/wiki/Attention_economy.

Barbara Rentschler, CMO and senior vice president of global marketing for K'NEX Brands, agrees with a social integration strategy. Rentschler says, "Social media is another tool in the marketing toolbox. We seldom use a single tool when reaching out to our fans and look for ways to combine traditional and digital tools to super charge our communication efforts."[9] Converged media demands converged strategy.

K'NEX knows traditional marketing must be maintained to compete and drive sales in the toy industry, but they also know the value of leveraging social media. For example, K'NEX sent a personal thank-you and free product to an influential blogger who used the product name in a blog post. The gift in return spawned a full post on the brand garnering further positive brand attention and awareness (see figure 6.1).[10]

However, knowing that integration among communication channels is important is simply the beginning. Making it happen is something completely different. To get there, marketers and advertisers should comprehend the full context of why integration has not been an easy process. To understand this further, take a step back and look at the background and context of the silos that make up the traditional communications disciplines. Integrating these specific areas of advertising, public relations, and interactive and social media represents both challenges and opportunities.

Figure 6.1. K'NEX sends thank-you to blogger.

Source: Trevor George, "K'NEX Lets Us Know 'We Are Being Heard,'" BlueWheelMedia.com (blog), January 25, 2012, http://bluewheelmedia.com/knex-lets-us-know-we-are-being-heard-2/. © K'NEX Brands, LLC

Think Like an Expert in All Fields

Traditionally, marketers have hired advertising agencies to plan and promote marketing communication. Inside the agencies, the advertising copywriter and art director came up with the "big idea" for an advertising campaign. **Copywriters** are simply the writers of advertising or publicity copy[11] and **art directors** are the professionals who execute or coordinate the type, photos, and illustrations used in advertising design.[12] Both copywriters and art directors are usually employed at advertising agencies and are often called the creative team.

After the creative team came up with the core campaign concept, then public relations and interactive professionals were brought in to help execute that main strategic concept. These are two important viewpoints that were not represented in the creation of the core driving idea of the campaign. PR and interactive were left to retrofit their plans to something already created. The copywriter and art director may have considered PR and interactive, but their focus was on more traditional, high-profile advertising vehicles like TV and print. Right or wrong, this is how it worked in both large international advertising firms and small regional creative boutiques.

In the best cases, public relations and interactive are in separate departments inside the same firm. But many times, advertising, public relations, and interactive or digital are completely separate companies in different cities hired by the marketing client. Perhaps this makes sense in terms of hiring the best in each field, but it certainly is not the best way to achieve integration. What further complicates integration today is that many social media departments are now found in-house with the marketing client. Again, this structure makes sense for those organizations, but represents a further segmenting and separation of discipline experts. Integration is much more effective when the process goes beyond the copywriter and art director. In the best cases, real integration happens when an expanded cross-disciplinary team works together on the big idea from the beginning, and in the same room, if possible (see figure 6.2).

One example goes back to the regional airport example mentioned in chapter 5. Not only did the big idea come from observational research, but a multi-disciplinary team helped create it. An expanded team strategy was used to create the truly integrated effort. The copywriter, art director, public relations specialists, interactive planner, and social media expert drove to the airport and met in the terminal together to come up with a "bigger" big idea. The idea was big because it was based on key consumer insights gained through observation. The idea was "bigger" because it truly drew from all disciplines, leveraging the strengths of each equally for a greater combined execution.[13]

Marketers and communications firms should strive to work in this type of expanded team whenever possible. If a marketer is creating a campaign by him- or herself, as within a small business or startup, or as a student, then it is possible to combine these skills individually. Study discipline-specific best practices and learn to think like an expert from each field. When brainstorming an idea, bring each discipline's perspective to bear in the formation of the integrated communications strategy.

One of the early advertising agencies to understand the concept of integrated disciplines was Crispin Porter + Bogusky. At an *Adweek* Creativity Conference, agency principal Alex Bogusky said his agency always strived for "PR-able advertising." The public

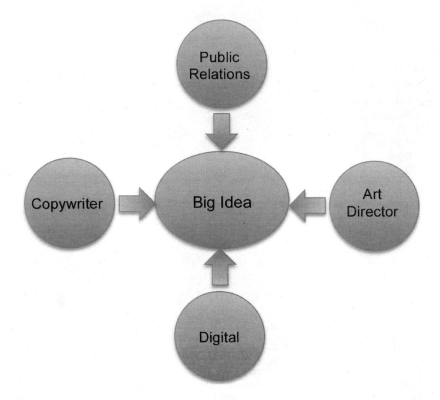

Figure 6.2. Brainstorm big ideas in multi-disciplinary teams.

relations aspect meant more than traditional press releases and events. Crispin Porter + Bogusky saw the power of the Internet and viral marketing before social media was big. In 2010, they were one of the first traditional advertising agencies to be named interactive agency of the year at the Cannes Lions Advertising Festival.[14] The amazing part is that their early viral success with Subservient Chicken for Burger King happened before and without the power of social media.

In thinking about PR-able advertising that comprises advertising, public relations, digital marketing, and social media, marketers and advertisers may find it useful to visualize social media as the glue that holds the other disciplines together. That is a good start, but in reality, social media represents much more. True integration is about having public relations, advertising, and social media "baked" into the big idea from the beginning.[15] It is about not forgetting the other communication touch points. That is why social media strategies should never be planned in isolation. The base strategic approach should work in interactive (social media), in earned media (public relations), and in paid media (advertising).

When forming a big idea, start by looking for consumer insights that are actionable across all three communication disciplines. Marketers and advertisers must ask themselves, "What is the big campaign concept that will lead to motivating and inspirational advertising, newsworthy public relations, and engaging social media?" Ideally the insight will lend itself to powerful advertising, be unique enough to be picked up by the press, and

MINI CASE

Burger King Subservient Chicken

In April 2004 a chicken dressed in garters emerged on the Internet responding to any command viewers typed. Subservient Chicken was the creation of Crispin Porter + Bogusky for marketing client Burger King. The viral campaign played off Burger King's "Have it your way" slogan and was created to help build awareness for the new TenderCrisp Chicken Sandwich. The agency and client decided to go with the more opt-in media of the Web versus traditional TV advertising, and agency employees first seeded the URL in a couple of chat rooms.

Within a year the microsite drew nearly 400 million hits, with visitors spending an average of six to seven minutes with the brand. This and the earned media coverage on major news outlets turned Subservient Chicken into a cultural icon. Further, sales of the sandwich increased 9 percent a week, with double-digit awareness, and total Burger King sales shot up 14 percent for the year after the campaign.[a] Bear in mind that the campaign managed to achieve these results before social media: Facebook was still limited to college students and Twitter wouldn't be created for another two years.[b]

---

[a] Mae Anderson, "Dissecting 'Subservient Chicken,'" Adweek.com, March 7, 2005, http://www.adweek.com/news/advertising/dissecting-subservient-chicken-78190f.

[b] Alex Alvarez, "Case Study: The Subservient Chicken," CMPMiami.com, August 31, 2012, http://www.cmpmiami.com/case-study-the-subservient-chicken.

---

interesting enough to engage the target audience in social media. Also in thinking about public relations specifically, try to come up with an idea that goes beyond a single launch event. Look for an idea that can be sustained and will garner attention over a longer period of time.

Three is the magic number when these disciplines work together. The magic comes from the increased attention and engagement that it can deliver. Marketing is now a two-way street, so a truly big idea should be big enough not only to integrate media, but also to engage people to talk and spread the message. Marketers must join conversations consumers are already having, or get consumers to start brand conversations. Maintaining separate specializations and training is still valuable. Marketers need to have experts in all fields, but bring them together at the idea level.

The *International Journal of Integrated Marketing Communications* research study highlighted in chapter 3 demonstrated the importance of integration. In 421 Effie Award–winning marketing campaigns studied, it was proven that an increase in the number of marketing communication touch points was needed over time to achieve award-winning results. The level of integration increased from an average of two marketing consumer touch points in 1998 to an average of six in 2010 in campaigns awarded for meeting business objectives.[16]

Part III of this book will now move into detail about selecting specific social media channels that fit the target audience and organization message, and that best execute a big idea. Before moving on to execution, make sure a big idea is integrated and sustainable for the long term. As a marketer or advertiser moves forward in the strategic process and focuses more directly on social media, it is important not to forget the traditional aspects of a marketing campaign. Including traditional marketing communications channels and campaigns will expand and leverage social media activity to achieve that magic integration. Many new social media efforts need traditional marketing and advertising to build awareness and jumpstart participation. Once the big idea has been developed, move on to the next chapter to explore the best social media ways and places to bring that idea to life for the target audience.

Theoretically Speaking: Corporate and Marketing Communication, PR, and Advertising

These concepts are all interrelated yet sometimes can be confused in practice. **Corporate communication** involves managing internal and external communications aimed at corporate stakeholders.[17] **Marketing communication** coordinates promotional messages delivered through channels like print, radio, television, and personal selling.[18] **Public relations** creates and maintains the goodwill of the public, such as customers, employees, and investors, through non-paid forms of media.[19] **Advertising** produces information for promoting the sale of commercial products or services.[20] **Integrated marketing communication** is the coordination of promotional methods to meet marketing objectives.[21] Think of corporate communication as focusing on the enterprise in dealing with issue management, mergers, and litigation. Marketing communications deals with the products and services and with creating demand or positioning. From crisis management to media outreach, PR can help meet both corporate and marketing goals. Advertising can be used for marketing and corporate communications when it is targeted to consumers and corporate stakeholders.

The BP oil spill in the Gulf of Mexico provides an example of how all these disciplines can work together. Following the spill, corporate communication was used for crisis management through both PR and corporate TV advertising to inform stakeholders and consumers what BP was doing to clean up. The BP TV ad was also aimed at BP employees; **internal marketing** promotes the firm and its policies to employees as if they are customers of the firm.[22] Integrated marketing communication's traditional definition limits the practice to synergistic efforts to meet marketing objectives, but as seen with the BP example, it is possible to create a larger integrated plan that uses advertising, PR, and internal efforts to meet both corporate and marketing communication objectives.[23]

There is another important reason to consider integration with traditional marketing methods—the amount of social media content is growing. Every minute it is estimated that there are 100,000 new tweets, 40,000 Facebook updates, 40,000 Instagram photos, and 30 hours of YouTube videos added to the Internet.[24] That is new content every minute of every day with much of it coming from marketers. In a recent Content Marketing Institute survey, 69 percent of marketers say they are creating more content than they did the previous year, and 59 percent expect their content marketing budget to increase the next year.[25]

With each social network becoming more flooded with content, reach is dropping. By 2014 Facebook reported that the average person saw more than 1,500 stories in their news feed whenever they logged in to their account. This was too many to possibly read. Facebook responded by adjusting their algorithm to show only about 300 stories.[26] This resulted in a drop of average organic reach to 3 percent for many business pages.[27] Many marketers and advertisers have shifted from a focus on reach to engagement. Social media may become more important for engaging current and prospective customers than for generating awareness, for which traditional advertising and public relations in mass media are still effective tools. As the social media landscape becomes more crowded, marketers should not abandon traditional marketing communication methods. One effort is not enough. Social media is more effective when you add advertising paid media and PR earned media to help meet goals.[28]

 SOCIAL PLAN PART 6

Integrate Traditional Marketing with Social Strategy

In this part of the social media plan, focus on integration of traditional marketing, advertising, PR, and digital marketing efforts with the new social media strategy. Collect and analyze information on all marketing efforts for the brand. What techniques are being used? What is the core message or promotion? Is there a common character, theme, or concept? Is there a brand or campaign tagline? Make note of current efforts and include what is being formed in the new social media plan, accounting for and explaining how current traditional efforts will be integrated into the new social effort. You may find that a new traditional marketing, advertising, and PR effort or campaign is needed, and thus your plan should make those recommendations. Report all findings and ideas in these areas:

1. Identify all traditional brand marketing, PR, advertising, and digital efforts.
2. Explain the current promotion, concept, character, theme, and tagline.
3. List ways in which the current effort could be integrated with the new social media big idea.
4. If a new traditional marketing or advertising campaign and promotion are needed, explain what they should be.

QUESTIONS FOR DISCUSSION

1. With the increased importance of integration, should marketers continue to hire separate PR, advertising, and digital firms? Or should every activity be brought in-house with the company? What are the advantages and disadvantages of each method?
2. Go back and look at the definitions and descriptions of integrated marketing communications and converged media strategy. What is the difference between these two models of thought? Which could be more effective and why?

3. Look more closely at the disciplines of PR and advertising. What do the practices have in common? What is substantially different? What are ways PR and advertising could work more closely together?
4. Why do you think Subservient Chicken was so successful? If Burger King launched the same campaign today, would it have the same results? How would social media play into the new launch effort?

ADDITIONAL EXERCISES

1. Find evidence of the attention economy and answer the following questions. Explain which businesses are succeeding and why. Which tech companies are succeeding at gaining attention and what methods are they using? How are companies that produce physical products competing in the attention economy? What best practices from marketing communications and advertising are organizations adapting into their business practices? Must every company now be interesting, or can attention still be bought?
2. Visit the American Association of Advertising Agencies website (www.aaaa.org). Look at the blogs and resources and note their emphasis and perspective. What is the purpose of advertising and what tools do ad professionals have at their disposal? Now visit the Public Relations Society of America's website (www.prsa.org). Do the same, by visiting their resources, research, and articles. What are the goals of PR and how do they achieve them? Finally, visit the Word of Mouth Marketing Association website (www.womma.org). Explore what they are talking about and are concerned with, and how they leverage social media to obtain their goals. Keep these professional perspectives in mind as you integrate and leverage each in the social media plan.

Notes

1. Henry Jenkins, *Convergence Culture: Where Old and New Media Collide.* New York: University Press (2006).
2. "Information Superhighway," Merriam-Webster.com, accessed February 17, 2015, http://www.merriam-webster.com/dictionary/information%20superhighway.
3. Norman Solomon, "SOLOMON: What Happened to the 'Information Superhighway'?" Alternet.org, April 25, 2000, http://www.alternet.org/story/587/solomon%3A_what_happened_to_the_%22information_superhighway%22.
4. "E-Commerce," Merriam-Webster.com, accessed February 17, 2015, http://www.merriam-webster.com/dictionary/e-commerce.
5. Cheskin Research, "Designing Digital Experiences for Youth," *Market Insights Series*, Fall 2002: 8–9.
6. "IP Convergence," *PC Magazine,* accessed February 17, 2015, http://www.pcmag.com/encyclopedia/term/57267/ip-convergence.
7. "Ad Agencies' Most Wanted: Integrated-Marketing Pros," *Wall Street Journal Online,* January 22, 2008, http://online.wsj.com/article/C50330NEEDLEMAN.html.
8. Jeremiah Owyang, "Altimeter Report: Paid + Owned + Earned = Converged Media," Web-Strategist.com, July 19, 2012, http://www.web-strategist.com/blog/2012/07/19/altimeter-report-paid-owned-earned-converged-media.

9. Rake Narang, "Barb Rentschler: Combine Traditional and Digital Tools to Super Charge Your Communication Efforts," PRWordAwards.com, accessed February 17, 2015, http://www.prworldawards.com/people/Barb-Rentschler.html#.UknSdSTFYnU.

10. Trevor George, "K'NEX Lets Us Know 'We Are Being Heard,'" BlueWheelMedia.com (blog), January 25, 2012, http://bluewheelmedia.com/knex-lets-us-know-we-are-being-heard-2.

11. "Copywriter," Merriam-Webster.com, accessed February 17, 2015, http://www.merriam-webster.com/dictionary/copywriter.

12. "Art Director," Merriam-Webster.com, accessed February 17, 2015, http://www.merriam-webster.com/dictionary/art%20director.

13. Keith Quesenberry, "Three Is the Magic Number," PostControlMarketing.com (blog), March 18, 2011, http://www.postcontrolmarketing.com/?p=236.

14. "Crispin Porter + Bogusky Awarded Interactive Agency of the Year at the Cannes Lions International Advertising Festival," PRNewswire.com, accessed February 17, 2015, http://www.prnewswire.com/news-releases/crispin-porter—bogusky-awarded-interactive-agency-of-the-year-at-the-cannes-lions-international-advertising-festival-97067799.html.

15. Alex M. Bogusky and John Winsor, *Baked-in: Creating Products and Businesses That Market Themselves.* Chicago: B2 Books (2009).

16. Keith A. Quesenberry, Michael K. Coolsen, and Kristen Wilkerson, "IMC in the Effies: Use of Integrated Marketing Communications Touchpoints Among Effie Award Winners," *International Journal of Integrated Marketing Communication* 4, no. 2 (2012): 60–72.

17. Cees Van Riel and Charles Fombrun, *Essentials of Corporate Communication: Implementing Practices for Effective Reputation Management.* New York: Routledge (2007).

18. "Marketing Communication," BusinessDictionary.com, accessed February 17, 2015, http://www.businessdictionary.com/definition/marketing-communications.html.

19. "Public Relations," BusinessDictionary.com, accessed February 17, 2015, http://www.businessdictionary.com/definition/public-relations.html.

20. "Advertising," BusinessDictionary.com, accessed February 17, 2015, http://www.businessdictionary.com/definition/advertising.html.

21. "Integrated Marketing Communications," BusinessDictionary.com, accessed February 17, 2015, http://www.businessdictionary.com/definition/integrated-marketing-communications-IMC.html.

22. "Internal Marketing," BusinessDictionary.com, accessed February 17, 2015, http://www.businessdictionary.com/definition/internal-marketing.html.

23. Keith A. Quesenberry, "Corporate Communications, Marketing, IMC, PR and Advertising, What's the Difference?" PostControlMarketing.com (blog), March 21, 2011, http://www.postcontrolmarketing.com/?p=243.

24. "What Happens in an Internet Minute?" DailyInfoGraphic.com, December 2013, http://www.dailyinfographic.com/wp-content/uploads/2013/12/Internet-minute.jpg.

25. Joe Pulizzi, October 15, 2014, "New Content Marketing Research: Challenged With Measurement," ContentMarketingInstitute.com, http://contentmarketinginstitute.com/2014/10/2015-b2c-consumer-content-marketing/

26. Brian Boland, "Organic Reach On Facebook: Your Questions Answered," Facebook.com (blog), June 5, 2014, https://www.facebook.com/business/news/Organic-Reach-on-Facebook.

27. Jamie Robinson, "Measuring Facebook Engagement," Wearesocial.com (blog), July 10, 2014, http://wearesocial.net/blog/2014/07/measuring-facebook-engagement.

28. Keith Quesenberry, "Can You Win the Content Marketing Arms Race?" SocialMediaToday (blog), May 1, 2015, http://www.socialmediatoday.com/social-business/2015-05-01/can-you-win-content-marketing-arms-race.

PART

III

Choose Social Options for Target, Message, and Idea

Social Networks, Blogs, and Forums

My best stories come from well-placed sources who point me in the right direction.[1]

—Wolf Blitzer

PREVIEW

Before Facebook there was a pioneering social networking site called Friendster. Launched in 2002, Friendster reached more than 3 million users within months and was considered the top social networking site, eventually reaching 115 million users.[2] Friendster's peak was around 2003–2004 when Google wanted to buy it for $30 million, but the site lost ground as Facebook grew. Friendster lost so much ground to Facebook that it relaunched as a gaming site in 2011 and discontinued its social network accounts. Peter Pachal of *PC Magazine* says the main reason Friendster failed was its lack of a news feed—the network never went much beyond user profiles.[3]

Ten years after Facebook, Friendster's founder Jonathan Abrams told his side of the story in a *Mashable* article. Abrams explained that early on there were a lot of copycat social networks spamming Friendster and poaching users. The site had plans for adding many of the features that made Facebook and MySpace popular, including Friendster College, a news feed, and music sharing, yet they faced numerous technology issues and the network lost a great number of users over stability problems. Now the Friendster founder is busy with Nuzzel, which he launched as a social news aggregator in 2012.[4] As this anecdote points out, social networks can come and go. That is why we will focus on social media categories and characteristics while exploring the main social media channels of today.

Choosing Social Options

Part III of this book will cover key characteristics of the main types or categories of social media channels and the major players in each space. Each section describes the general size of the channel, who is talking in that space, and what type of information they are sharing. This part of the book will also look at global and mobile use of each social channel plus possible key performance indicators (KPIs).

Entire books have been written on each of these social channels. The purpose here is not to explain all the details about the specific channel, such as how to set up a Facebook business page. A quick Google search should reveal plenty of guides. Instead, this section is designed to provide the information necessary to choose the best social channels for a specific social media strategy. Choosing channels based on these key characteristics represents a systematic strategic process that can be applied to any current social network or new one that emerges. In case today's Facebook becomes yesterday's Friendster, you will still have a solid social strategy that works.

Now that the business objectives, target audience, key consumer insight, and big idea are in place, it is time to select the optimal social channels to implement the social strategy and decide how to execute it. Like Wolf Blitzer putting together a news story, marketers and advertisers should look for the best place and way to tell a story. Think of each social channel as a well-placed source to launch a social media campaign in the right direction.

What follows are descriptions of the central characteristics of key social channels (size, content, and users) in several categories. To gain a full appreciation of each, join the channel as a user and become a firsthand witness to the unique social experience delivered by each option. With monthly global social-network use surpassing two billion, there is no denying that social networks will only increase in importance to marketing.[5]

In reading through each category and channel, marketers should keep the objectives, target audience, and key insight with big idea in the front of their minds. Look for the ideal vehicles to deliver brand messages and engage the target audience. "Try on" each social outlet, imagining the kind of content the social strategy idea could create from the organization, its employees, and consumers.

What would the motivation be for consumers to create and share the content? Look for ideal channels to deliver the right message to the right people. This method will keep social efforts strategically focused and prevent wasted effort chasing every new social channel that makes headlines. This strategic approach provides a framework to avoid wasted effort, but also to add new channels that make sense for the content and consumer as they emerge. If any of these social channels sound as if they may be a good fit for your strategy, I encourage you to search online for further details and the latest stats and channel-specific best practices.

This book is focused on social media marketing, which is about attracting an audience by creating valuable content and encourage sharing via social media. Social media marketing is earned media, in that it doesn't cost the marketer money for the space or time. However, as social media channels have grown more crowded and have gone public, many have started selling native ads. **Native advertising** is paid marketing that delivers useful, targeted content along with and in a form that looks like the social media site's or app's non-ad content. Native ads can take the form of promoted listings in Twitter, sponsored updates on LinkedIn, or promoted Facebook posts or articles on Buzzfeed. When considering social media channels in the chapters that follow, consider adding native advertising to the channels that offer it. It may be a good way to reach a targeted audience, to jumpstart a new effort, or to boost specific promotions.[6]

Social Networks

Of all the types of social media, social networks seem to have drawn the most hype, and for good reason. Social channels such as Facebook and LinkedIn are big. Facebook may be known as "The Social Network" because of the famous movie about its founding, but it is not the only social network. A **social network** is any website where one connects with those sharing personal or professional interests.[7]

Social networks usually allow people to set up a profile and offer various ways to join groups and interact with other users through updates or posts. This is a good start for a definition, but today mobile access plays an ever-increasing role in social-network activity. Networks, which started on websites, are accessed more and more via mobile devices in optimized websites and apps on smartphones and tablets. In fact, Facebook has made a concerted effort to reinvent itself as a mobile-first company and it worked. For example, Facebook reported a 51 percent increase in monthly active mobile users from 2012 to 2013 alone.[8]

Facebook

Founded in 2004, **Facebook** is an online social networking service where users create profiles, connect to other users as "friends," and exchange messages, photos, and videos. Facebook made big news when it surpassed one billion monthly users and is soon predicted to surpass 1.5 billion. For marketers, that number is hard to ignore. The majority of those users are global, with United States users comprising slightly less than 20 percent of that one billion.[9] If a marketer's business objectives are focused on the US, much of that audience will not apply, yet it's still slightly more than half of the total US population of 314 million.

Facebook started as a social network for college students, but now its demographic makeup is much more broad. Roughly 71 percent of adult Internet users in the US are on Facebook.[10] The social network is made up mostly of thirty- to forty-nine-year-olds (36 percent), followed by eighteen- to twenty-nine-year-olds (27 percent), fifty to sixty-four-year-olds (25 percent) and a growing group of users aged sixty-five and older (12 percent). The social network maintains its college roots. Two-thirds of Facebook users (66 percent) have at least some college education and 37 percent of Facebook users have a college degree.

Facebook users are diverse when it comes to income with just over a third (35 percent) making more than $75,000 a year and just under a third (30 percent) making less than $30,000 a year with the rest (35 percent) falling in between, earning $30,000 to $74,900. It is important to note that there is also strong Facebook use by a younger school-age population from thirteen to eighteen years old. Facebook users also tend to be more suburban and urban than rural. In general, Facebook is most appealing to young to early middle-age women.[11]

Every person on Facebook has a profile page and a home page. The profile page is built on the Timeline design, in which users' most recent activity is shown first and users can scroll down—and back in time—to birth. The home page is where they view the activity of friends or pages they have liked via the news feed of recently posted updates.

Facebook also allows users to create and join groups of common interests where photos and videos can be shared and discussions can take place. Pages or fan pages are where businesses and other entities exist on Facebook. Profiles are reserved for individual people. When an organization posts content on its fan page, it shows up in the news feeds of people who have liked it. It also shows up in a friend's news feed if someone liked the content.

It is important to note that not all friends or fans see all updates. This is called organic reach. **Organic reach** is the number of unique individuals who see a post from your social media page or account through unpaid distribution. Organic reach is expressed in terms of a percentage of fans or followers who see a person's or organization's published content. The percent of updates that are seen varies, but it has been declining as Facebook becomes more crowded and adjusts its news feed algorithm.[12]

Facebook has mobile apps, including iOS (iPhone) and Android, and includes a mobile-optimized website. In 2012 they officially declared themselves a mobile company when for the first time the number of daily active mobile users surpassed the number of users checking Facebook from a computer.[13] A survey has also reported that Facebook is the second-most-used smartphone app behind Google Maps.[14]

Marketing strategies for Facebook should include sharing information that fans of the brand would find interesting, entertaining, and sharable. Early strategies should focus on building fans/likes to increase the audience exposure for later efforts. Many brands have done this by running contests and special promotions where consumers must like the brand page to enter the contest. Facebook apps exist that can make contest entry through the social network easy.

Many have found that updates with photos and video garner the most views and engagement. Other strategies include encouraging customers to upload content, such as photos of themselves using the product, and awarding prizes by voting on the best submission. The Alouette Cheese Facebook page encourages fans to upload food they have created with the brand's products (see figure 7.1).[15] Hashtags can be used on Facebook, but are more central to channels such as Twitter and Instagram. Straightforward promotions and product news can be shared on Facebook, but don't get too promotional. Remember, this is a social medium.

Marketers may feel good boasting about the number of likes their organization has on Facebook, but it also represents a real metric of how many potential eyeballs content is reaching with every update. This exposure can multiply quickly, considering the average

Figure 7.1. Strive for a balance of brand promotion and fan content.

Source: Alouette Cheese Facebook page, accessed January 18, 2015, https://www.facebook.com/AlouetteCheese. © 2015 Alouette Cheese USA LLC.

Facebook user has 224 friends.[16] However, updates in Facebook's news feed algorithm has produced a drop in organic reach and the network now sells sponsored posts to make up for the drop.[17] Marketers should consider native ads or paying to boost posts and/or promote pages to gain more reach. The Facebook Ads Manager or Power Editor enables some specific audience-targeting features to optimize your buy. Another option to boost reach is by Facebook tagging. Encourage fans to tag your page in their posts, or a brand can tag other company or organization pages and people. Depending on the match of audiences, this could extend reach to another page's or person's followers.

Facebook Insights provides a wide array of measurement options, but possible key performance indicators (KPIs) to focus on could include number of fans, page likes, status likes, posts, shares, tags, and comments, and don't forget to indicate sentiment when appropriate.

LinkedIn

Launched in 2003, **LinkedIn** is a business-focused social networking service that allows users to create professional profiles of work experience and form connections with other professionals. LinkedIn can be thought of as the professional side of social networking. It has surpassed 300 million users, and like Facebook, more than half of those users are outside the US.[18] Yet over a quarter of the US population is on LinkedIn. LinkedIn promotes itself as the world's largest professional network, and that focus shows up in the type of people it attracts.

Twenty-eight percent of US adult Internet users are on LinkedIn.[19] Users of this professional network are nearly evenly split between men (53 percent) and women (47 percent). People in their prime working years of thirty to sixty-four are key users of the site (72 percent). A sizable group of LinkedIn's users are mid- to high income with

49 percent making more than $75,000 a year and 42 percent earning $30,000 to $74,999 a year.

Not surprisingly, LinkedIn users are also highly educated, with 91 percent having some college education or a degree. More than 68 percent of LinkedIn users have a college degree or higher. It seems LinkedIn attracts its main users during or right after college graduation, and is used by both men and women who are starting or are in the midst of their professional careers.[20]

LinkedIn has always been a business-oriented social-networking site, and that remains the focus of its users' activities. Like other social networks, LinkedIn is built around profile pages, but here users list information such as job experience, education, and professional skills—the kind of information listed on a resume. Instead of "friends," this community focuses on building a professional network through "connections." The emphasis here is on coworkers, bosses, former bosses, clients, and other professional contacts people have made over the years.

LinkedIn also offers groups where professionals in the same field or with the same interests can share content, ask questions, or post and search for industry jobs. Job search is a major activity on the site, which has become a valuable tool for job searchers and recruiters alike. Users are able to apply for positions through LinkedIn, and recommendations attached to users' profiles function much like letters of recommendation.

Similar to Facebook fan pages, LinkedIn offers organizations the option to create a company page that can function like a corporate website with social-interaction features. Fresh content is delivered via status updates that appear under the activity feed of user's profiles or as discussion posts in groups. Like the rest of the site, the content shared favors industry or professional topics.[21] LinkedIn Pulse is a new publishing platform with basic blogging capabilities available via posts. Now users can publish their own content for further connection and reach in addition to regular updates.[22] Pulse is helping to turn LinkedIn into a news discovery engine and has the potential to increase social engagement (see figure 7.2).[23]

Like Facebook, LinkedIn has seen a dramatic increase in mobile use with 27 percent of visits happening via mobile devices. The company reports that 30 percent of members view jobs on the network from mobile devices. The latest version of the iOS and Android apps allows users to submit job applications via mobile devices. Much of the current job-search activity may move to LinkedIn, considering a mobile application process can take less than a minute with no need to attach a resume file. LinkedIn has also created a new CheckIn mobile app specifically to help recruiters keep track of job-candidate information during events and conventions.[24]

Because of LinkedIn's professional focus, it can be especially beneficial for business-to-business efforts, helping salespeople find leads and sell trade-oriented products. Recruitment advertisers and marketers with an emphasis on personal sales should also consider this an invaluable social media tool for their efforts. To grow connections or followers, publish quality content in bloglike posts. Also consider the native advertising option of purchasing audience reach with targeted sponsored updates in the LinkedIn feed. A business professional or salesperson might track key performance indicators (KPIs) such as connections, followers, groups, updates, posts, searches, and views.

Figure 7.2. LinkedIn Pulse offers new publisher tools.

Source: Keith A. Quesenberry, "How Social Media Can Hurt or Help Your Career," LinkedIn.com, November 29, 2014, https://www.linkedin.com/pulse/20141129153637-9796156-how-social-media-can-hurt-or-help-your -career?trk=mp-reader-card.

Google+

Founded in 2011, **Google+** is a social networking and identity service that adds a social layer to other Google properties and also serves to link web content directly with its author. Google+ is a latecomer to the social- networking space, considering that both Facebook and LinkedIn are now more than ten years old. This is Google's latest venture into social network- ing following other attempts. Google grew this social network quickly, with 540 million monthly active users, but critics claim that only half of those users actually visit the social network because most users starting a Gmail account were signed up for Google+ automatically.[25] Like the first two social network sites, most of the users (between 75 and 85 percent) are based outside of the US.[26]

For now, users on Google+ are not very active with slightly less than a quarter (22 percent) visiting the network monthly.[27] The data available on the network does show some insights into Google+. Users of this social network are mostly male (73 percent) and skew relatively young with an average age of twenty-eight years old. Google+ users are more technical and more likely to be in fields such as engineering and web development.[28] Users are also wealthy, with nearly a third of Google+ users having a household income of $100,000 or more.[29] Education-level data is not available, but it is safe to assume education level is high to go with salary and technical professional occupations.

Like other social networks, Google+ is built around user profiles and sharing of information. Here users have personal networks, called circles, of which content shows up in news feeds. Instead of likes, Google+ users can click "+1." A unique feature is Google Hangouts, which offers live streaming video for chats of more than two people. Google+ focuses on user content, and the most shared content on Google+ consists of pictures, video, long posts, and status updates.[30]

To further its emphasis on user content, Google has released two tools to help authors and publishers build a bigger audience. Author Attribution automatically links content from websites and apps like WordPress.com and TypePad to author name, picture, and a link to the author's Google+ profile when content appears in search, news, and other Google products. Publishers can also embed posts into web pages to allow readers to click +1, comment, or follow.[31]

Like Facebook, more people access Google+ from mobile devices than desktops.[32] Some expect Google+ to achieve much of its growth through mobile use via its Android devices. Reports have indicated that Google+ is used by 30 percent of smartphone users, behind Facebook's 44 percent but ahead of Twitter's 22 percent, making it the fourth-most-used smartphone app.[33]

Google+ is still fairly new as far as social networks, but there may be good reasons to consider its use in social media plans. If the target skews toward younger males and is perhaps in a technical field, this may be a good place to reach the audience. Despite rumors that come and go pronouncing Google+ dead, the platform is here to stay for now and provides a base for valuable products such as Google Photo and Hangout. Google+ is secretive in its plans, but changes could grow the user base quickly. Plus, because this is a Google product, being on this social network could impact search engine optimization (SEO) strategy. Similar to Facebook, marketers should track KPIs such as +1s, circles, views, shares, and their corresponding sentiment.

Social Network Considerations

In sharing the brand, product, or service story, what social network will be the best source? Match objectives, target audience, and the type of content the big idea (insight) lends itself toward creating. These three social networks are some of the most popular, but are not the only options.

Explore more social networks with a simple Google search of "Top Social Networking Sites." There may be a smaller, focused community that is much more appropriate for an organization's target audience or message. For example, MySpace may be ideal for music promotion. The social network Orkut may not be as popular in the US, but is very popular in certain global markets. There has also been a surge in physician-only social networks that could be very valuable for healthcare organizations.[34]

Blogs and Forums

Seth Godin's book *Poke the Box* says, "The cost of being wrong is less than the cost of doing nothing."[35] One of the best ways to "poke the box" is to test and get ideas by publishing a blog. **Blog** is an abbreviated version of Weblog, which describes websites that contain a reverse chronological order of entries or posts. They feature diary-type commentary or stories on specific subjects that range from personal to political.[36] Blogs include hyperlinks to other websites and also allow easy embedding of multimedia content such as photos, video, and audio. Readers can "talk back" to the author through comments listed under each post. The unique characteristics of blogs are that anyone can publish one easily on any topic, and that blogs are interactive. The rise in popularity of blogs has helped remove the gatekeeper from professional media publishing.

However, a non-professional label for this social medium can be misleading. Top blogs have mass media appeal. For example, *The Huffington Post* blog now pulls in 54 million unique views a month and has secured a coveted seat in the White House briefing room.[37] To put this in perspective, *Time* magazine's monthly circulation is now only 3.3 million.[38]

But a marketer does not need to reach millions to be successful. A mommy blogger with 20,000 monthly views can be worth a marketer's attention for the right product or service because her viewers are segmented and very focused.[39] Blogs often form active communities of common interests, and authors can be very influential in those areas.

Before moving on, it is worth discussing the term mommy blogger. **Mommy blogger** is defined as a mother who blogs about her children, motherhood, parenting, and other related topics.[40] This term has become standard in marketing and media. However, it should be noted that many women find this term condescending, stating that they are moms, but also writers, bloggers, business owners, website owners, and entrepreneurs. Critics argue that the term doesn't represent the professionalism of moms who own blogs, they don't call each other by this term, and not all moms blog about child-related subjects. Others ask why there is no related term such as "daddy blogger."

How many blogs are there? In 2008 *The Blog Herald* reported roughly 200 million blogs.[41] By 2014 *Technorati*'s Top 100 directory contained more than 1.3 billion blogs listed by category.[42] Unfortunately Technorati shut down its blog ranking index in May 2014 to focus on its advertising platform. Of the blogs out there Nielsen reports that 6.7 million people publish blogs on blogging websites and 12 million are writing blogs using social networks.[43]

We will first look at each of the major blogging platforms: Blogger, WordPress, and Tumblr. Each of these blogging platforms has unique users, content, and characteristics.

C MINI CASE

GM Fastlane Blog

At the turn of the century, General Motors was struggling to win back customers lost to foreign automakers. GM first fixed the product problem by hiring Bob Lutz, a rock star in product development. Yet the company felt the new cars were not getting a fair chance from the automotive press. So they launched the Fastlane blog to get the company's message directly to customers, enthusiasts, and media.[a]

Introduced in January 2005, the blog featured direct access to the candid thoughts of then-vice chairman Bob Lutz and other GM executives. These higher-ups in the organization challenged the public to take a new look and test-drive their new cars and trucks. The effort helped GM overcome its dinosaur image, reach customers quickly, and attract web traffic through other sites and blogs linking to Fastlane. The results included millions of visitors and thousands of comments with more than five hundred other blogs linking to Fastlane. The blog was covered by mainstream press such as the *New York Times*, the *Wall Street Journal*, the *Financial Times*, and *Business Week*. The effort won a PRSA Bronze Anvil Award[b] and Forrester Research reported that the yearly value of the blog in consumer research insight alone was $180,000.[c]

---

[a] "GM Fastlane Blog: A Corporate Giant Fights Back," PRSA.org, accessed February 18, 2015, http://www.prsa.org/SearchResults/view/6M-063005/0/GM_Fastlane_Blog_A_Corporate_Giant_Fights_Back#.VLo968b91UQ.

[b] Manning Selvage & Lee BlogWorks, "GM Fastlane Blog: A Corporate Giant Fights Back." PRFirms.com, accessed February 18, 2015, http://prfirms.org/resources/gm-fastlane-blog-a-corporate-giant-fights-back.

[c] Charlene Li, "New ROI of Blogging Report from Forrester." Empowered (blog), January 25, 2007, http://forrester.typepad.com/groundswell/2007/01/new_roi_of_blog.html.

Then we will explore forums. Similar to blogs, yet different, forums are online discussion sites that form around common needs or interests. There is usually a moderator, but no one person or group of people are responsible for creating content. Posts are more like informal conversations versus more formal articles that you tend to find on blogs.

Blogger

Blogger is a blog-publishing service that allows free user accounts hosted at the subdomain of blogspot.com. This free blogging system is very clean, fast, and streamlined. It is the oldest of the three major blogging platforms. It started in 1999 and was acquired by Google in 2003.[44] Perhaps that is why it is the largest blogging platform, with roughly 65 to 70 million unique visitors a month.[45] Again, it is important to look at those numbers in the context of country usage. Blogger.com is highly global with only 15 percent of visitor traffic coming from the US. Top individual countries include India (17 percent), Indonesia (11 percent), and Brazil (6 percent).[46]

Blogger users are close to the US average in terms of age, but do skew slightly older with higher percentages in the eighteen- to thirty-four- and fifty-five- to sixty-five-year-old categories. Based on the top blog subjects, Blogger seems to attract bloggers who are talking about parenting-related subjects and engaging coupon and discount seekers.[47] The ease of use and limited custom options also make it more the domain of casual bloggers (see figure 7.3).[48]

With Blogger's ease of use come limitations in design choices, and it does not support plug-ins for advanced features and customization.[49] Because Blogger is owned by Google, it does provide easy integration with Google+, Google Adsense, and other Google properties.[50]

For ease of use and its integration with Google+ and other Google accounts, Blogger may be the ideal tool to get an organization blog up quickly. Depending on target audience, it may also be a place to search for influential individual bloggers with sizable subscriber lists who appeal to a niche audience for the product or service. Packaged-goods companies may find appropriate mom or dad bloggers here.

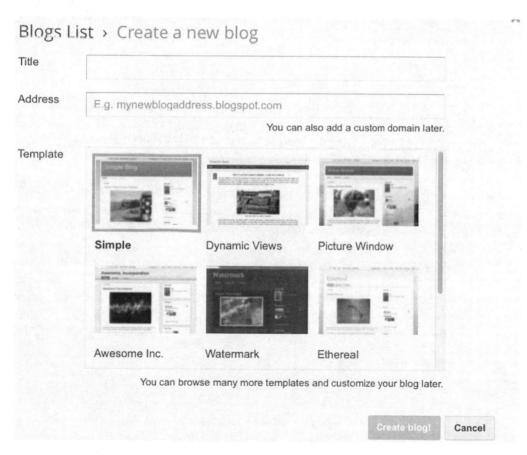

Figure 7.3. Blogger's advantages are ease of use and simplicity.

Source: Blogger.com, accessed January 18, 2015, https://www.blogger.com/home. © Google Inc.

Google likes to keep stats private, so specific numbers on Blogger mobile usage are not available. However, Blogger does have mobile apps for users to post and edit blogs or share photos, links, and even location. Blogger blogs are also optimized for easy viewing on mobile devices.[51] For key performance indicators (KPIs), marketers should consider tracking posts, comments, likes, links, views, engagement, referrals, and sentiment.

WordPress

 WordPress is a free open-source blogging and content-management system first launched in 2003. WordPress averages 30 to 35 million unique visitors a month.[52] These numbers may be lower than Blogger's, but WordPress is used by close to half (48 percent) of the top 100 blogs worldwide.[53] WordPress also reports that they generate more than 35.4 million posts and 61 million comments a month.[54]

WordPress seems to draw a broader audience. The demographics of its visitors are close to US Internet averages, with the highest number of WordPress users being twenty-five to thirty-four years old. Users skew slightly more female. WordPress top blog subjects suggest that it engages people interested in stories.[55] Income levels are evenly spread with slightly more people making under $50,000 a year. Yet WordPress visitors are highly educated, slightly more than average in the categories of having college and graduate-school educations.[56] Despite its professional spin, most views still come from home (roughly 70 percent) versus computers at work (roughly 30 percent).[57]

WordPress is known for its flexibility, with many different design themes and functional plug-ins to customize blogs.[58] WordPress.com offers free blogs with hosting and WordPress.org allows free download of the software to install on other hosting services. Most large blogs are hosted on WordPress, so it is more a platform for professional bloggers, media businesses, and companies than Blogger.[59]

Some examples of the high-profile companies on WordPress include *People* magazine, *Harvard Business Review*, the *New York Times* Company, and Eddie Bauer. Eddie Bauer's blog features photos and stories about living an adventure lifestyle. Direct links send readers to the retail website (see figure 7.4).[60]

WordPress blogs are gaining in mobile activity with nearly 30 percent of views coming from mobile devices. WordPress also has mobile applications that allow posting, commenting, liking, and replying. In addition, the blogging platform includes a plug-in that optimizes its blogs for viewing on mobile devices.[61] WordPress has key performance indicators (KPIs) similar to Blogger, including posts, comments, likes, links, views, engagement, referrals, and sentiment.

Tumblr

 Tumblr is a blogging platform and social-networking website that allows users to post multimedia content in a short-form blog. Tumbler is a later entry, beginning in 2007, but has grown quickly to roughly 420 million users with 206 million registered blogs.[62] Tumblr blogs are also unique in keeping their audience's attention, with average stays up to twice that of

Figure 7.4. Eddie Bauer's WordPress blog provides interesting content.

Source: "Live Your Adventure," EddieBauer.com (blog), accessed January 18, 2015, http://blog.eddiebauer.com. © Eddie Bauer LLC.

Blogger and WordPress.[63] In 2013, Tumblr was acquired by Yahoo, so marketers should expect easy integration with other Yahoo services.[64] Tumblr is also globally focused. However, roughly 43 percent of its unique visitors come from the United States. Other top countries include Brazil, the UK, Canada, and Germany.[65]

Tumblr is unique in that its focus is on simple, quick posts that highlight images and videos. In fact, it could technically be considered a microblogging platform with social-networking features. For strategic purposes, Tumblr has been categorized as a highly visual, short-form blog. This blogging platform also emphasizes social media activities where users follow blogs, as they do on Twitter, and like content as they do on Facebook. Users can also share content by reblogging it, much like a retweet on Twitter.[66]

Another social-networking feature to be added is including "@" in posts to directly mention and tag other users. This is a feature that is popular on Twitter.[67] Of the three blogging platforms covered here, Tumblr has the most social-networking features.

Tumblr user demographics skew younger, drawing the largest percentage of users in the eighteen- to twenty-four-year-old range (46 percent) with the next largest group aged thirty to forty-nine (30 percent). The social media channel is fairly evenly split between men (47 percent) and women (53 percent). Users' income levels are diverse with nearly a third (28 percent) earning under $30,000 a year, yet close to half (45 percent) earning over $75,000 a year. Nearly a third (31 percent) have a high-school education or less, yet close to half (43 percent) have a college degree.[68]

It should be no surprise that Tumblr's content focuses on multimedia such as photos and video, but also engages users interested in games and Internet memes.[69] Look for unique content such as infographics, comics, and links. Tumblr is not ideal for text-heavy entries, and the emphasis on sharing means less original content. This environment lends itself toward casual bloggers looking for something between Twitter and WordPress, and businesses that are more focused on visual content.[70] However, many media outlets have opened Tumblr accounts as another venue to share their program content.

Tumblr can be an ideal channel for a brand, product, or service that is highly visual. It is a great way to feature high-quality graphics for users to share quickly. Tumblr can also be seen as the right network for blogger outreach if the target audience is in a niche fashion, graphic, craft, or design industry.

By far Tumblr has more views from a computer (roughly 90 percent) versus mobile devices (roughly 10 percent).[71] Tumblr has a mobile app that allows easy posts with photo and video, likes, and comments, as well as search via hashtags (using the # sign) and mentions (using the @ sign) much like Twitter. Tumblr blogs are also optimized for viewing on mobile devices.[72] Tumblr key performance indicators (KPIs) are slightly different than the other blogging platforms and could include posts, comments, likes, links, views, engagement, referrals, and sentiment, but also follows and reblogs.

Forums

 Forums are online discussion sites where people hold conversations on related topics via posted messages. Forums differ from chat rooms in that the messages are usually longer than one line of text, and chat rooms happen in real time, more like a phone call, versus forum discussion that functions more like an email conversation. Some estimates indicate there are millions of Internet forums, which are also called message boards or bulletin boards. TheBiggestBoards.com has a list of the top boards and provides some search capabilities. Forums are similar to blogs in that they provide digital meeting places for people interested in common subjects so they can discuss the topics together. Forums may also be called discussion boards, threaded discussions, or discussion groups.

On forums, people can create discussions by starting a new thread or subject and others respond with replies to those threads. Threads can be anything from simple statements and questions to longer opinions, stories, or how-tos. Unlike chat rooms, forums keep archives of discussions with many users linking to archived entries.[73]

One popular use for forums is learning how to repair items or troubleshoot computers and software. Forums have sprung up around products, services, and brands. On these forums fans provide tech support to each other and discuss brand activities. They can be consumer-run forums like forums.tdiclub.com or brand-supported like discussions.apple.com. Marketers should find the forums relevant to their organization or industry.[74]

Forums have owners who administer them, build discussion categories, create moderators, and manage users. The moderators are assigned to monitor a certain category or categories and are given the power to delete messages or even ban individuals from the forum. Users are the individual members who have public access.[75]

Forums tend to have strict rules on behavior and policies on posting threads and replies. Participants can be scolded or banned for posting off-topic messages or for inappropriate activity such as personal attacks. Marketers must be aware that on most forums, overt sales messages are especially not tolerated. Be careful not to be labeled a spammer and thus be banned from the community. This could especially be harmful on a forum centered around a brand. Try to be helpful, not pushy.

Perform searches around the brand, product, service, industry, and target audience to find relevant forums. You probably already found many during the social media audit. Now go back to those sites to look at their size, the kind of users the forum attracts, and the type of content they share. Is there potential for participation to help meet organizational objectives? Are the users in the target market? Does the content shared lend itself to the main message, key insight, or big idea? If so, those forums may need to be a key part of the social media strategy. If no forums currently exist, could the brand benefit from starting one? Based on the characteristics of forums described above, could a brand-sponsored forum help meet objectives or even help overcome some obstacles identified in the audit, such as poor product support?

Blog and Forum Considerations

Why engage bloggers or members of forums? Seth Godin has it right in his quote about poking the box. The emphasis should be presence over perfection. Failing to contribute to vibrant communities engaged in discussion about a brand, product, service, or industry costs organizations. As in any personal relationship between friends, spouses, or coworkers, silence is deadly. A well-meaning personal statement, if not perfect, goes a long way in the consumer's mind versus polished push-marketing campaigns.

Consider the **1% rule** or the 90-9-1 principle, first coined by bloggers Ben McConnell and Jackie Hunt. It states that in collaborative sites such as blogs and forums, 90 percent of users view the content, 9 percent contribute infrequently, and only 1 percent actively create new content.[76] As a marketer, this is good news. If a brand can engage the 1 percent of bloggers or forum participants, they will spread the word to the other 99 percent.

Like you did with social networks, join some brand, fan, or industry forums and poke around. Key performance indicators (KPIs) for forums can include posts, comments, members, views, threads, and links, and don't forget to indicate positive or negative sentiment when appropriate.

Marketers should know that people are out there talking about their organization. Start reading, posting, and commenting on these blogs and forums or start your own. The cost of not engaging in that conversation can be huge, such as a missed opportunity to stop an angry protest before it gets out of hand or an opportunity to fuel a viral campaign. Find the right fit for social media campaign objectives, target, and big idea.

SOCIAL PLAN PART 7

Select Social Networks, Blog Platforms, and Forums

In this part of the social media plan, explore all the major social media networks. Research each, looking at the size and makeup of the users. Does the target audience match the main users of the network? What kind of content is popular? What is the culture of the network? Do these characteristics match brand, product, service, and big idea? Do the same exploration and comparison for blogs and forums. Could the brand benefit from a blog? Which platform would be best? What about a forum? Should the organization start its own, or participate in existing forums? Report all findings and ideas in these areas:

1. Identify the top social networks where the target audience is active.
2. For each social network, describe the main type of content and culture.
3. Find existing brand, product, or service blogs and forums. How could the brand participate?
4. Is there a need for a customer-support forum or other type of forum?

QUESTIONS FOR DISCUSSION

1. Facebook is by far the largest and most dominant social media network. Do you feel all organizations must have a Facebook page? Can you think of an example where it wouldn't make sense?
2. How could a B2B (business-to-business) company use LinkedIn as a marketing tool? What strategies could be used on LinkedIn to build qualified leads and secure sales?
3. Compare WordPress blogs to blogs on Blogger and Tumblr. What are the main differences? List examples of how a brand would use a WordPress or a Blogger blog versus Tumblr.
4. The GM Fastlane corporate blog is a success. Find another company blog that is doing well. What business objectives is the blog helping to meet? Can you find any ROI data to report?

ADDITIONAL EXERCISES

1. One of the best ways to learn about social-network options is to join them. This exercise challenges you to join these top social networks and others you feel may apply to the target audience of your brand. This doesn't mean launch an official business presence. Join them personally to get a firsthand look at the environment, how it works, and what content tends to be liked. Also, notice the posted and unposted community rules. Make note of them for later efforts. Have fun and think like a consumer enjoying these social networks, while observing them for strategic business insight.
2. As with social networks, one of the best ways to learn about blogs and forums is to join them. Do a search to find some of the most active forums in and around the brand, product, or

service. Look for the most active contributors and identify them as possible influencers. Find some top blogs in your field and subscribe to them. Or perhaps start your own blog. Learn firsthand the characteristics and possibilities of this channel. Also, as with social networks, make a note of the community rules for your later efforts. Again, have fun and think like a consumer, while observing for strategic business insight.

Notes

1. "Right Direction Quotes," BrainyQuote.com, accessed February 18, 2015, http://www .brainyquote.com/quotes/keywords/right_direction_2.html.

2. "Friendster," Wikipedia, last modified January 10, 2015, http://en.wikipedia.org/wiki/ Friendster.

3. Peter Pachal, "Why Friendster Died: Social Media Isn't a Game," PCMagazine.com, April 28, 2011, http://www.pcmag.com/article2/0,2817,2384588,00.asp.

4. Seth Fiegerman, "Friendster Founder Tells His Side of the Story, 10 Years After Facebook," Mashable.com, February 3, 2014, http://mashable.com/2014/02/03/jonathan-abrams-friendster -facebook.

5. Simon Kemp, "Global Social Media Users Pass 2 Billion," We Are Social (blog), August 8, 2014, http://wearesocial.net/blog/2014/08/global-social-media-users-pass-2-billion.

6. Joe Pulizzi, "Hey WSJ—Content Marketing is NOT Native Advertising," Content Marketing Institute (blog), November 6, 2014, http://contentmarketinginstitute.com/2014/11/ wsj-content-marketing-not-native.

7. "Social Network," Dictionary.com, accessed February 18, 2015, http://dictionary.reference .com/browse/social+network.

8. Donna Tam, "Facebook Earnings by the Numbers: 819M Mobile Users," CNET.com, July 24, 2013, http://news.cnet.com/8301-1023_3 57595333 93/facebook-earnings-by-the-numbers -819m-mobile-users.

9. Maximillian Nierhoff, "Facebook Country Stats February 2013—Top 10 Countries Lose Users Due to the Ongoing Account Cleanup," Quintly.com (blog), February 4, 2013, http://www .quintly.com/blog/2013/02/facebook-country-stats-february-2013-top-10-countries-lose-users.

10. "Social Media Site Use by Year," PewInternet.org, January 8, 2015, http://www.pew internet.org/2015/01/09/social-media-update-2014/pi_2015-01-09_social-media_01.

11. Maeve Duggan and Joanna Brenner, "The Demographics of Social Media Users—2012," PewInternet.org, February 14, 2013, http://pewinternet.org/~/media//Files/Reports/2013/PIP _SocialMediaUsers.pdf.

12. Emeric Emoult, "Guide to Facebook Reach: What Marketers Need to Know," SocialMe diaExaminer.com (blog), March 3, 2014, http://www.socialmediaexaminer.com/facebook-reach -guide.

13. Luke Brown, "Facebook Mobile Usage Outstrips Web for the First Time Ever," TechRa dar.com, January 30, 2012, http://www.techradar.com/us/news/internet/facebook-mobile-usage -outstrips-web-for-first-time-ever-1128489.

14. Cooper Smith, "Google+ Is the Fourth Most-Used SmartPhone App," BusinessInsider. com, September 5, 2013, http://www.businessinsider.com/google-smartphone-app-popularity -2013-9#infographic.

15. Alouette Cheese Facebook page, accessed January 18, 2015, https://www.facebook.com/ AlouetteCheese.

16. Sara Goo, "Facebook: A Profile of its 'Friends,'" PewResearch.org, May 16, 2012, http://pewresearch.org/pubs/2262/facebook-ipo-friends-profile-social-networking-habits-privacy-online-behavior.

17. Keith A. Quesenberry, "If You're Simply Adding to the Noise, Facebook Will Now Turn Off Your Organic Reach," PostControlMarketing.com (blog), February 6, 2014, http://www.postcontrolmarketing.com/?p=1468.

18. Sarah Perez, "LinkedIn Hits 300 Million Users," Techcrunch.com (blog), http://techcrunch.com/2014/04/18/linkedin-hits-300-million-users.

19. "Social Media Site Use by Year," PewInternet.org.

20. Matt McGee, "Social Network Demographics: Pew Study Shows Who Uses Facebook, Twitter, Pinterest & Others," MarketingLand.com, September 14, 2012, http://marketingland.com/social-network-demographics-pew-study-shows-who-uses-facebook-twitter-pinterest-others-21594.

21. Stephanie Buck, "The Beginner's Guide to LinkedIn," Mashable.com, May 23, 2012, http://mashable.com/2012/05/23/linkedin-beginners.

22. Michael Stelzner, "LinkedIn Publishing Platform: What Marketers Need to Know," SocialMediaExaminer.com, April 19, 2014, http://www.socialmediaexaminer.com/linkedin-publishing-platform-with-stephanie-sammons.

23. Keith A. Quesenberry, "How Social Media Can Hurt or Help Your Career," LinkedIn.com, November 29, 2014, https://www.linkedin.com/pulse/20141129153637-9796156-how-social-media-can-hurt-or-help-your-career?trk=mp-reader-card.

24. Lauren Mobertz, "Now You Can Apply to Jobs on LinkedIn Using Any Mobile Device," DashBurst.com, August 5, 2013, http://dashburst.com/linkedin-mobile-apply-jobs.

25. Rebecca Borison, "Google+ Is Still Struggling Three Years Later," BusinessInsider.com (blog), June 28, 2014, http://www.businessinsider.com/google-plus-three-years-later-2014-6.

26. Amir Efrati, "ComScore: Google+ Makes Gains Worldwide But Struggles on Mobile," Digits (the tech blog of the *Wall Street Journal*), January 3, 2013, http://blogs.wsj.com/digits/2013/01/03/google-makes-gains-worldwide-but-struggles-on-mobile.

27. Borison, "Google+ Is Still Struggling Three Years Later."

28. "Google Plus Demographics & Statistics," Statisticsbrain.com (blog), March 4, 2015, http://www.statisticsbrain.com/google-plus-demographics-statistics.

29. Bianca Bosker, "Facebook vs. Google+ Searchers: How Their Demographics Differ," HuffingtonPost.com, August 30, 2011, http://www.huffingtonpost.com/2011/08/30/facebook-vs-google-plus-searchers_n_941682.html.

30. Stephanie Frasco, "Google+ Overview: Breaking Through Misconceptions," SocialMediaToday.com, April 2, 2013, http://socialmediatoday.com/stephaniefrasco/1332761/google-plus-overview.

31. Guynn, "Google+ Rolls Out Features."

32. Efrati, "ComScore."

33. Cooper Smith, "Google+ Is the Fourth Most-Used SmartPhone App," BusinessInsider.com, September 5, 2013, http://www.businessinsider.com/google-smartphone-app-popularity-2013-9#infographic.

34. Deanna Pogoreic, "In a Popularity Contest of Physician-Only Social Networks, Doximity Pulls Ahead with 200K Users," MedCityNews.com, August 27, 2013, http://medcitynews.com/2013/08/in-a-popularity-contest-of-physician-only-social-networks-doximity-pulls-ahead-with-200k-users.

35. Seth Godin, *Poke the Box: When Was the Last Time You Did Something for the First Time?* Delaware: The Domino Project (2011).

36. "What Is a Blog?" WordPress, accessed February 18, 2015, http://codex.wordpress.org/Introduction_to_Blogging.

37. "Top 15 Most Popular Blogs," eBizMBA.com, accessed February 18, 2015, http://www.ebizmba.com/articles/blogs.

38. Katerina-Eva Matsa, Jane Sasseen, and Amy Mitchell, "Magazines: By the Numbers," State oftheMedia.org, accessed February 18, 2015, http://stateofthemedia.org/2012/magazines-are-hopes-for-tablets-overdone/magazines-by-the-numbers.

39. Larissa Faw, "Is Blogging Really a Way for Women to Earn a Living?" Forbes.com, April 25, 2012, http://www.forbes.com/sites/larissafaw/2012/04/25/is-blogging-really-a-way-for-women-to-earn-a-living-2.

40. "Mommy-blogger," YourDictionary.com, accessed June 24, 2015, http://www.yourdictionary.com/mommy-blogger.

41. Anne Helmond, "How Many Blogs Are There? Is Someone Still Counting?" BlogHerald.com, February 11, 2008, http://www.blogherald.com/2008/02/11/how-many-blogs-are-there-is-someone-still-counting.

42. "Blogs Directory," Technorati, accessed January 18, 2014, http://technorati.com/blogs/directory.

43. "Buzz in the Blogosphere: Millions More Bloggers and Blog Readers," Nielsen.com, March 8, 2012, http://www.nielsen.com/us/en/newswire/2012/buzz-in-the-blogosphere-millions-more-bloggers-and-blog-readers.html.

44. "Blogger," Wikipedia, last modified February 13, 2015, http://en.wikipedia.org/wiki/Blogger_%28service%29.

45. Mark Lindsey, "Round 2 of Tumblr vs. WordPress vs. Blogspot: Fight!" Compete.com (blog), February 8, 2012, https://blog.compete.com/2012/02/08/round-2-of-tumbr-vs-wordpress-vs-blogger-fight.

46. Jeffry Darwis, "Infographic—Blogger," DarwisZone.com, December 16, 2012, http://www.darwiszone.com/p/infograpic.html#.Uk8JAyTFYnU.

47. Lindsey, "Round 2 of Tumblr vs. WordPress vs. Blogspot: Fight!"

48. Kasia Mikoluk, "Best Blogging Platform: WordPress, Blogger, Tumblr, SquareSpace, or Typepad?" Udemy.com (blog), June 30, 2013, https://www.udemy.com/blog/best-blogging-platform.

49. "Blogger Features," Blogger, accessed February 18, 2015, https://www.blogger.com/features.

50. Mark Saric, "Blogger, WordPress, or Tumblr: Where Should I Blog?" HowToMakeMyBlog.com, February 23, 2013, http://www.howtomakemyblog.com/popular/blogger-wordpress-tumblr.

51. "Blogger," Wikipedia.

52. Lindsey, "Round 2 of Tumblr vs. WordPress vs. Blogspot: Fight!"

53. "WordPress Completely Dominates Top 100 Blogs," Pingdom.com, April 11, 2012, http://royal.pingdom.com/2012/04/11/wordpress-completely-dominates-top-100-blogs.

54. "WordPress Stats," WordPress.com, accessed October 15, 2013, http://en.wordpress.com/stats.

55. Mikoluk, "Best Blogging Platform."

56. "WordPress.com," Quantcast, accessed October 15, 2013, https://www.quantcast.com/wordpress.com.

57. "WordPress," Wikipedia, last modified February 17, 2015, http://en.wikipedia.org/wiki/WordPress.

58. Saric, "Blogger, WordPress or Tumblr?"

59. Mikoluk, "Best Blogging Platform."

60. "Live Your Adventure," EddieBauer.com (blog), accessed January 18, 2015, http://blog .eddiebauer.com.

61. "WordPress.com," Quantcast.

62. Cynthia Boris, "Tumblr Announces 40 Percent Growth and a Fancy New Video Player," October 24, 2014, http://www.marketingpilgrim.com/2014/10/tumblr-announces-40-percent -growth-and-a-fancy-new-video-player.html.

63. Lindsey, "Round 2 of Tumblr vs. WordPress vs. Blogspot: Fight!"

64. "Tumblr," Wikipedia, last modified February 1, 2015, http://en.wikipedia.org/wiki/ Tumblr.

65. Lauren Hockenson, "Tumblr Numbers: The Rapid Rise of Social Blogging [INFO-GRAPHIC]," Mashable.com, November 14, 2011, http://mashable.com/2011/11/14/tumblr -infographic/.

66. Saric, "Blogger, WordPress or Tumblr?"

67. Samantha Murphy Kelly, "Tumblr Introduces @Mentions for Users." Mashable.com, January 15, 2014, http://mashable.com/2014/01/14/tumblr-adds-mentons.

68. "Tumblr Blog Network," Quantcast, accessed October 15, 2013, https://www.quantcast .com/tumblr.com?qcLocale=en_US.

69. Lindsey, "Round 2 of Tumblr vs. Wordpress vs. Blogspot: Fight!"

70. Mikoluk, "Best Blogging Platform."

71. "Tumblr Blog Network," Quantcast.

72. "Tumblr," Wikipedia.

73. The Institution of Engineering Technology, "What Is a 'Forum'?" accessed February 18, 2015, http://www.theiet.org/forums/blog/help/english/What_is_a_forum.htm.

74. TDI Club Internet Forum, accessed October 15, 2013, from http://forums.tdiclub.com.

75. The Institution of Engineering Technology, "What Is a 'Forum'?"

76. "1% rule (Internet Culture)," Wikipedia, last modified July 11, 2014, http://en.wikipedia .org/wiki/1%25_rule_%28Internet_culture%29.

Microblogging and Media Sharing

Be sincere; be brief; be seated.[1]

—Franklin D. Roosevelt

PREVIEW

"Standing beneath this serene sky, overlooking these broad fields now reposing . . ."[2] Remember what speech these words are from? Do the following words sound more familiar? "Four score and seven years ago our fathers brought forth . . ." Most people probably know the second quote as the beginning of the Gettysburg Address given by Abraham Lincoln on November 19, 1863.[3] The first quote is from Edward Everett, who was to be giving the main Gettysburg Address on that day. Everett's speech was a two-hour, nearly fourteen-thousand-word oration on the event of the US Civil War. Right after Everett's speech, Lincoln spoke just ten sentences in two minutes and accomplished much more than Everett.[4]

When *Time* magazine published a Top 10 List of greatest speeches, Abraham Lincoln's Gettysburg Address was included among those of other greats such as Socrates, Martin Luther King Jr., and Winston Churchill. It is also interesting to note that Winston Churchill's famous "Blood, Toil, Tears and Sweat" speech of 1940 lasted a mere five minutes.[5] The lesson here is that clear and concise communication is often the most powerful and memorable.

Microblogging

In the Franklin D. Roosevelt quote, he may have been giving his son instructions for making a speech, but this way of thinking is behind some of the fastest-growing and most influential social media channels. Even as we spend more and more time engaging with social media, placing limits on those individual interactions has spawned two of the most popular social media icons: Twitter and Pinterest.

Microblogging is a form of traditional blogging where the content is smaller in both file size and length of content. Microblogs limit exchange to smaller bits of information such as short sentences, single images, or video links that can be called microposts. Like traditional blogs, users post on topics from what they are doing and seeing right now to motorcycles or chocolate or television programs like *The Voice*.[6] The difference may seem small, but microblogs are used in very different ways than traditional blogs or other social media channels.

There are many microblogging services, including Twitter, Pinterest, Vine, Weibo, and Plurk. Some also consider Tumblr to be a microblog. Social networking websites such as Facebook, MySpace, LinkedIn, and Google+ also have microblogging features in the form of status updates.[7]

The other key characteristic of microblogging is the real-time reporting that has emerged from the short nature of updates that allows users to post items quickly. Twitter has developed into a source of news for crisis situations such as the Mumbai terror attacks, Iran protests, and Boston Marathon bombing. Citizens have become sources of information outside formal journalism to influence or even cause mass media coverage. Microblogging also creates an enormous amount of data that can then be analyzed for trends with services such as Trendsmap.[8]

In addition, microblogging has potential for collaborative work in organizations where email has become slow and inefficient. There are many free and open-source software services that act as hosted microblogging platforms for private organizational use.

Why do people microblog? The findings of a study by Emily Pronin and Daniel Wegner suggest a link between short bursts of activity and feelings of elation, power, and creativity.[9] Is there some connection between these feelings and the organization's brand, product, or service? Can microblogging be leveraged in the social media plan? Find out by looking at the two main microblogging platforms, Twitter and Pinterest, in further detail.

Twitter

Twitter is an online social networking service that enables users to send short, 140-character messages. Launched in 2006, Twitter has grown to over 300 million monthly active users and is called by some "the pulse of the planet."[10] Marketers may want to consider the global aspects of Twitter. Only 49 million or 25 percent of those monthly active users are from the US, despite 88 percent of Twitter's advertising revenue coming from US organizations. Twitter grew enormously at first, doubling in size from 2010 to 2013, but its growth has slowed more recently. Yet more than 23 percent of the total US population is tweeting.[11]

Who are Twitter users? Twitter use is most common among those eighteen to forty-nine with 73 percent of all users in that age range. Most are highly educated with 71 percent having some college or a college degree. They are much more likely to live in suburban or urban areas rather than rural. The largest group of Twitter users makes more than $75,000 a year (35 percent), but marketers are almost just as likely to find users making less than $30,000 a year (27 percent). Roughly another third are in between, earning $30,000 to $74,999 a year.[12]

What do these users share? They share thoughts, news, information, jokes, pictures, and links in 140 characters or less—not words or letters. These message updates are called tweets. Mashable's "Beginner's Guide to Twitter" says it "makes global communication cheap and measurable." Like the social networks, users have profiles, but on Twitter most are public for anyone to see. In addition to a profile, each user is assigned a handle, which is their username. Usernames vary wildly, from real names and abbreviations to nicknames or even organizations. Organizations can open Twitter accounts with profiles. They are not restricted to separate pages like they are on Facebook.[13]

Users follow other users that interest them so that their tweets appear in the other user's feed, or stream of tweets (updates), on their home page. The more people following, the more people see the updates. That is why early marketing efforts on Twitter should concentrate on building followers. If a user sees a tweet they like in their feed, they can "retweet" (RT), or reshare, the message, giving credit to the original author, but then having it appear in the feed of everyone following them.

Another way to acknowledge another user and separate specific tweets from all conversation is with a mention (using the @ symbol). For example, adding @Kquesen to a tweet notifies the author of this book, initiating a discussion in this public space. Twitter users could also direct-message (DM) another user to conduct private messages back and forth—still in 140 characters. Yet users can only direct-message a user who follows them.

Companies such as Verizon are now providing customer service via Twitter. These companies try to get angry customers off the public feed by encouraging them to follow and then send a direct message. Other companies such as airlines have opened separate Twitter accounts dedicated to customer service. With some 500 million tweets a day, users find related messages by including a hashtag (#) to designate a topic of conversation such as #TheVoice or #startup.[14] Hashtags are the main search tool for Twitter that allows users to find all tweets about a given subject—even from users they don't follow. Twitter has also created the social media app Vine, which emphasizes short video content in the form of seven-second clips, and the app Periscope, which streams live video.

One of the main attractions of Twitter is its real-time reporting. Marketers like HGTV use the channel to share interesting content, but also to promote their shows in real-time (see figure 8.1).[15] Twitter is very mobile, with apps available on both iOS and Android devices. One survey reports that Twitter is the sixth-most-used app, accessed by 22 percent of all smartphone users. With 80 percent of Americans owning a smartphone or tablet, they are now accessing Twitter while watching television at the same time, which has made TV programming a more interactive experience.[16] Native advertising is an option for Twitter. Marketers should consider purchasing promoted tweets to boost reach and jumpstart efforts.

Figure 8.1. HGTV leverages the real-time aspect of Twitter.

Source: HGTV Twitter, accessed January 18, 2015, https://twitter.com/hgtv. © Scripps Networks, LLC

More and more media companies are creating profiles to allow fans to follow shows and sporting events, make live comments, and vote via hashtags that can also be published on the television screen. The NBA especially has leveraged the third screen, with two-thirds of its players engaging fans on Twitter, reaching more than 130 million people.[17]

Despite its slowed growth Twitter users are highly influential and a large number of journalists use the network for story leads. Nearly 60 percent of all journalists worldwide use Twitter, and more than 50 percent use it to gather news stories.[18] Twitter could especially apply to public relations efforts to garner earned media coverage.

Key performance indicators (KPIs) for Twitter could include tweets, retweets, mentions, direct messages, and referrals. Don't forget to analyze sentiment. Twitter has become a favorite place for angry customers to complain about products and services, and a growing number expect a quick response from organizations. The challenges and opportunities of social media customer service will be discussed further in part IV of the book.

Pinterest

Pinterest is a web and mobile social network that enables visual discovery, collection, and sharing and serves as a storage tool. An even newer phenomenon than Twitter, Pinterest began only in 2010, but grew to over 70 million unique monthly users quickly. This online pin board

has a high amount of business activity with roughly 500,000 business accounts, which may help explain why only 20 percent of Pinterest images contain faces.

This channel is focused on products, designs, and ideas. It is not a family-photo-sharing service. An interesting statistic is that nearly 70 percent of online consumers have found an item they have bought or wanted to buy on Pinterest, versus only 40 percent on Facebook.[19] Another distinguishing characteristic is that unlike the other channels touting a larger overall user number, 70 percent of Pinterest users are in the US.[20] This could be an important factor to consider depending on organizational objectives and target audience.

Twenty-eight percent of US adult Internet users are on Pinterest.[21] Like many of the social channels, Pinterest has younger users, but the majority are between thirty and forty-nine years old (42 percent) with another quarter age eighteen to twenty-nine (25 percent) and fifty to sixty-four (27 percent). They are well educated, with half of the users having an undergraduate or graduate college degree (50 percent) and another third with some college (29 percent). Pinterest users have higher income with most making more than $75,000 a year (37 percent) and another quarter earning between $50,000 and $74,999 a year (26 percent). One of the key characteristics of Pinterest is that the site skews heavily female. Women are about five times as likely to be on the site as men, the largest difference of gender in any channel (85 percent).[22]

Pinterest may be thought of as a highly visual form of Twitter. Some describe its main activity as "virtual scrapbooking," but this scrapbook enables users to collect and share photos, videos, and articles of their interests. Like other social sites, this channel starts with a profile where users place their name, bio, and photo. The main action is to pin. A pin is a post or update that is shared on the public network. It is similar to a tweet, but is image based. Each pin added is automatically linked back to the website from which it came. A collection of pins is linked by a topic and collected on a board. A board of "Famous Chili" could have pictures of different chilis with links to the recipes.[23] Campbell's food leverages the recipe and themed boards well for their Campbell's Kitchen recipe content (see figure 8.2).[24]

Like other social channels, users select other users to follow. Being a follower means the person can follow all of another user's pins or just certain boards. When following, those pins show up on the Pinterest home page under the following board. This activity functions like a Facebook or Twitter stream. Similar to a retweet on Twitter, users can repin an image they like and add it to their own board, but it still gives credit to the original author and maintains the source link. Authors can also add captions to their images but are limited to five hundred characters and are not allowed to include hyperlinks in the text.[25]

Pinterest also enables users to like pins that they approve of, but this will not place it on that user's board the way a repin does. Similar to Twitter hashtags, Pinterest's pins and boards can be tagged by category, such as Food & Drinks or Gifts. Gifts may be categorized with price tags and users can search for gifts by price range. The site has also added price alerts that automatically send an email when the price of a pinned product drops.[26]

It is easy to see why this channel is popular with businesses. Websites such as Postris can help marketers stay on top of what is trending on Pinterest. In addition, Pinterest provides a robust web analytics system for business.[27] Native advertising is available on Pinterest and could be a way to increase reach by purchasing promoted pins.

Figure 8.2. Campbell's leverages themed cooking boards on Pinterest.

Source: Campbell's Kitchen Pinterest Account, accessed January 18, 2015, http://www.pinterest.com/campbell kitchen. © CSC Brands LP.

Pinterest is mobile with apps for many devices designed to allow pinning right from the smartphone's camera. In fact, 35 percent of visitors come from a mobile device.[28] Unlike other social channels, Pinterest seems to have had an eye toward business from the beginning and probably deserves a good look for many organizations. But marketers should consider its size, capabilities, and the small percentage of male users. With Pinterest key performance indicators (KPIs), look at boards, pins, repins, likes, and followers, and don't forget sentiment and referrals.

Microblogging Considerations

The leaders in the microblogging channel are fairly young and the size of content and the user base is smaller. But the type of content, type of users, and channel capabilities might be perfect for the right big idea, target audience, and business objective. As FDR told his son, being brief can be much more powerful than being big. Also remember the lesson learned from Everett's and Lincoln's Gettysburg addresses. Short can be impactful. Be sure to explore the top microblogging platforms as social strategy options.

MINI CASE

Pharrell's "Happy"

The song "Happy" by Pharrell was originally produced for the animated hit *Despicable Me 2*, but the artist and producers wanted to broaden its appeal. The world's first twenty-four-hour video was created and launched at 24hoursofhappy.com. The song played and replayed for twenty-four hours while viewers could tune in any time to see people going about their jobs dancing to "Happy."[a] The music video featured an interactive sequence showing Pharrell and three hundred people, famous and not, dancing around Los Angeles over the course of a day.

The viral video took the top prize, a Grand Prix in Cyber Craft, at Cannes Lions.[b] The idea spawned imitations, of which some became viral hits of their own. Clips of the video and these imitations spread via social sites like YouTube. After the viral release, sales of the single rose sharply by 14,000 percent. This promotion was one of the biggest hits of all time, drawing close to 10 million visitors from around the world. The UN even named March 20 as Happiness Day, sponsored by Pharrell.[c]

---

[a] Ed Owen, "24 Hours of Happy Wins Cannes Cyber Grand Prix," Global Academy of Digital Marketing, June 24, 2014, http://www.gogadm.com/24-hours-of-happy-wins-cannes-cyber-grand-prix.

[b] Ann-Christine Diaz, "Pharrell's 24-Hour 'Happy' Video, Chipotle's 'The Scarecrow' and Volvo's 'Live Tests' Take Cyber Grand Prix at Cannes," AdAge.com, June 18, 2014, http://adage.com/article/special-report-cannes-lions/pharrell-happy-chipotle-volvo-cannes-cyber-grand-prix/293773.

[c] Owen, "24 Hours of Happy Wins Cannes Cyber Grand Prix."

Media Sharing

Virginia Woolf said in *The Common Reader*, "For pleasure has no relish unless we share it." She tells us that her intention is for her essays to be read by the "common reader" who reads books for personal enjoyment.[29] Perhaps that is why social media sharing has become so popular on the Internet and through apps on mobile devices. It is a common desire for people to share and read for enjoyment. When asked, 70 percent of Internet users say they have shared some type of content on social media sites within the previous month. With the growing popularity of visually focused sites such as Flickr and Instagram, it is no surprise that pictures are the most popular type of content shared by 43 percent of Internet users. Beyond that, the next four most popular types of content shared are people's opinions, status updates, links to articles, and recommendations.[30]

Video clips may be the tenth most likely type of content users share, but video is certainly popular in terms of views and powerful in terms of message. Only 17 percent of Internet users share video online, but three-fourths (78 percent) watch or download online videos on video-sharing sites such as YouTube or Vimeo. Online video watching is highest among those under fifty, with the highest viewing rates in the eighteen- to twenty-nine-year-old demographic. Online video watchers are also more likely to have attended or graduated college and have higher incomes. Eighty-seven percent of online

US adults with annual incomes of $75,000 or more watch online videos compared to 74 percent of middle-income households ($30,000 to $74,999).[31]

Internet users under thirty-five years old are most likely to share content (81 percent) followed by those thirty-five to forty-nine years old (70 percent). Women are more likely (74 percent) to share content than men (69 percent) and the likelihood of sharing rises with income and education level.[32] The top reasons people post content are to share interesting things (61 percent), important things (43 percent), and funny things (43 percent). People also want to let others know what they believe in (39 percent), want to recommend a product or service (30 percent), and want to provide support to a cause or organization (30 percent) that they believe in.[33]

These survey results give organizations an idea of the type of content to create that will most likely get shared through social media word-of-mouth. Another important point is to make sure sharing is easy by adding social media share buttons to all content. Take a look at the top media-sharing sites online and on mobile apps to see how YouTube, Flickr, and Instagram could possibly fit with organizational objectives, target, or campaign idea.

YouTube

YouTube is a video-sharing website that enables users to upload, view, and share user-generated and corporate-media video. YouTube is the top video-sharing website with over one billion unique monthly visitors. That is nearly one out of every two Internet users. Founded in 2005, and bought by Google in 2006, the video-sharing site has attributed its most recent growth to increased use among younger audiences, such as Generation Y, or eighteen- to thirty-four-year-olds. Increased viewing on mobile devices has also fueled growth. Generation Y is reported to watch just as much YouTube content on smartphones as they do on PCs.[34]

More than one hour of video is uploaded to YouTube every second.[35] YouTube generates a lot of the content that is shared on other channels, with more than seven hundred YouTube videos shared on Twitter each minute and five hundred years' worth of YouTube video watched on Facebook every day. Similar to other social channels, YouTube is very global, with roughly 70 percent of YouTube traffic coming from outside the US. The introduction of YouTube in 2005, and later Vimeo, has driven video use up from 33 percent to 72 percent in less than ten years. Some have dubbed this incredible increase the "YouTube Effect."[36]

YouTube reports that 30 percent of its users are under thirty-four, but that does not include users under eighteen years old. In total, 41 percent of YouTube's audience is twelve to thirty-four years old. The Nielsen company notes that YouTube reaches more eighteen- to thirty-four-year-olds than any cable network. Teenagers may also prefer the video site to other popular social channels, visiting this social channel more per week than Facebook, Twitter, and Google+.[37] This may be changing with the introduction of native video capabilities being added to social networks such as Facebook, Twitter, and Instagram. YouTube skews slightly toward females over males, with middle-class income levels. Most YouTube users make $25,000 to $75,000 per year, with more in the range of $50,000 to $75,000 a year. They are also educated or currently enrolled in school with most having some college education.[38]

More than simply a video-hosting site, YouTube has many of the features and characteristics of a social network. Users have a profile where they can list occupation and hobbies and upload a picture. They upload videos and mark them as public or private. Videos are separated by content that is organized into channels, from brand channels to channels on interests such as comedy videos, how-to videos, or business videos. Channels also follow other channels with mutual interests and content. Each video allows users to enter a title, description, and category. Popular categories include home improvement, fitness, sketch comedy, travel, beauty, and cooking.[39] The Dove brand has used its YouTube channel to distribute Dove Films for years. These videos draw viewers in and provide positive messages to consumers that are transferred to the beauty brand (see figure 8.3).[40]

Viewers are able to like or dislike a video as a general rating, enter comments, and offer video shout-outs. People can also reply to commenters directly or add to the general conversation. It is important to note that videos get positive and negative comments, but may also get extremely negative, callous, anonymous remarks. These negative commenters simply enjoy bullying and are called trolls. **Trolls** intentionally post inflammatory, extraneous messages in online communities to provoke emotional responses. YouTube users can engage trolls with witty remarks, block their accounts, or simply ignore them and let other commenters defend them.[41] Note that trolls are not a problem limited only to YouTube. Marketers and advertisers should also watch out for them in forums and in the comments sections of blogs and online articles.

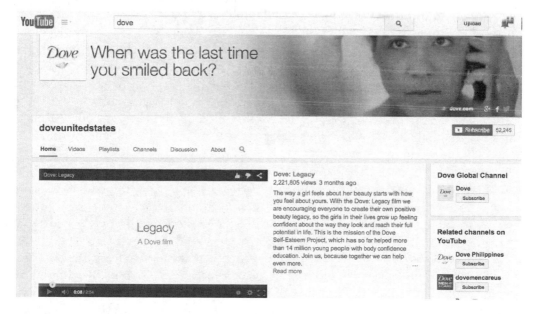

Figure 8.3. Dove's Branded YouTube Channel

Source: "Dove United States YouTube Channel," Dove, accessed January 18, 2015, https://www.youtube.com/channel/UC0uGC_EBwAxw3ljqeGjy2qw. © UNILEVER

A popular video version of blogging has emerged on YouTube. A **video blog,** or vlog, is a combination of video, images, and text that can be thought of as a form of web television. Vloggers talk about anything from politics to pop culture. Some are random personal thoughts and chronicles of their lives. Others are comedy sketches or fictional dramas. Many a vlogger has amassed millions of views and subscribers by doing product and service reviews. It may be worth a marketer's time to find the top reviewers in their category or industry and seek a positive review through outreach.[42]

YouTube has mobile apps for all major mobile platforms and is accessed on millions of devices. The site reports that 25 percent of all YouTube views happen via a mobile device.[43] YouTube's mobile app is the third most used mobile app behind Google Maps and Facebook, with 35 percent of people indicating they have used it in the past month.[44] Key performance indicators for YouTube could be views, comments, shares, subscribers, referrals, favorites, likes, and dislikes. YouTube Analytics also provides information about activity, such as audience retention, demographics, traffic sources, minutes watched, and playback location.

Flickr

Flickr is an imaging and video-hosting online community that allows users to share and embed photos in blogs and social media. Flickr is the top photo-sharing site with over 92 million users.[45] Each visitor spends an average of 2.7 minutes per visit, and about 4.5 million new photos are uploaded daily. Flickr was started in 2004 and was purchased by Yahoo in 2005. Like many of the other social channels, Flickr is truly global, with more users outside the US. Yet a quarter (25 percent) come from the US.[46]

Flickr attracts more women (57 percent) than men (43 percent) who skew older than many other social networks. In fact, 65 percent of Flickr users are thirty-five years old and older, with only 31 percent between eighteen and thirty-four years old, and 5 percent under eighteen. The younger photo-sharing crowd may be using Instagram, as will be seen in the next section.[47] Despite the older user base, income is lower than other social media channels, with 34 percent earning between $25,000 and $50,000 and 27 percent earning between $50,000 and $75,000. The photo site also attracts mostly users who have some college education (54 percent).[48]

Flickr is an image- and video-hosting site that provides web services and supports a robust online community. In addition to being a popular place for users to share personal photos, Flickr is widely used by professional photographers for their portfolios. Many bloggers use Flickr to host their images for embedding in blogs and social media.[49]

Photos and videos can be accessed from Flickr without the need to register an account, but an account must be made in order to upload content onto the website. Registering an account allows users to create a profile page containing photos and videos that the user has uploaded and grants the ability to add another Flickr user as a contact. Professional and amateur photographers alike can upload their images and sell them as stock images through the network. The site includes a terabyte of free storage for all users.[50]

Flickr members organize their images with tags that searchers use to find images along with descriptions. Photos under the same collection can be organized within sets, which can also apply geotagging and be connected to a Google map via the tool imapflickr. Photos can be designated as public or private, with private photos only being visible to the uploader or to other users such as friends and family.

Similar to other social sites, Flickr enables groups to be formed around similar photo interests. After joining a Flickr group, recent uploads appear on a user's homepage. Flickr also allows "faves," comments, and easy sharing to other social sites.

Interestingly, Flickr has entered into partnerships with institutions such as the Library of Congress, the National Archives, and the Smithsonian Institution to "first show the hidden treasures of the world's public photography archives."[51]

Flickr can be an especially useful tool for small business, startups, or nonprofits. For example, visuals are a top trend in tourism. Hosting photos on Flickr makes it easy to embed in other social media networks such as blogs, Facebook, and Twitter, or on a website for search engine optimization (SEO) benefits. Flickr allows posting links in photo descriptions to help target audiences find the brand, product, or service. Descriptions can be turned into testimonials, progress reports, event reporting, new product announcements, or even employee profiles.[52]

Flickr mobile use is robust. Flickr has mobile apps for iOS, Android, Windows Phone, and PlayStation Vita. Flickr's mobile app is the fifteenth-most-used mobile app with 5 percent of people indicating they have used it in the previous month.[53] Key performance indicators for Flickr could be views, faves, shares, downloads, group members, and sentiment.

Instagram

 Instagram is an online mobile social networking service that enables users to take photos and videos and share them on a variety of social networking platforms. Instagram was only launched in 2010, but this photo- and video-sharing social-networking service has grown tremendously via its mobile app. Instagram has more than 300 million active users.[54] Nearly 26 percent of online adults use Instagram, up from 13 percent in 2012.[55]

Like other social networks, Instagram's amazing growth (100 million users in nine months) has come from a global audience with 70 percent of Instagram users outside the US.[56] Facebook acquired Instagram in 2013, so integration with the popular network is another added benefit.

Instagram is very popular with teens and young adults. Nielsen reports Instagram is the top photo site among twelve- to seventeen-year-olds.[57] Of online US adults, nearly half of Instagram users are eighteen to twenty-nine years old (48 percent) with another 40 percent in the thirty- to forty-nine-year-old range. From there, older usage drops off quickly. More women than men use Instagram (64 percent versus 36 percent) with the largest group of users having some college education or a college degree (66 percent).[58] Instagram users are less wealthy than other social media outlets, with 27 percent of online users earning less than $30,000 a year. This makes sense, considering many users are younger, in college or high school. By far most users dwell in suburbs or cities (86 percent) versus rural.[59]

Instagram is unique in that it enables users to take pictures and videos, apply digital filters, and share on other social sites, such as Facebook, Twitter, Tumblr, and Flickr. Instagram photos are distinctive in that they are a square shape, similar to the old-time Kodak Instamatic. The service also supports video by allowing up to fifteen-second short clips. This feature was added to compete with Twitter's Vine.

Users can create a social media profile with recently shared photos and a biography. Instagram users follow other users, like and comment on their photos, and share them. Instagram also uses hashtags to categorize photos and videos like Twitter does, and added "direct," which allows users to send photos only to a specific user or group, to compete with other popular services such as Snapchat.[60]

Marketers should look at Instagram as a way to reach a younger targeted audience. From there it can be used in similar ways, such as embedding Instagram photos and videos in a blog or website for improved SEO. Instagram could be used to post photos of products, employees, store environment, or events. Mobile-only Instagram serves as a great channel for engaging photo or video contests to gain user-generated content. Trending hashtags relevant to the social media strategy can be found and used to participate in the discussion to gain followers and attention for an organization. Benefit Cosmetics UK, for example, creates custom photos for Instagram to attract likes, shares, and comments (see figure 8.4).[61]

Instagram is also unique from all the channels discussed in that it started as a mobile-only app and not an online website. There is a website, but it is merely a simpler version of the app. Instagram's mobile app is supported on iOS, Android, and Windows Phone and is the tenth-most-used app, with 11 percent of smartphone users indicating they have used in it in the last month.[62] Instagram also offers native advertising opportunities where marketers and advertisers can purchase in-feed advertisements. Key performance indicators for Instagram could be views, shares, downloads, likes, comments, and sentiment.

Media-Sharing Considerations

Virginia Woolf wanted to reach the "common reader" with her writing. Never since the invention of the printing press has such an explosion in technology enabled more reading and sharing of stories and information. Which of the top three media-sharing channels is right for your audience, message, and big idea?

Other social media channels to consider are the video site Vimeo, which is more oriented toward artistic videos with an older, more adult demographic, and Slideshare, which has many business or B2B opportunities as a place to share presentations and generate leads. Last.fm is an online music database where users' profiles display what they like.[63] Snapchat is a photo- and video-sharing service that has quickly grown in popularity among younger high-school and college-age users due to the anonymity of messages being deleted after ten seconds.[64] As they grow, live-streaming video apps like Periscope and MeerKat could be viable options for the right effort. Search Google for ways marketers are leveraging this new channel to see if it may be the right fit for brand efforts.

Figure 8.4. Benefit Cosmetics UK Custom Instagram Photos

Source: "Benefit Cosmetics Instagram Post," Benefit Cosmetics UK Instagram account, accessed January 18, 2015, https://instagram.com/benefitcosmeticsuk.© Benefit Cosmetics LLC.

SOCIAL PLAN PART 8

Choose Most Strategic Content Sharing

Explore and choose content-sharing channels that best fit your social media plan. Consider all the top social media sharing networks. Research each, looking at the number and makeup of the users to ensure a match with your target audience. Do the brand, product, or service and the big idea fit the type of content that is shared on the channel? How can the organization leverage the real-time, seasonal, and topical characteristics of microblogging? What type of content is ideal for sharing—text, photo, or video? Report all findings and ideas in these areas:

1. Identify microblogs where the target audience is active.
2. Describe the type of content that is shared and popular on each.
3. Find photo- and video-sharing networks that match the target audience.
4. Explain what content the brand could create.

QUESTIONS FOR DISCUSSION

1. "Tweets per minute" is a measure of total activity on Twitter. It is known to spike during large events, such as the 2013 Super Bowl blackout. How could a brand take advantage of these spikes in Twitter activity?
2. Pinterest is unique in its user base and content. Make a list of brands that would work well on the microblog and a list of brands for which Pinterest is not a good fit. Explain your answers.
3. Everyone talks about viral videos. Do some research and develop a list of characteristics or ingredients that make a video go viral.
4. Look at the difference between Facebook posts and Instagram posts. Do some research and explain how a brand should adjust their content to be popular on each platform.

ADDITIONAL EXERCISES

1. For this exercise, join the top microblogs and get an idea of what is happening in this social space. Follow some industry leaders on Twitter, follow your competition, search for some trending topics. What are people doing and saying on the site? Is content mostly text or pictures or are they sharing video? Do they provide links? Do the same for Pinterest. Who knows? You may discover a brilliant business idea, or simply a great new BBQ recipe. Have fun, but also look for strategic business opportunities. How could your business engage consumers, influencers, and the media through microblogging?
2. Jump into the content-sharing sites and look for characteristics your brand, product, or service can leverage. Start with YouTube. You have probably viewed hundreds of videos here, but ask yourself, "What makes a video popular or of interest to me?" Also, consider what type of

consumer-oriented video your organization could produce to help meet your plan objectives. Do the same on Instagram and Pinterest. You are simply exploring here. If these sites are not right for your plan, then don't include them. You want to try them all, but cannot and should not implement them all.

Notes

1. "'Be sincere. Be brief. Be seated.' Public speaking's best advice?" GingerPublicSpeaking.com, accessed February 18, 2015, http://www.gingerpublicspeaking.com/be-sincere-be-brief-be-seated-public-speakings-best-advice.

2. "Edward Everett, 'Gettysburg Address,'" VoicesofDemocracy.com, accessed February 18, 2015, http://voicesofdemocracy.umd.edu/everett-gettysburg-address-speech-text.

3. "The Gettysburg Address," AbrahamLincolnOnline.com, accessed February 18, http://www.abrahamlincolnonline.org/lincoln/speeches/gettysburg.htm.

4. "Gettysburg Address," Wikipedia, last modified February 13, 2015, http://en.wikipedia.org/wiki/Gettysburg_Address.

5. "Top 10 Greatest Speeches," Time.com, accessed February 18, 2015, http://content.time.com/time/specials/packages/completelist/0,29569,1841228,00.html.

6. "Microblogging," Wikipedia, January 18, 2015, http://en.wikipedia.org/wiki/Microblogging.

7. "Microblogging," Wikipedia.

8. "Trendsmap," Trendsmap.com, accessed October 18, 2013, http://trendsmap.com.

9. Emily Pronin and Daniel Wengner, "Manic Thinking: Independent Effects of Thought Speed and Thought Content on Mood," *Psychological Science* 17, no. 9 (2006): 807–813.

10. Nicole Lee, "Twitter Has Over 300 Million, But Still Losing Money," April 28, 2015, http://www.engadget.com/2015/04/28/twitter-q1-2015.

11. "Social Media Site Use by Year," PewInternet.org, January 8, 2015, http://www.pewinternet.org/2015/01/09/social-media-update-2014/pi_2015-01-09_social-media_01.

12. Maeve Duggan and Aaron Smith, "Social Media Update 2013," PewInternet.org, December 30, 2013, http://pewinternet.org/Reports/2013/Social-Media-Update/Main-Findings.aspx.

13. Brandon Smith, "The Beginner's Guide to Twitter," Mashable.com, June 5, 2012, http://mashable.com/2012/06/05/twitter-for-beginners.

14. "Twitter Usage Statistics," InternetLiveStats.com, accessed June 26, 2015, http://www.internetlivestats.com/twitter-statistics.

15. HGTV Twitter account, accessed January 18, 2015, https://twitter.com/hgtv.

16. Smith, "The Beginner's Guide to Twitter."

17. Carl Quintanilla, "CNBC's #TwitterRevolution Premiers on Wednesday, August 7th at 9pm," July 25, 2013, http://www.cnbc.com/id/100915.

18. Allison Stadd, "59% of Journalists Worldwide Use Twitter, Up from 47% In 2012 [STUDY]," MediaBistro.com, June 26, 2013, http://www.mediabistro.com/alltwitter/journalists-twitter_b45416.

19. Craig Smith, "By the Numbers: 23 Amazing Pinterest Stats," Digital Marketing Ramblings (blog), accessed September 4, 2013, http://expandedramblings.com/index.php/pinterest-stats.

20. "Pinterest Has 70 Million Users. More than 70% Are in the U.S.," Semiocast.com, July 10, 2013, http://semiocast.com/en/publications/2013_07_10_Pinterest_has_70_million_users.

21. "Social Media Site Use by Year," PewInternet.org.

22. Duggan and Smith, "Social Media Update 2013."

23. "How to Use Pinterest: A Beginner's Guide," BeeLiked.com, accessed September 4, 2013, http://beeliked.com/resources/how-to-use-pinterest-a-beginner-s-guide.

24. Campbell's Kitchen Pinterest account, accessed February 18, 2015, http://www.pinterest.com/campbellkitchen.

25. "How to Use Pinterest: A Beginner's Guide," BeeLiked.com.

26. Donna Tam, "Pinterest, Now with Price Alerts, Panders to Shoppers," CNET.com, August 1, 2013, http://news.cnet.com/8301-1023_3-57596521-93/pinterest-now-with-price-alerts-panders-to-shoppers.

27. "Pinterest for Business," Pinterest.com, accessed October 8, 2013, http://business.pinterest.com/analytics.

28. Smith, "By the Numbers: 23 Amazing Pinterest Stats."

29. Virginia Woolf, *The Common Reader.* New York: Harcourt (1984).

30. "What Internet Users Like to Share on Social Media Sites," MarketingCharts.com, September 19, 2013, http://www.marketingcharts.com/wp/online/what-internet-users-like-to-share-on-social-media-sites-36804.

31. Kristen Purcell, "Online Video 2013," PewInternet.org, October 2013, http://pewinternet.org/Reports/2013/Online-Video/Main-Findings/Online-video-2013.aspx.

32. "What Internet Users Like to Share on Social Media Sites," MarketingCharts.com.

33. Ayaz Nanji, "Why People Share on Social Media." MarketingProfs.com, http://www.marketingprofs.com/charts/2013/11564/why-people-share-on-social-media.

34. Stan Schroeder, "YouTube Now Has One Billion Monthly Users," Mashable.com, March 21, 2013, http://mashable.com/2013/03/21/youtube-one-billion.

35. Eric Larson, "The Beginner's Guide to YouTube," Mashable.com, October 5, 2013, http://mashable.com/2013/10/05/youtube-beginner-guide.

36. Jeff Bullas, "35 Mind Numbing YouTube Facts, Figures and Statistics—Infographic," Jeffbullas.com (blog), May 23, 2012, http://www.jeffbullas.com/2012/05/23/35-mind-numbing-youtube-facts-figures-and-statistics-infographic.

37. Purcell, "Online Video 2013."

38. Sam Gutelle, "As Early Adopters Grow Up, Will YouTube's Audience Age in Place?" Tubefilter.com, April 2, 2013, http://www.tubefilter.com/2013/04/02/youtube-age-in-place-audience-demographics.

39. Larson, "The Beginner's Guide to YouTube."

40. "Dove United States YouTube Channel," YouTube.com, accessed January 18, 2015, https://www.youtube.com/channel/UC0uGC_EBwAxw3ljqeGjy2qw.

41. Larson, "The Beginner's Guide to YouTube."

42. Larson, "The Beginner's Guide to YouTube."

43. Brian Chappell, "2012 Social Network Analysis Report Demographic Geographic and Search Data Revealed," IgniteSocialMedia.com, July 31, 2012, http://www.ignitesocialmedia.com/social-media-stats/2012-social-network-analysis-report.

44. Gutelle, "As Early Adopters Grow Up, Will YouTube's Audience Age In Place?"

45. "Social Media Active Users by Network [INFOGRAPHIC]," TheSocialMediaHat.com (blog), May 26, 2015, http://www.thesocialmediahat.com/active-users.

46. "Flickr," Yahoo Advertising, accessed October 18, 2013, http://advertising.yahoo.com/article/flickr.html.

47. Michelle Meyers, "How Instagram Became the Network for Tweens," CNET.com, September 8, 2012, http://news.cnet.com/8301-1023_3-57508430-93/how-instagram-became-the-social-network-for-tweens.

48. Chappell, "2012 Social Network Analysis Report Demographic Geographic and Search Data Revealed."

49. "Flickr," Wikipedia, last modified February 12, 2015, http://en.wikipedia.org/wiki/Flickr.

50. "Flickr," Yahoo Advertising.

51. "Flickr," Wikipedia.

52. Becky McCray, "How a Small Business Can Use the New Flickr," SmallBizSurvival.com, June 25, 2013, http://smallbizsurvival.com/2013/06/how-a-small-business-can-use-the-new -flickr.html.

53. Cooper Smith, "Google+ Is The Fourth Most-Used SmartPhone App," BusinessInsider .com, September 5, 2013, http://www.businessinsider.com/google-smartphone-app-popularity -2013-9#infographic.

54. Josh Constine, "Instagram Hits 300 Million Monthly Users To Surpass Twitter, Keeps It Real With Verified Badges," Techcrunch (blog), December 10, 2014, http://techcrunch.com/ 2014/12/10/not-a-fad.

55. "Social Media Site Use by Year," PewInternet.org.

56. Constine, "Instagram Hits 300 Million Monthly Users to Surpass Twitter, Keeps It Real With Verified Badges."

57. Meyers, "How Instagram Became the Network for Tweens."

58. "Social Media Site Use by Year," PewInternet.org.

59. Duggan and Smith, "Social Media Update 2013."

60. "Instagram," Wikipedia, last modified February 15, 2014, http://en.wikipedia.org/wiki/ Instagram#cite_note-instagram1-8.

61. "Benefit Cosmetics UK Instagram Post," Instagram.com, accessed January 18, 2015, https://instagram.com/benefitcosmetics/?hl=en.

62. Smith, "Google+ Is The Fourth Most-Used SmartPhone App."

63. Debbie Hemley, "26 Tips for Using Instagram for Business," SocialMediaExaminer.com, September 10, 2013, http://www.socialmediaexaminer.com/instagram-for-business-tips/.

64. "Snapchat," Wikipedia, last modified February 5, 2015, http://en.wikipedia.org/wiki/ Snapchat.

Geo-location, Ratings, and Reviews

Not all those who wander are lost.[1]

—J. R. R. Tolkien

PREVIEW

Many people like "checking in" online and giving reviews and ratings. How much of a difference can they make? Business professor Michael Luca set out to measure this in his research, "Reviews, Reputation and Revenue." In a study of Seattle Yelp restaurant reviews from 2003 to 2009, the researcher found that a one-star increase in Yelp rating led to a 5 to 9 percent increase in revenue. However, the increase was only found with independent restaurants, not chain restaurants. In fact, the study found that chain-restaurant market share declined as Yelp penetration increased.[2]

A negative result of this powerful influence on business is that it has created an intense incentive to post fake reviews. Michael Luca teamed up with Georgios Zervas in a follow-up Yelp study. They found that businesses without many existing reviews and those that face intense competition are more likely to engage in review fraud. How big is the overall problem? In a site-wide measurement of suspicious reviews, the researchers found that roughly 16 percent of all reviews are filtered or removed by Yelp for being fake.[3] These findings are important to keep in mind. Where there is money to be made, some will try to cheat the system. Yet marketers and advertisers must always consider the ethical consequences. In the end, getting caught is far worse for a business than the initial economic gain.

Geo-location

J. R. R. Tolkien is best known for his fantasy books *The Hobbit* and *Lord of the Rings*, which have since been made into a very successful Hollywood film series. His quote can be applied to social location networks where users discover new adventures and earn rewards for wandering to new locations.

As smartphones have grown in popularity, so has the use of real-time location data, which has enabled sharing a user's location with friends or the public in the form of a check-in. **Check-in** is defined as self-reported positioning to share one's physical location through a social networking service.[4] Foursquare is the big social player and innovator in this category that built a social community around checking in to locations and earning points and badges for doing so. Not to be outdone, social media services such as Facebook, Instagram, and Twitter have since added optional location layers to their channels.

Roughly 12 percent of all smartphone owners used geo-location or geosocial services such as Foursquare to share their location with friends. **Geosocial** is a type of social networking in which user-submitted location data allow social networks to connect and coordinate users with local people, businesses, or events. It is interesting to note that after an initial increase in usage Pew Research Center reports that social checking in actually declined from 18 percent in 2012 to 12 percent. Marketers will have to wait and see if this is a long-term trend.[5]

Foursquare may have been the innovator in checking in, but other social services have taken some of this activity from them. Facebook actually has the largest percent of geosocial users with 39 percent, followed by Foursquare with 18 percent, and Google+ at 14 percent. Other useful mentions are Instagram at 5 percent and Yelp with 5 percent of check-ins.[6]

Geo-location still offers many opportunities for businesses to further engage target consumers and drive participation at physical locations. The top three location-based social services are Foursquare and location layers on Facebook and Google+, and these could be the optimal fit for an organization's objectives, target audience, or big idea.

Foursquare

Foursquare is a personalized local search-and-discovery-service mobile app that enables users to find friends and read recommendations. Like Instagram, Foursquare is a social networking service first developed for mobile devices. Foursquare has 50 million registered users with some 6 million check-ins per day.[7] The social service is split between US and global participants with 50 percent of users outside the US.[8]

Foursquare has slightly more male users (60 percent) than female (40 percent) users. The social media service is most popular with eighteen- to twenty-nine-year-olds (40 percent) making up the largest age group. They are slightly less affluent than some other social services with nearly half (49 percent) earning less than $50,000 a year. Forty-three percent of Foursquare users have some college education and 40 percent have no college education.[9]

Foursquare's community is based on users connecting with friends and checking in at venues to earn points and badges. Different amounts of points are earned for different categories, such as 1 point for checking in to a place a user has been before and 4 points for checking in to a new category. Users who check in the most at a venue become the "mayor," which can become a heated competition. Check-ins get very specific within certain areas of buildings, and many users indicate participating in a specific activity at the venue. Venue tags are used in Foursquare, as well as private to-do lists and public tips that give suggestions on what to see, eat, and do at a location.[10]

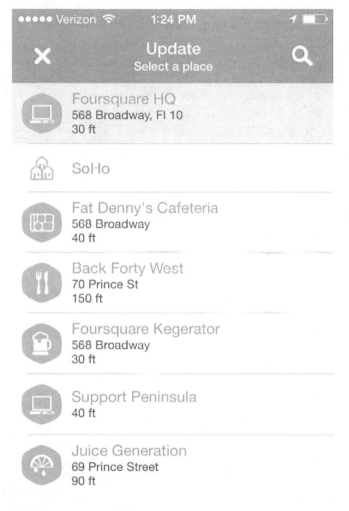

Figure 9.1. Swarm still pulls in Foursquare business information.

Source: "Swarm for Business," Foursquare Help Center, accessed January 18, 2015, https://support.foursquare.com/hc/en-us/articles/202005800 -Swarm-for-Merchants.

The Explore function allows users to browse locations by category or search words. Foursquare added a like button similar to Facebook, a ratings system similar to Yelp, and a "recently opened" feature. Many marketers have used Foursquare check-ins as a key promotional tool to drive in-store local and regional traffic.

Businesses can offer specials such as discounts and free offers when users check in. A good tool to promote these offers is a Foursquare door sign. Like other social services, Foursquare also allows organizations to create pages of tips and allows users to follow the company to get special tips for checking in. Companies can allow users to unlock badges for completing a specific number of check-ins. Organizations have also included Add to My Foursquare buttons on websites to direct visitors to add a location to their to-do lists.[11]

In 2014 Foursquare made a bold move by dividing its social network into two apps based on its two most popular functions: a new version of Foursquare and Swarm. Swarm is the more personal app for locating friends and checking into venues. With this update, Foursquare became more focused on mobile local searches and activity recommendations. For business, Foursquare is still the app for connecting with users. People check-in through the Swarm app, but tips, photos, and location information are still based in Foursquare. Marketers are still able to see a list of active customers.[12] People now use Swarm as the personal side of Foursquare to "keep up and meet up" with friends, but can still check-in to let friends know they are at a business. Businesses show up as a check-in option if a user is nearby (see figure 9.1).[13]

Foursquare's mobile app works on a large variety of platforms including iOS, Android, Symbian, Series 40, MeeGo, WebOS, Windows Phone, Blackberry, and PlayStation Vita. In a smartphone user survey Foursquare's mobile app was the ninth-most-used mobile app with 6 percent of people indicating they had used it in the previous month.[14] Foursquare key performance indicators could be views, shares, check-ins, likes, followers, badges, and sentiment.

Facebook Places

Facebook is a major player in the social media scene that is hard to ignore with more than one billion monthly global users[15] and nearly half of the total US population.[16] The information previously covered on Facebook will not be repeated, but instead this section will focus on the social network's location-service features.

Facebook Places started as a mobile app that is no longer available. Now location-tagging is integrated into Facebook itself. This feature enables users to tag or check-in to a specific place or business, which then shows up as a status update, image, or video post and appears in the user's news feed. Facebook users can tag friends in specific locations within an update or post, which then appears in the friends' news feeds. These features have been added to emulate the features available in Foursquare.[17]

Another important feature is that when users click on "check-in," businesses and organizations nearest to their current location will appear as options for the post. Organizations should make sure the business's physical location is in their Facebook page description to automatically be included in the Facebook Places directory to show up in search results. A post tagged with the business location will lead those who click it to the business's Facebook page. Location tagging on Facebook adds another way for organizations

Figure 9.2. Facebook Places allows users to find businesses nearby.

Source: "Connect to Your Customers with Facebook WiFi," Facebook Business, accessed January 15, 2015, https://www.facebook.com/business/facebook-wifi. © Facebook.

to appear in news feeds, but also allows businesses to publish promotions and discounts on the Facebook page after users click on the tag in a news feed.[18]

Other Facebook location features take their cue from Yelp. In addition to checking in, Facebook users now can also "Recommend This Place" with a description and five star rating. It isn't hard to see how this feature is important for business. Users can make reviews to be seen by all and share with friends. This feature also has enabled Facebook users to make restaurant reservations, which can be seen as an attempt to compete with other social services such as OpenTable.[19] In addition, the Nearby tab on the Facebook mobile app can help users find businesses (see figure 9.2).[20]

The addition of these features has pushed Facebook into the area of local search and entertainment discovery. With Facebook's size, businesses should pay attention and be sure to monitor and manage their presence there. The addition of user-generated reviews and ratings gives Facebook page owners less control over what will appear on their pages. Be sure to monitor for positive and negative sentiment and check-ins as key additional Facebook KPIs. But these features also represent ways for an organization to get exposure on the social network through graph search and news feed distribution.[21]

Google+ Locations

Google+ is a fairly new social network, only launched in 2011, but Google has grown this network quickly to 540 million monthly active users.[22] Adding location services to Google+ was a way to further the network's growth.

When updating mapping for mobile devices, Google retired its location service Google Latitude near the end of 2013. At the same time Google added location-sharing and check-in features to Google+ as a way to compete with Foursquare, Facebook, and Yelp.

Google+ Locations provides another reason for organizations to pay attention to the Google+ social network and optimize a presence there. One advantage of Google+ is the tight control that circles offer users. This applies to location sharing in that a user may choose to add location sharing to only specific circles, such as family or friends versus public. This could encourage increased adoption for people with privacy concerns about check-ins and everyone knowing where they are.[23]

For organizations that leverage location, Google+ Locations may be a valuable tool in addition to the mainstays of Foursquare and Facebook. Other business uses to consider are using Google+ Locations to locate and view company representatives in a city, or find coworkers, clients, and leads during conferences and conventions.[24] For Google+ Locations, an additional KPI to measure could be location shares.

Geo-location Considerations

As Foursquare says on its opening screen, geo-location social services are all about trying to "keep up & meet up with friends on-the-go." These services really bridge the gap between fantasy digital worlds and real physical places. J. R. R. Tolkien would probably have been inspired by this combination. What kind of brand story can the brand tell to engage and encourage participation from the target audience? If driving consumers to a location supports the organization's goals, geosocial may be an ideal channel in the social media plan.

Ratings and Reviews

Mark Twain once said, "The public is the only critic whose opinion is worth anything at all."[25] Mark Twain wrote *Adventures of Huckleberry Finn*, which has been called the great American novel. His quote above is truer today than ever before. As seen in the early chapters of this book, social media has turned every individual into a publisher with the potential influence and reach of a professional. An organization may get a rave review in the *New York Times*, but angry consumers publishing negative comments through ratings and reviews can stagnate sales.

Reviews are reports that give someone's opinion about the quality of a product, service, or performance. **Ratings** are also a measurement of how good or bad something is, but expressed specifically on a scale that is a relative estimate or evaluation.[26] Five-point rating scales are popular and can be expressed as straight numbers, stars, or even spoons. Reviews are longer descriptions of a critic's opinion of a product or experience with a service. Back in Mark Twain's day, most critics were professional and only a few were published. Here we are talking about social media–powered ratings and reviews where any amateur critic is able to voice his or her opinion on numerous social channels.

How important are social ratings and reviews? According to a survey by Dimensional Research, 90 percent of respondents who remembered reading online reviews said positive online reviews influenced buying decisions and 86 percent said negative reviews

MINI CASE
C
McDonald's Q&A

In 2012 McDonald's Canada made a bold move when it launched a Q&A social media campaign that truly embraced transparency. The company knew that consumers were active with ratings and reviews of the restaurant and asking tough questions online about how the company made its food. They launched a website to answer user-submitted questions head-on about ingredients, prep, food sourcing, and advertising. Answers appeared via text, photos, and video allowing the brand to address rumors, misinformation, and myths. The campaign was a success, attracting global media attention fielding more than fourteen thousand questions within months and spawning an integrated traditional advertising campaign of TV, digital, and outdoor ads.[a]

In 2014 McDonald's expanded the Q&A campaign to the US with the help of MythBusters TV show cohost Grant Imahara. The "Our Food. Your Questions" campaign used TV commercials showing real people's questions and inviting consumers to pose more via social media. The effort also used webisode videos (short online-only TV shows) by Imahara addressing consumers' main doubts and questions about McDonald's food. The brand said this was their first big effort into two-way dialogue with consumers giving them a behind-the-scenes view.[b]

[a] Paula Bernstein, "Would You Like to See How We Make Our Fries With That? Behind McDonald's Big Transparency Play," FastCompany.com, November 6, 2012, http://www.fastcocreate.com/1681832/would-you-like-to-see-how-we-make-our-fries-with-that-behind-mcdonalds-big-transparency-play.

[b] "McDonald's, 'MythBuster' Launch Food Q&A," HuffingtonPost.com, October 13, 2014, http://www.huffingtonpost.com/burgerbusiness/mcdonalds-mythbuster-laun_b_5976250.html.

influenced their buying. Where do these reviews happen? Reviews can be found on online review sites, retail sites, Facebook, company sites, Yelp, and Twitter.[27]

This trend is growing, as 58 percent are more likely to share customer service experiences today than five years ago. This sharing now occurs more on social media (45 percent) than online review sites (35 percent). Interestingly, nearly 100 percent of those in high-income brackets (over $150,000) said they share customer service experiences with others. What's more, this sharing is not limited only to B2C (business-to-consumer) goods, with 62 percent saying they purchase more products or services from a B2B (business-to-business) company after reading a positive review, which is higher than the 42 percent response for B2C.[28]

In a survey conducted during the holiday shopping season, consumers indicated that online ratings and reviews influenced both their online (48 percent) and in-store (37 percent) purchases more than other factors, such as email (35 percent online, 27 percent in-store) and Google search (31 percent online, 20 percent in-store). Display advertising only influenced purchase by 16 percent online and 15 percent in-store. Additionally, respondents indicated mobile advertising only influenced 11 percent of online and 9 percent of in-store purchases.[29] Social ratings and reviews can be very influential in purchase decisions. While organizations cannot and should not directly create reviews and ratings, they need to be monitored, influenced, and optimized to help meet organization goals.

This section will look at three ratings-and-reviews services to give an overview of how these channels could possibly fit into a social media plan, target audience, and big idea.

Yelp

 Yelp is a website and mobile app that publishes crowd-sourced ratings and reviews about local businesses. Yelp is an early innovator into social recommendations, first founded in 2004. Yelp has grown to 142 million unique visitors per month with over 77 million user-generated reviews.[30] Because Yelp is location-specific it has expanded city by city, first starting in the US, but now in cities across the world.[31] Still Yelp remains a US-focused social channel with only 18 percent of traffic coming from outside the country.[32]

Yelp users are more female (54 percent) than male (46 percent) and middle-aged, with 62 percent of visitors between the ages of twenty-five and fifty-four. Yelp users are on average middle income, yet 38 percent earn over $100,000 a year. Yelp users are also highly educated with nearly three-quarters (71 percent) having attended college or graduate school.[33]

Yelp encourages users to review and rate businesses using their five-star rating system. The system filters these ratings and reviews to remove unhelpful, biased, or fraudulent reviews.[34] To encourage and reward good reviews, the service offers a Yelp Elite Squad designation to those who offer well-written reviews, offer great tips, have a full profile, and communicate nicely with other Yelp users. Yelp emphasizes to businesses that people love to talk about the things they love. Statistics show that 66 percent of all reviews on Yelp are four stars or higher.[35]

Depending on the type of business, Yelp ratings can significantly impact performance. Yelp restaurants in Seattle were found to increase revenue 5 to 9 percent per one-star increase in Yelp rating.[36] Yelp users can review any local business, service, or place, such as restaurants, shops, bars, salons, spas, dentists, mechanics, parks, and museums.

In addition to reviews, Yelp allows users to find local events, from music fests and parties to dance lessons and networking opportunities. Users also submit lists, which can be, for example, top dinners, favorite places, wedding venues, or fitness hot spots. In 2010 Yelp added a location-sharing check-in feature that includes badges with regular rankings such as duke, baron, or king.[37]

Businesses can use Yelp's check-in feature for promotions and events, and it can be a great way to jumpstart traffic through public relations. In addition, Yelp has added restaurant reservations as a feature through its Yelp SeatMe and free Yelp Reservations, integrated with OpenTable. Yelp also offers local city discussion forums where users can talk about various local interests under various categories. To participate, a user must register and create a user profile similar to other social networking sites.

A business can set up a free account with a profile to post offers and photos and to directly message customers. Yelp offers robust analytics with an alert system so business owners can respond right away to negative or positive comments. Yelp helps organizations identify where customers are coming from and also identifies the most vocal fans and critics for outreach.[38] Yelp now offers businesses ways to entice regular and new customers to purchase with Yelp Deals and Gift Certificates (see figure 9.3).[39]

Figure 9.3. Yelp offers incentives to drive traffic to business.

Source: Morgan Remmers, "Get Ready for Holiday Shoppers with Yelp Deals and Gift Certificates!" Yelp Blog for Business Owners (blog), October 31, 2014, https://biz.yelp.com/blog/get-ready-for-holiday-shoppers-with-yelp-deals-and-gift-certificates. © Yelp Inc.

Yelp started as a website, but over the years it has become increasingly mobile. By 2012 45 percent of Yelp's traffic was coming from mobile devices. Yelp mobile apps are available for iOS, Android, Windows Phone, and Blackberry.[40] Yelp's mobile app is the twelfth-most-used mobile app, with 3 percent of people indicating they have used it in the past month.[41] Key performance indicators for Yelp could be views, shares, comments, ratings, check-ins, reservations, lists, number of reviews, and sentiment of reviews.

Citysearch

 Citysearch is an online city guide that provides information about businesses in the categories of dining, entertainment, retail, travel, and professionals services. Citysearch is one of the oldest and best-known review sites. Started in 1995, this online city guide has grown over the years by purchasing competitors such as Sidewalk.com from Microsoft. Citysearch's parent company, CityGrid Media, also owns Insider Pages and Urbanspoon.[42] Citysearch has more than 14.5 million business listings with user reviews and ratings. CitiGrid has roughly 2 million unique US users visit the site every month down from a high of nearly 4 million visitors. Much of this traffic seems to have been lost to the popular competitor Yelp.[43] Citysearch has no global presence and is limited to major cities across the US.

User statistics are hard to locate for Citysearch, but in general more women than men use the site. Most users have completed some college with a smaller number completing a bachelor's degree. Most browsing of the site occurs from school or work.[44]

Citysearch was launched as online local directory that provides information about dining, entertainment, travel businesses, and professional services. But in response to new social media competitors such as Yelp, in 2012 it redesigned and repositioned itself as a recommendations site. Scrapping its old star ratings system, the site now allows users to give a basic thumbs-up or thumbs-down, which are then turned into percentage scores for comparison among businesses. In addition, the site now encourages more user-generated content via user-written tips and user-uploaded photos. They also include additional professional editorial content from local experts called scouts.[45]

Other Citysearch features include opportunities for local or regionally focused businesses. Best of Citysearch is a feature that gives local people a chance to vote for favorite businesses in categories such as Restaurants, Nightlife, Hotels, and Services. Nominations for Best of Citysearch come from editors, and throughout the voting period visitors cast votes for their favorite local business. Then top ten businesses in each category are revealed to their cities. Top businesses get Best of Citysearch badges displayed on their listings.[46] Best of Citysearch is a way to build awareness of a local business or regional location.[47]

Claiming a business's page is free, but upgrades let marketers enhance the listing page with a bio, photos, video, and extra text. Upgraded accounts can also add deals and special offers, respond to reviews, and run targeted ads on the site. Pricing is performance-based, and Citysearch does not release that information publicly. Spam is moderated via both humans and machine.[48] The future of Citisearch could be up in the air. Significant layoffs at the company and losses in website traffic to Yelp indicate the company could be struggling to find its unique selling point.[49]

Citysearch has also transitioned from an online website to becoming more mobile-friendly. Currently it offers full-feature mobile apps for iOS and Android. By 2012, 30 percent of Citysearch's traffic came from mobile devices.[50] Key performance indicators for Citysearch could be views, shares, votes, photos, tips, and sentiment of tips.

Google+ Local

Once again, Google appears with an effort to get a foothold in another area of online business. In 2012 Google+ Local replaced Google Places and is integrated into the new Google Maps.

Through Google+, users submit reviews and five-star ratings for businesses that appear on Google Maps. In addition, users can upload photos. These reviews and photos will help others when they are checking out a place, and are integrated into the aggregate score that other people see. Google has also acquired Zagat and features Zagat reviews in Google+ Local for a combination of listing, Zagat, and Google+ user content.[51]

It is important for businesses to claim their listings and ensure information is correct. To make a Google+ Local listing stand out, add additional content of up to ten photos and five videos directly linked from YouTube. Monitoring user comments is also a good idea, considering the enormous amount of search traffic directed by Google each month. Business owners can still mange local listing information through Google Places for Business.[52]

Google+ Local is mobile through the Google+ app, but also through the Google Maps app, which is the world's most popular app for smartphones with more than 54 percent of global owners using it at least once during the previous month in a recent survey.[53] Key performance indicators for Google+ Local could be views, shares, ratings, reviews, and sentiment of reviews.

Ratings and Reviews Considerations

Other rating and review social channels to consider are Insider Pages, which is more oriented toward service businesses; Angie's List, which is a paid member review site focused on contractors and doctors; and TripAdvisor, which specializes in travel and essential for hotels and restaurants that cater to tourists. If a marketer's or advertiser's product is sold on your own website or on top online retailer websites such as Amazon.com, ratings and reviews there should be monitored as well. Mark Twain may have been more right than he knew. The power of public opinion (amateur critics) is undeniable in today's social media environment.

Depending on the type of organization, product, and service, ratings-and-reviews social channels should be considered. Where is the brand target audience expressing their opinions about the brand and its competitors? Has the organization optimized its brand presence in that channel, and are they monitoring it, ready to engage both the positive and negative ratings and reviews? Or perhaps the brand doesn't have much of a presence, but needs to encourage comments and content from the most loyal fans. In what ways can happy customers be encouraged to share their opinions?

SOCIAL PLAN PART 9

Strategic Use of Location, Ratings, and Reviews

Take an in-depth look at geo-location channels and features in social networking sites. Also analyze ratings and review sites and features on social networks. How can these features benefit the brand and campaign? Where is the target audience? Are they checking in or looking up ratings and reviews about the products and services? Where are they doing it? What can the brand do to leverage these features and influence conversation and discovery? What type of content (text, photo, or video) is needed to best take advantage of these social services? Report all findings and ideas in these areas:

1. Identify geo-location channels or social networks with geo-location features where the target audience is participating.
2. Describe the type of activity and content that is popular on each.
3. Find the rating and review networks where the target audience is most active. In what social networks or retail websites are they discovering ratings and reviews?
4. Discover and explain how the organization can best leverage this information about the brand to help meet business objectives.

QUESTIONS FOR DISCUSSION

1. Facebook has added geo-location features such as checking in and the Nearby tab. How many Facebook members are actually using these features? Is activity large enough to warrant business activity?
2. Conduct additional research into the Foursquare split into two apps with Swarm. Has the split been a success? What do businesses need to know to take advantage of the new features?
3. Yelp can make or break a local business. How accurate are ratings and reviews on the website? Do some research into the real impact of Yelp on local business, both positive and negative.
4. Google+ has added geo-location and ratings and reviews integrated with Google Maps. Dig deeper into all aspects of Google+. What are some best practices for organizations to leverage a social network that seems to be including it all?

ADDITIONAL EXERCISES

1. Go onto Facebook and Google+ and explore their check-in features. Whether you are comfortable checking in yourself or not, see the rich information location-sharing offers. Also, join Foursquare. This network is the innovator and still important. If your organization has a physical location, location-based social media could be a key part of your strategy. Perhaps the business is already on Facebook but has not thought about taking advantage of location-based features. Take some time and brainstorm ways the brand could use location information for a business advantage.
2. Reviews are powerful. Have you taken the time to read them? Find all the ratings and reviews written about your organization, brand, product, or service. Start with key ratings and reviews sites in the industry and then move into the social media channels highlighted here. What did you discover? If there are few reviews, what do you need to do to get people writing? Are the reviews negative? What do you need to fix? Are reviews positive? How do you leverage them in other social channels and encourage more?

Notes

1. "Lost," BrainyQuote.com, accessed February 18, 2015, http://www.brainyquote.com/quotes/keywords/lost.html.

2. Brad Plumer, "How Yelp Is Killing Chain Restaurants," WashingtonPost.com (blog), October 3, 2011, http://www.washingtonpost.com/blogs/wonkblog/post/how-yelp-is-killing-chain-restaurants/2011/10/03/gIQAokJvHL_blog.html.

3. Kevin Li, "Research: Underdog Businesses Are More Likely to Post Fake Yelp Reviews," *Harvard Business Review,* August 30, 2013, https://hbr.org/2013/08/research-underdog-businesses-a.

4. "Check-in," Wikipedia, last modified April 30, 2015, https://en.wikipedia.org/wiki/Check-in.

5. Kathryn Zickuhr, "Location-Based Services," PewInternet.org, September 12, 2013, http://pewinternet.org/Reports/2013/Location/Main-Report/LocationBased-Services.aspx.

6. Zickuhr, "Location-Based Services."

7. Sarah Frier, "Checking Into What's Behind Foursquare's $41 Million Infusion," Bloomberg Business.com, April 11, 2013, http://go.bloomberg.com/tech-deals/2013 04 11-checking-into -whats-behind-foursquares-41-million-infusion.

8. "Foursquare," Wikipedia, last modified February 15, 2015, http://en.wikipedia.org/wiki/ Foursquare.

9. Brandon Gaille, "26 Great Foursquare Demographics," BrandonGaille.com, January 13, 2015, http://brandongaille.com/26-great-foursquare-demographics/.

10. "Foursquare," Wikipedia.

11. "Foursquare," Wikipedia.

12. Evan Lepage, "Foursquare vs. the Swarm App: What's the Difference?" Hootsuite.com (blog), accessed February 18, 2015, http://blog.hootsuite.com/foursquare-vs-the-swarm-app -whats-the-difference.

13. "Swarm for Business," Foursquare Help Center, accessed January 18, 2015, https://support .foursquare.com/hc/en-us/articles/202005800-Swarm-for-Merchants.

14. Cooper Smith, "Google+ Is the Fourth Most-Used SmartPhone App," BusinessInsider .com, September 5, 2013, http://www.businessinsider.com/google-smartphone-app-popularity -2013-9#infographic.

15. Donna Tam, "Facebook Earnings by the Numbers: 819M Mobile Users," CNET.com, July 24, 2013, http://news.cnet.com/8301-1023_3-57595333-93/facebook-earnings-by-the-numbers -819m-mobile-users.

16. Maximilian Nierhoff, "Facebook Country Stats February 2013—Top 10 Countries Lose Users Due to the Ongoing Account Cleanup," Quintly.com (blog), February 4, 2013, http://www .quintly.com/blog/2013/02/facebook-country-stats-february-2013-top-10-countries-lose-users.

17. Wilson Alvarez, "Foursquare versus Facebook Places," WilsonAlvarez.com (blog), February 14, 2013, http://www.wilsonalvarez.com/foursquare-versus-facebook-places/.

18. Alvarez, "Foursquare versus Facebook Places."

19. "Find Places Nearby and Check In," Facebook Help Center, accessed October 10, 2014, https://www.facebook.com/help/461075590584469.

20. "Connect to Your Customers with Facebook WiFi," Facebook Business, accessed January 15, 2015, https://www.facebook.com/business/facebook-wifi.

21. Brittany Darwell, "Facebook Lets Users Rate Any Place and Change Their Ratings from Desktop Pages," InsideFacebook.com, May 5, 2013, http://www.insidefacebook.com/2013/05/15/ facebook-lets-users-rate-any-place-and-change-their-ratings-from-desktop-pages/.

22. "Social Media Active Users by Network [INFOGRAPHIC]," TheSocialMediaHat.com (blog), May 26, 2015, http://www.thesocialmediahat.com/active-users.

23. Jennifer Beese, "Search Giant Retires Latitude, Readies Google+ Location Services," Sproutsocial.com (blog), July 11, 2013, http://sproutsocial.com/insights/google-plus-latitude.

24. Greg Finn, "Miss Google Latitude? Google+ With Location Sharing Is Now Be [sic] a Suitable Alternative," CyprusNorth.com, November 27, 2013, http://cypressnorth.com/social-media/ miss-google-latitude-google-location-sharing-now-suitable-alternative.

25. "Critic," BrainyQuote.com, accessed February 18, 2015, http://www.brainyquote.com/ quotes/keywords/critic.html.

26. "Review," Merriam-Webster.com, accessed February 18, 2015, http://www.merriam -webster.com/dictionary/review?show=0&t=1389524908.

27. Amy Gesenhues, "Survey: 90% of Customers Say Buying Decisions Are Influenced by Online Reviews," MarketingLand.com, April 9, 2013, http://marketingland.com/survey -customers-more-frustrated-by-how-long-it-takes-to-resolve-a-customer-service-issue-than-the -resolution-38756.

28. Gesenhues, "Survey: 90% of Customers Say Buying Decisions Are Influenced by Online Reviews."

29. "Ratings and Reviews a Top Shopping Influencer During the Holiday Season," Marketing Charts.com, January 9, 2014, http://www.marketingcharts.com/wp/online/ratings-and-reviews -a-top-shopping-influencer-during-the-holiday-season-39087/?utm_campaign=rssfeed&utm _source=mc&utm_medium=textlink.

30. "10 Things You Should Know About Yelp," Yelp.com, accessed June 26, 2015, http:// www.yelp.com/about.

31. "Yelp, Inc.," Wikipedia, last modified February 12, 2015, http://en.wikipedia.org/wiki/ Yelp.

32. Samantha Shankman, "Yelp Brushed Off the Competition with a Focus on Mobile and Global Expansion," Skift.com, October 13, 2013, http://skift.com/2013/10/30/yelp-brushes-off -the-competition-with-a-focus-on-mobile-and-global-expansion.

33. "Audience: Who's On Yelp," Yelp.com, accessed June 26, 2015, http://www.yelp.com/ advertise/agency/audience.

34. "Yelp, Inc.," Wikipedia.

35. "Yelp Common Questions," Yelp.com, accessed October 10, 2014, https://biz.yelp.com/ support/common_questions.

36. Michael Luca, "Reviews, Reputation, and Revenue: The Case of Yelp.com," Harvard Business School, September 16, 2011, http://www.hbs.edu/faculty/Publication%20Files/12-016.pdf.

37. "Yelp Common Questions," Yelp.com.

38. "Introduction to Ratings and Review Sites," SocialQuickstarter.com, accessed October 10, 2014, http://www.socialquickstarter.com/content/78-introduction_to_ratings_and_review_sites.

39. Morgan Remmers, "Get Ready for Holiday Shoppers with Yelp Deals and Gift Certificates!" Yelp Blog for Business Owners (blog), October 31, 2014, https://biz.yelp.com/blog/get -ready-for-holiday-shoppers-with-yelp-deals-and-gift-certificates.

40. "Yelp, Inc.," Wikipedia.

41. Smith, "Google+ Is the Fourth Most-Used SmartPhone App."

42. "Citysearch," Wikipedia, last modified February 14, 2015, http://en.wikipedia.org/wiki/ Citysearch.

43. "Citysearch," Crunchbase.com, accessed February 18, 2015, http://crunchbase.com/company/ citysearch.

44. "Citysearch," Alexa.com, accessed October 10, 2014, http://www.alexa.com/siteinfo/ citysearch.com.

45. Greg Sterling, "Citysearch Redesigns and Repositions as Recommendations Site," Screen werk.com, June 28, 2012, http://screenwerk.com/2012/06/28/citysearch-redesigns-and-repositions -as-recommendations-site.

46. "Citysearch," Wikipedia.

47. "Best of Citysearch," Citysearch.com, accessed January 18, 2015, http://www.citysearch .com/best.

48. Christopher Null, "Yelp Alternative: Which User Review Services Matter?," PCWorld .com, http://www.pcworld.com/article/249770/beyond_yelp_which_user_review_services_matter _.html.

49. Ingrid Lunden, "CityGrid, Parent of CitySearch and Urbanspoon, Lays Off Two-Thirds of Staff, as Local Ad Push Bites," Techcrunch.com (blog), July 1, 2013, http://techcrunch.com/ 2013/07/01/iacs-citygrid-parent-of-citysearch-and-urbanspoon-lays-off-two-thirds-of-staff -as-local-ad-push-bites.

50. "Citysearch," Wikipedia.

51. "Local—Now with a Dash of Zagat and a Sprinkle of Google+," Google Official Blog, May 30, 2012, http://googleblog.blogspot.com/2012/05/localnow-with-dash-of-zagat-and.html.

52. "Introduction to Ratings and Review Sites," SocialQuickstarter.com.

53. Smith, "Google+ Is the Fourth Most-Used SmartPhone App."

Social Bookmarking and Social Knowledge

Organizing is what you do before you do something, so that when you do it, it is not all mixed up.[1]

—A. A. Milne

PREVIEW

What value is there in being perceived as being "in the know"? The concept of **social capital** has been defined as the actual or virtual resources accrued by an individual or group by mutual acquaintance and recognition.[2] Social capital benefits people because they can draw upon resources shared by other members of the social network, such as information and connections for personal and career networking. Thus belonging to a social network and sharing knowledge benefits both the receiver and giver. As individuals and a group build up social capital, everyone in the network benefits.[3] Perhaps that can partially explain the rise of social bookmarking and social-knowledge sites.

Another reason people like to share knowledge is that it simply makes them feel better. Psychology researchers have found that forms of social capital have been related to well-being, such as increased self-esteem and satisfaction with life.[4] Why do people share information and answer questions online for free? It benefits them personally as well as professionally, and simply makes them feel good.

Social Bookmarking

No one really knows how many web pages make up the Internet, but Kevin Kelly, founder of *WIRED* magazine, wrote that there are at least a trillion web pages and growing.[5] Keeping track of all that information is difficult, to say the least. A. A. Milne, most famous for his *Winnie-the-Pooh* series, understood the importance of organization. A main feature in Pooh books is the map of the Hundred Acre Wood. Without it one might get mixed up in the story. The same can be applied to the Internet. The information age can become useless if we have no way of saving and organizing all that data. Bookmarking management systems were developed for this reason.

Social bookmarking is an online service where users can save, comment on, and share bookmarks of web documents or links. These types of services have been around since 1996, but the founding of Delicious in 2003 helped the words "social bookmarking" and "tagging" catch on. **Tagging** is the way social-bookmarking programs organize links to resources.

Tagging in social-bookmarking systems has also created **folksonomy**, which refers to a simple form of shared vocabularies. **Collaborative tagging** can be used to analyze trends and determine popularity of content over time as different sources converge. Examining different social-bookmarking tags can also reveal correlations to identify community or shared vocabularies as a form of crowdsourcing.[6]

Social-bookmarking systems enable users to save links to web pages to access later or share with others. Bookmarks can be viewed via search, tags (categories), or chronologically. Web feeds enable users to become aware when new bookmark links are saved under specific tags. This activity allows users with similar interests to network and collaborate. Over the years these bookmarking management systems have added comments, ratings, web annotation (layered web-page comments), and groups with social networking features.[7]

For individual users, social bookmarking is useful for collecting bookmarks from various computers, organizing them, enabling access to those links from anywhere, and easily sharing with others. Organizations can use social bookmarking as a way to increase information-sharing between members. Social bookmarking can also benefit organizations in terms of search engine optimization (SEO). Sharing generates more than 10 percent of all Internet traffic. What's more, social channels such as bookmarking and blogs comprise 34 percent of that traffic.[8]

Curating content is one way to do this. An organization can be seen as a resource for valuable information by aggregating and sharing the top developments and strategies in its industry. Also consider social bookmarking as a tool to collect testimonials in one place where the brand can send potential customers. Finally, creating folders and tags for marketing and PR campaigns can make it easy to track success by collecting stories, blog posts, and tweets that have been written about it.[9]

The social media site Delicious was one of the earliest to popularize social bookmarking and it pioneered tagging, so it should be considered. However, the three most popular sites by number of users are Reddit, StumbleUpon, and Digg.[10] A key to success in social bookmarking is joining one community and being active. Submit links, write reviews, rate other stories, and start networking with others who share the same interests. The more active a user is, the better their reputation and the more trusted their links will become.[11]

Reddit

Reddit is defined as a social news and entertainment company. Founded in 2006 and acquired by Condé Nast Publications in 2006,[12] Reddit has roughly 32 million unique monthly visitors, making it the top social bookmarking site.[13] Nearly half of Reddit's traffic comes from the US (46 percent). The next largest countries include India at 12 percent and Canada and the United Kingdom at 5 percent.[14]

Research reports that 6 percent of all US online adults are Reddit users. Overall, men are more likely (63 percent) to use Reddit as women (37 percent). Those under fifty are significantly more likely to use Reddit (81 percent) with nearly half (43 percent) aged eighteen to twenty-nine. The service is much more common among suburban and urban residents than rural. Nearly half (48 percent) of Reddit users have an undergraduate college degree or higher with just over a quarter having some college educations (27 percent). Household income is fairly evenly split with just over a third (35 percent) earning over $75,000 a year and a quarter earning under $30,000 a year (26 percent). The rest (49 percent) earn between $30,000 and $74,999 a year.[15]

Reddit is often referred to as "the front page of the Internet." To be effective on Reddit, organizations must get involved with the community of users called Redditors. This social site is about bookmarking web links, but the most important part is sharing. Users post things they find interesting, cool, horrible, and strange. Then they comment on the posts and upvote or downvote them, which moves items up or down in ranking. Ranking is also based on age of the submission, feedback ratio, and total vote count. From the front page, shared content is organized by Subreddits, which are communities centered on a topic, from Mobile to Minecraft. Marketers and advertisers can create their own Subreddit or participate in others and keep track of updates by subscribing.[16]

Like many communities, Reddit has its own language. OP refers to an original poster. TIL means "today I learned," which is a very common abbreviation. Many posts are TIL observations and realizations. Among the most popular abbreviations are IAmA and AMA, referring to the Ask Me Anything thread. Well-known people have done AMAs, including President Barack Obama, astronaut Chris Hadfield, Madonna, and Bill Gates. Obama's AMA was so popular, the increased traffic brought down many parts of the website.[17]

As on other social channels, each Reddit user creates a profile, but here two numbers indicate how much Karma a user has earned. Redditors get Karma points for both posts and comments that have been upvoted by other users. Increased link and comment Karma points help boost a user's influence in the Reddit community. For a small amount (about $30 a year) users can purchase a premium Gold membership to get access to secret Subreddits and other features.[18] Organizations should be aware of the Reddit or Slashdot Effect, when a smaller website suddenly gets a huge influx of traffic due to Reddit. Be prepared so that this immense traffic won't crash an organization's website.[19]

Social Media Examiner suggests several ways organizations can use Reddit to grow their businesses. First, organizations should find brand enthusiasts through Subreddits or create new ones related to the product or service. Next, encourage user submissions such as pictures of their dog or car or motorcycle. Finally, feature the best submission that week. Reddit is also a place to monitor customer questions, suggestions, and complaints. Be sure to get these customers to the right internal channels for customer service.[20] It is important for marketers to approach this social channel from the right perspective. Reddit cannot be seen as simply another advertising promotion channel. Reddit actually offers guidelines for successful marketing on Reddit called "brandiquette." Their advice to brands on what not to do for Reddit marketing can be seen in figure 10.1.[21]

Brands can also use Subreddits to keep fans updated with organization news and events. The Major League Baseball team Philadelphia Phillies uses the sidebar to feature an updated team schedule and league ranking board. Brands can also leverage the popularity of AMAs to hold interviews with key employees or supporters of the organization, brand, product, or service.[22]

Specific Reddit mobile user statistics were unavailable. However, in 2012 Reddit launched a redesigned interface to be more mobile-friendly. There are several unofficial apps available for Reddit content on Android and Windows Phone, and Reddit has its own official app for iOS.[23] Key performance indicators for Reddit could be views, shares, upvotes, downvotes, ranking, subscribers to a Subreddit, Karma, and sentiment of comments.

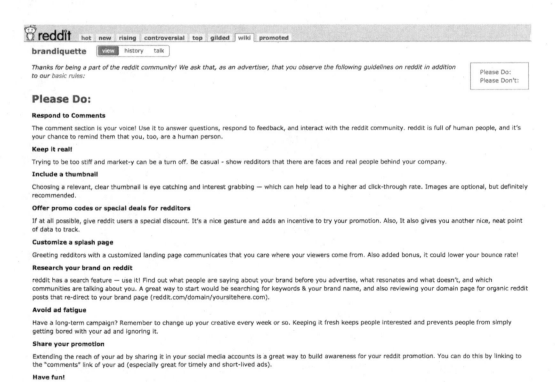

Figure 10.1. Wiki on "Brandiquette" for Advertisers on Reddit

Source: "brandiquette," Reddit.com, accessed March 12, 2015, https://www.reddit.com/wiki/brandiquette © Reddit Inc.

StumbleUpon

 Founded in 2001, **StumbleUpon** is billed as a discovery engine that finds and recommends web content to users. The site has social-networking features that allow users to find and rate web pages, photos, and videos via categories of their interests and peer-sourcing.[24] The social site has more than 28 million visitors a month, only slightly lower than Reddit.[25] Yet StumbleUpon is much more global, with 70 percent of that user traffic coming from outside the US. However, 30 percent is still a sizable amount of US traffic at over 8 million.[26]

StumbleUpon is also different from Reddit in that more of its users are women (55 percent) versus men (45 percent). StumbleUpon users are middle-aged, with the majority between thirty-five and forty-four years old and roughly 68 percent between twenty-five and fifty-four years old. Income is on the lower side with 41 percent earning between $25,000 and $50,000 and only 23 percent earning between $50,000 and $75,000. Most of the social site's users have some college education (64 percent of Internet users on StumbleUpon) with an additional 18 percent having earned a bachelor's degree.[27]

StumbleUpon can be thought of as a bookmarking site and search engine that uses collaborative filtering to create communities of web surfers interested in similar topics via the Stumble Button. StumbleUpon automates word-of-mouth sharing of peer-approved websites. Like other social sites, users create a profile with a brief bio and share and rate websites to create peer networks of common interests that distribute content stumbled upon by recommendations. User profiles also include a blog-style record of sites they have rated, but also keep track of likes, lists, following, followers, interests, and channels. Users rate sites with a thumbs up or thumbs-down and can leave additional comments on the review page, which then appears in their user's blog-style profile.[28]

Types of content can be organized with interest filters such as Home Improvement, Entrepreneurship, or Humor. Content filters can be used to show only stumbles with audio, video, flash, or images. What users stumble upon is influenced by the interests of the people they follow, and previous content they have rated as a thumbs-up. In 2006 the social channel launched StumbleUponVideo that allows users to "stumble" through and rate video content from YouTube, Vimeo, CollegeHumor, Google, MySpace, Funny-OrDie, Hulu, and TED.[29]

StumbleUpon allows organizations to curate content, promote their own content, and connect with communities of common interests. The channel can be valuable for B2B and B2C organizations as long as the content created and shared can entertain, be informative, and connect with the target audience. *Forbes* uses StumbleUpon as a content feed and as a way to gain followers through their company page or StumbleUpon channel. TV shows, such as *2 Broke Girls*, have channels to engage fans of the show and draw new viewers. And the charity World Wildlife Fund has nearly twenty thousand followers staying up to date on the nonprofit's developments, actions, and ways to support their efforts.[30]

Lists are a popular feature with StumbleUpon users and can be a powerful tool. There are nearly 10 million lists on the channel with topics from Design Your Space and Body Is a Temple to Places to Go Immediately and Killer Recipes. Getting on these lists could help the brand, product, or service. Organizations should include StumbleUpon widgets on brand websites and blogs for easy sharing. Identify influential StumbleUpon users in the industry, follow them, and get on their radar. A couple thumbs-up from power users can draw a lot of attention quickly.[31]

StumbleUpon has been redesigned to be mobile-friendly and has launched a new mobile app. The app is available on iOS, Android, and Windows Phone.[32] Since these changes in 2012, mobile activity increased rapidly to 40 percent of all StumbleUpon's users accessing the site from a mobile device.[33] Key performance indicators for Stumble-Upon could be views, shares, followers, thumbs-up, recommends, likes, and sentiment.

Digg

 Digg is a social news website that aggregates or collects news and publisher's streams via peer evaluation of voting up content, and also supports easy sharing of content to other social platforms such as Twitter and Facebook.[34] The social channel has 6 million unique visitors a month, which is significantly lower than Reddit and StumbleUpon but still three times the number of social-bookmarking innovator site Delicious, which has 1.5 million monthly visitors. Digg does have slightly more US users than StumbleUpon (40 percent), yet is more global than Reddit.[35]

Digg users are nearly evenly split between men and women, with males slightly more likely (53 percent) to be on the site than females (47 percent). As with the other two social-bookmarking channels, users tend to be middle-aged, with nearly 70 percent of online users between twenty-five and fifty-four years old on Digg. Income level is lower, with 38 percent of users earning $25,000 to $50,000 and nearly 60 percent earning under $50,000. However, 60 percent of Digg users have some college education with another 21 percent who have completed their bachelor's degree.[36]

This social channel lets users discover, share, and recommend website content, describing itself as "What the Internet is talking about right now." Digg members submit a web page on Digg.com and then other members vote the page up to Digg It or vote it down to Bury It. Digg has since gotten rid of the Bury It option. Voting also takes place across the web through Digg button widgets added to other sites that allow visitors to vote as they browse. Additional features include categories such as science, business, entertainment, and technology, plus an editorially driven front page. Digg has enhanced mobile features, and with the shutdown of Google Reader has launched its own Digg Reader.[37]

Digg has had a bumpy road from being an early innovator to losing traffic to competitor Reddit. As a result, Digg was torn apart in 2012. The site was recreated with a new staff, design, and interface. Since the relaunch, Digg has slowly regained users. Stories with the most "Diggs" make their way to the homepage, but the Digg Score also factors in Facebook shares and tweets.

Digg moderators add a human factor that consists of Digg Editors who decide what and where stories should appear.[38] The new home page has big photos and minimal text, and comments have been eliminated (see figure 10.2).[39] The focus of Digg is now on quality content that users want to read, with a goal of highlighting sixty to seventy posts a day. Digg wants the home page to be a calm and clear place that is not noisy.[40]

Figure 10.2. Digg emphasizes large photos, quality content, and less clutter.

Source: "Digg Homepage," accessed January 18, 2015, http://digg.com. © New.me Inc.

For organizations Digg represents a way to spot trends, collect and distribute content, and build awareness. Digg is a great way to fuel PR campaigns by spreading earned media coverage. Publishers like Digg because it drives traffic to their stories. Digg could also drive traffic spikes to organization websites. Open an account and submit links every time an organization creates a new piece of content or is featured in an article from another news source.

The Digg widget button should also be added to business websites and blogs to enable easy Digg voting. Another strategy is to monitor the Digg home page and write a blog post or create content about the topics that have made it to the front page of Digg. This can generate search from what may be a hot topic, but also will provide links to direct traffic and improve search engine optimization (SEO). Getting popular within the site will boost search engine rankings and traffic.[41]

Digg is also mobile friendly and has launched mobile apps. Specific mobile-use numbers were not available, but Digg has made it a priority with apps available for iOS and Android. Digg also launched a Digg Reader app for easy mobile access of their RSS Reader.[42] Key performance indicators for Digg could be views, votes or Diggs, shares, and saves.

C **MINI CASE**

Behr Paints BuzzFeed

In 2013 Behr Paints decided to go after a younger crowd by partnering with the social news-content site BuzzFeed. Behr sponsored the new DIY BuzzFeed content vertical to offer household solutions and share ideas. Instead of buying traditional advertising, brands partner with BuzzFeed to offer value-added programs.[a]

Behr partnered with Burson-Marsteller to create eighteen custom editorial posts about painting and decorating tips and tricks from Behr's director of color marketing, Erika Woelfel. The native advertising effort kicked off with Behr giving the BuzzFeed office a DIY makeover that generated more custom posts. The five-month campaign resulted in nearly 60 million impressions.[b]

[a] Karl Greenberg, "Behr Paints BuzzFeed," MediaPost.com, April 9, 2013, http://www.mediapost.com/publications/article/197671/behr-paints-buzzfeed.html.

[b] "Case Study: Behr's BuzzFeed Campaign," Burson-Marsteller.com, accessed February 18, 2015, http://www.burson-marsteller.com/case-studies/behrs-buzzfeed-campaign.

Social Bookmarking Considerations

The Hundred Acre Wood was a big place, and readers of *Winnie-the-Pooh* needed a map to get around. A. A. Milne knew a little organization can go a long way. That is the goal of bookmarking sites and news aggregators for the vast amount of information found on the web.

Public attention is hard to garner with so much clutter, but a cohesive social bookmarking strategy could be a way for brands, products, and services to direct that attention their way. Besides the three social channels presented here, also consider Delicious and BuzzFeed for social media plans.

Social Knowledge

Brian Eno said, "Every collaboration helps you grow."[43] Brian Eno is an innovator in ambient music, but what most of the public is probably more familiar with is Eno's collaborative efforts with well-known artists such as David Bowie, Talking Heads, U2, Coldplay, and Paul Simon.[44] Collaboration can improve organizations and their social media through wikis and social-knowledge channels that make it easier than ever.

Writing is normally the solo act of a single person collecting knowledge and then individually sharing it with others. This is true for interpersonal communication, articles, books, and even encyclopedias. A **wiki** is simply a website that allows collaborative editing by multiple contributors. The word "wiki" comes from WikiWikiWeb, a website that first introduced this style of programming in 1995.[45]

Encyclopedia salesmen used to go house to house selling parents the key to knowledge for their children to succeed in life. Today, this type of knowledge is no longer held by a few. No matter a person's opinion of the quality and accuracy of Wikipedia, most cannot argue with its influence. Before discussing Wikipedia, it is important to first consider private wikis.

Internal communications can improve organization performance through integrated employee communication. Most businesses are separated into silos that make up the company's collective knowledge. This institutional memory or knowledge can get locked up with specific employees, on individual hard drives, or lost completely when an employee leaves.

Private wikis provide access to a business's most up-to-date collective knowledge. **Company wikis** can bring together global divisions and partners who may not be in the same building, city, or country.[46] The main reasons an organization would use a wiki include: documentation (19 percent), knowledge base (19 percent), project management (17 percent), tacit knowledge (17 percent), meeting management (14 percent), and encyclopedia (12 percent).[47]

Employee-only wiki's can be run on a company's own servers or outsourced to an online wiki provider. The key to success is defining the goal of the wiki. Goals would be to provide or house anything from supply orders and entertainment spots for clients to ways to operate specialized equipment and valuable marketing knowledge about key competitors. Aggregate questions and answers to the public wiki to cut down on answering the same question over and over. The new level of transparency and collaboration will help make efforts much more efficient and timely. Competitive advantage may come from the shared knowledge gained from a corporate wiki. It is working for IBM, which runs 56,000 internal wikis that have more than a million page views a day.[48]

Beyond private wikis, public **social-knowledge channels** are Internet-based information exchanges where users can ask questions and get answers from real people. These services have become social as they base answers on the wisdom of the crowd, user ratings, followers, commenting, and sharing. Users of these services see themselves as influencers making a difference in their areas of expertise.

Here we will look at the top public wiki, Wikipedia, and how it can influence organizations for business. Then we will discuss Yahoo! Answers and Quora, two of the top social-knowledge channels. Question-and-answer sites can be an effective way for organizations to connect with a target audience, build a brand, and improve search engine optimization (SEO).

Wikipedia

Wikipedia is a collaboratively edited, free Internet encyclopedia supported by the nonprofit Wikimedia Foundation. There are now nearly 5 million English language articles and more than 35 million articles total on Wikipedia. Many of these articles are centered on businesses.[49] How should marketers interact with Wikipedia? If they do not already have an article about their business, should they create one?

First, find out if the business or organization qualifies. Anyone can make a Wikipedia article, but if it does not meet the social site's guidelines, a moderator will delete it. Wikipedia is not a directory, and its guidelines state that businesses must meet certain requirements. The main qualification is reputation. If an organization is a startup or small business, it may not be eligible.[50] High-level media exposure is the main hurdle to having a Wikipedia page, and that requires coverage in large media outlets.

For businesses that do meet the guidelines, a Wikipedia article can help add legitimacy to the organization. Users know the site is not marketing- or advertising-driven and is more factually based. Wikipedia is social media–driven, yet still an encyclopedia. Opinions are not allowed, and a Wikipedia article offers a place to present the facts about an organization. It is also great for exposure, since nearly all Google searches return Wikipedia's listings in the top links.[51]

There are negative aspects to being on Wikipedia. Moderators do not like employees or business owners making updates. Organizations normally need to find someone unassociated with the business to update content and be active on the Talk page.[52] That said, there is little control once an article is up. See figure 10.3 for the IBM Wikipedia Talk page.

Anyone, from disgruntled customers to neighbors and competitors, can go in and update a business page. This means the page needs to be constantly monitored. A Wikipedia entry can significantly boost the reputation of a business, but can also seriously hurt it through a piece of misinformation.[53] Key performance indicators for Wikipedia could be views, comments, and sentiment.

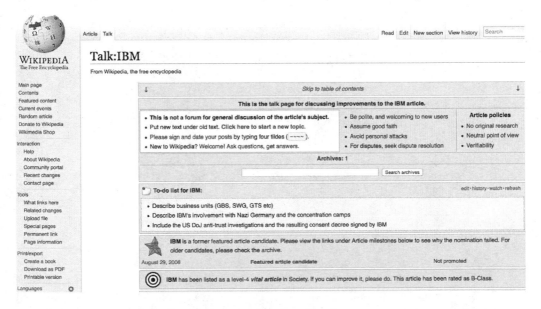

Figure 10.3. The IBM Talk Page on Wikipedia

Source: "Talk: IBM," *Wikipedia.com*, accessed January 18, 2015, http://en.wikipedia.org/wiki/Talk:IBM. © Wikimedia Foundation, Inc.

Yahoo! Answers

Yahoo! Answers is a community question-and-answer website or social-knowledge channel started by Yahoo! in 2005. The site generates roughly 24 million unique users per month in the US, and Yahoo staff claim 200 million users worldwide. In fact, the site is available in twelve different languages.[54] Demographic information on Yahoo! Answers users was unavailable.

Yahoo! Answers users can ask any question, as long as they do not violate the community guidelines. Contents of answers are owned by users, but Yahoo! has a royalty-free right to publish the information. Misuse or misinformation is monitored by users, who report abuses. Some subject areas are based more on personal opinion, but most answers must be based on fact, and users are required to mention their sources. Posts are removed if a significant number of trusted abuse reports are received. To ask and answer questions, users must have a Yahoo! ID. Questions are assigned to a category and remain open for four days, but the window can be extended to eight.[55]

Social points encourage users to answer questions and help limit spam. They can receive 10 points for giving the Best Answer designated by the asker of the question or voted by the community. Points are divided from Level 1 (1–249 points) to Level 7 (25,000+ points), which designate how active a user has been and provide more access to the site. Badges are used to designate Yahoo! Answers contributors with Top Contributor, Staff, and Official, which is used for celebrities or government departments. Knowledge Partners badges designate organizations that share their personal knowledge and experience.

It is important to note that Yahoo! Answers has been criticized for its answers not always being factual or very deep. Some claim this stems from a reward system based on activity and not quality. However, the community guidelines do require factual information with sources and users monitor answers that can be removed.[56]

Many celebrities have appeared on Yahoo! Answers to promote causes and organizations. During the 2008 US presidential campaign, Hillary Clinton, John McCain, Barack Obama, and Mitt Romney posted questions. For a nonprofit awareness campaign, UNICEF ambassadors asked questions to garner support.[57] In 2013, a new version of the site was released and promoted as being better, faster, and simpler. Features include a personalized home page, content activity streams, and the ability to add photos and video.[58]

Participation in Yahoo! Answers can help organizations drive traffic, generate awareness, or establish a brand reputation. Providing helpful, significant answers can help generate qualified leads. Monitoring questions in key categories is also a great consumer-research tool. Knowing what people are looking for can help improve business offerings.[59]

Open an account and fill in the user profile with a website link and bio that emphasizes expertise in a specific area. Find a niche by answering questions that can be answered well to build authority and drive traffic. Including a website link in every answer could be labeled as spam. Deliver real value and users will find the organization via the account bio.[60]

Contribute to the community. Don't just add content. The individual must also engage with other users. Vote on other contributors' answers and make helpful comments. Take off the "marketing hat" to start connecting, leading, and influencing. Contributing highly valued answers builds credibility and boosts image as an industry leader.

Search engines try to find the best answer to questions typed in the search box. Even Google returns a high number of Yahoo! Answers pages. This can lead to high visibility for an organization to build brand awareness and traffic.[61]

Yahoo! Answers was redesigned to be more mobile-friendly. Yahoo! Answers Mobile has a cleaner, simplified interface, but Yahoo! does not currently have mobile apps for the service. Mobile traffic numbers were not available. Key performance indicators for Yahoo! Answers could be views, shares, follows, links, points, Best Answers, questions, and top contributors.

Quora

Quora is a question-and-answer website where questions are submitted and answered by its community of users. This social-knowledge channel was founded only in 2009, but has grown quickly.[62] Quora has 2.9 million unique visitors a month.[63] Interestingly, Quora's India traffic (39 percent) has surpassed its US traffic (25 percent) on a global scale.[64]

Quora users are slightly more male (58 percent) versus female (42 percent) and tend to be middle-aged (35 percent of online users that are thirty-five to forty-four years old are on the site). Income levels are evenly split with half of Quora users (50 percent) earning under $50,000 a year and the other half earning more than $50,000 a year. Quora users are highly educated with nearly 45 percent holding a bachelor's or graduate degree and nearly half (48 percent) indicate some college education.[65]

Quora was started by two former Facebook employees to build a better question-and-answer site. Promoted as "Your best source for knowledge," this social site collects user-submitted questions and answers like Yahoo! Answers. Content is organized in more than 400,000 topics for information discovery and easier navigation. Users collaborate by editing questions and suggesting edits to other users' answers like they do on Wikipedia. Users can also upvote or downvote answers like they can on Digg.

Quora includes full-text search and a blogging platform to create and follow blogs.[66] Quora also has a Stats feature described as a dashboard for authors. The Quora question-and-answer site and blogging platform was built to enable anyone sharing great content to gain a big audience.

Like Digg, Quora's home page highlights content from across the service rather than just people users follow. As Techcrunch says, "You don't have to be a celebrity or have built up a personal following to make a splash." Quora Stats helps track that traffic through views on questions, answers, and blog posts over time. It also tracks upvotes and shares.[67]

Unlike Yahoo! Answers, Quora requires users to register with their real name versus a screen name. Despite being a new social site, it has attracted high-profile users such as Jimmy Wales, Michael Dell, Steve Case, Marc Andreessen, and Ashton Kutcher. The social channel has also managed to receive positive stories in the high-profile press.[68]

Quora attracts a higher quality of experts than other question-and-answer sites. Big-name CEOs, Hollywood producers, and well-known journalists have been answering questions, but people don't need to be famous to get big exposure on Quora. Users vote for quality answers. Make sure contributions are thoughtful, intelligent, and interesting.

For success on Quora, company representatives should start by establishing credibility by announcing who they are, what their background is, and their job title. Instead of giving a predictable, straightforward response, try to take answers in a unique, yet related direction. People love stories. Stats are great, but support an opinion with a story that brings it to life, is entertaining to read, and makes the answer memorable.[69]

Quora offers an opportunity to build a brand as an expert or thought leader in an industry. Set up an account for a key employee and fill out the bio section that also connects the account to jobs the individual had, education institutions attended, and cities where he or she has lived. Include a link to the company website or blog.[70]

Answering questions increases links and search engine optimization. By keying in on relevant topics, an organization can reach its target audience and engage them where they are looking for solutions. Helpful, informed answers can generate qualified leads back to organizational websites or blogs. Yet don't be pushy, or contributions could be labeled as spam.[71]

Specific mobile statistics are not available, but Quora is more mobile than Yahoo! Answers in that it has official mobile apps for both iOS and Android.[72] Key performance indicators for Quora could be views, shares, upvotes, downvotes, comments, and sentiment.

Social Knowledge Considerations

There are numerous social-knowledge channels on the Internet, from Wikipedia to question-and-answer sites. In addition to the sites covered here, also consider Answers .com, ChaCha, Ask.com, and WikiAnswers. As with other social media channels, no marketer can do it all. The key to success is to choose one or two, contribute quality content, and build real engagement. The next section will cover a topic related to social knowledge. Podcasts and RSS feeds enable social knowledge to be sent automatically to subscribers.

Podcasts

George Carlin said, "The reason I talk to myself is that I'm the only one whose answers I accept."[73] Yet podcasts have grown immensely based on the truth that we do like to hear answers, insights, and stories from others. Whether it is delivering comedy skits, newscasts, poetry, or business tips, a **podcast** is a series of episodes of audio or video content delivered digitally. Podcasts are subscribed to and downloaded through web syndication or streamed online through a computer or mobile device.[74]

Instead of a user checking for new content, new episodes are automatically delivered when released. The term *podcast* is a combination of *broadcast* and *pod,* referring to the iPod as the main delivery device of audio podcasts. Files are user-selected and downloaded onto the device, and then can be taken anywhere for listening or viewing later offline.[75]

Podcasting follows the main characteristic of social media in that it bypasses the traditional gatekeepers in broadcast media such as radio stations. No one owns the technology and it is free to create and listen to content. Considering the broad array of devices that can use the medium, another generic term that can be used is netcasting. Podcasting was around before, but gained its big start in 2005 when Apple released iTunes 4.9 with native support for podcasts. A version of podcasts is a **video podcast**, which consists of video clips or web television series. Video podcasts are now delivered via iTunes, but can also refer to video distributed through the Internet on websites or social channels such as YouTube.[76]

In the summer of 2013, Apple announced that it had surpassed one billion subscriptions for podcasts via its iTunes app. *USA TODAY* has reported a resurgence in podcast contributors and listeners. The mainstream is heading to podcasting with actors and comedians such as Alec Baldwin, Joan Rivers, and Tom Green starting shows along with CBS, NBC, ABC, and FOX, which are now offering audio versions of their TV news shows. Top podcasts are attracting millions of listeners, but marketers and advertisers can be successful with a smaller number by attracting the right niche.[77] Audiences for all podcasts should grow as iTunes podcast software will now start to be integrated into car audio systems.

Podcasting has also grown past its iTunes roots to reach new audiences on apps such as TuneIn Radio, SoundCloud, Stitcher, and iHeartRadio. With the growth of smartphones and Bluetooth in cars, some see podcasts as a serious threat to traditional broadcast radio. Clear Channel, the largest radio broadcaster in the US, has responded by allowing consumers to record their own podcasts and submit them to iHeartRadio alongside professional shows from ABC, NPR, and Ryan Seacrest (see figure 10.4).

The lesson here is that anyone can produce a hit show and the outlets for distribution are growing. Podcasts can be a great tool and distribution channel for content marketing efforts. Figure 10.4 is the search bar for finding podcasts on iHeartRadio, which are called Shows On Demand.[78]

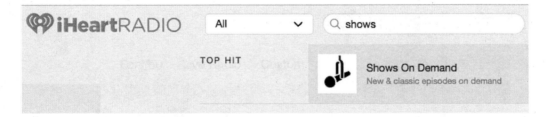

Figure 10.4. iHeartRadio features podcasts as Shows On Demand.

Source: iHeartradio.com, accessed March 14, 2015, http://www.iheart.com. © iHeartMedia, Inc.

RSS Feeds

 RSS or rich site summary is a convenient way for people to listen to and read what others are saying and writing. RSS, also known as "really simple syndication," uses standard web feed formats to publish frequently updated information including blog entries, news, audio, and video. Feeds started as early as the late 1990s, but the now ubiquitous RSS icon was created in 2004 for use first in Mozilla's Firefox browser.[79]

RSS channels or feeds contain full or summarized text and metadata such as author and date information. RSS allows authors to syndicate or publish content automatically to subscribers who want to receive current updates from favorite websites on their computers or mobile devices. This makes it easier for users who do not have to check a site to see if new content is available. Users subscribe by entering their feed's URL into their RSS reader or by clicking the feed icon. The important consideration for business use of RSS is to make sure organization of content is easy to share and easier to collect.[80]

Brand websites and blogs should offer an RSS feed to ensure updated content is automatically delivered via email or a feed reader. A feed reader is also a convenient way to keep up to date on competitor activity and industry developments.

With the shutdown of the popular Google reader in 2013, millions of RSS users had to switch to alternatives. Readers are available to use on computers and mobile apps. Top RSS readers include Feedly, AOL Reader, and Digg Reader. Digg Reader is the most social reader in that it blends social news with RSS subscriptions. If any of the articles in a feed are trending on Digg.com, one to three dots appear next to it, indicating how popular it is with other readers on the web.[81]

iTunes

iTunes is the Apple media player used to play, download, and organize digital audio and video on computers and mobile devices, including iPhone, iPod Touch, and iPad. First released in 2001, iTunes had grown to over 800 million iTunes accounts.[82] Podcasts through iTunes are now available in more than 150 countries worldwide, making iTunes the top podcast distributor in the US and the world.[83]

An Edison Research and Arbitron study shows that nearly a third of Americans have listened to a podcast, including audio listening and video watching. Podcast consumers are evenly split between men (54 percent) and women (46 percent), but skew slightly male. They tend to be younger than some of the other social channels, with half of podcast consumers between twelve and thirty-four years old. Podcast consumers are wealthier, with 44 percent earning more than $75,000 a year. Podcast subscribers are also very social, with 78 percent indicating they have social media accounts.[84]

Beyond using a quality microphone and recording and editing equipment, a good podcast has "intros" and "outtros," with music and voice-overs announcing the show title, host, organization, and call to action to drive traffic to other social channels or corporate websites and blogs. In the beginning, podcasts should tell the audience what they can expect in terms of content, frequency, and format. Consider having guest interviews of employees or industry experts to keep content fresh and interesting.[85]

In each episode enter title, artist, and album information, including keywords as relevant tags to be found in search. The iTunes format divides podcasts into sixteen categories, from business and health to government and technology. List your podcast in the right categories to be discovered by the organization's target audience. Social features of iTunes include ratings and reviews, so it is a good idea to regularly ask listeners to rate and review the podcast to help new listeners discover it.

Podcasting can be a useful channel for a business to connect with a target audience on a personal level in their car, in the gym, or in the office while performing other activities. Podcasting is really a one-on-one medium that can build engagement with existing clients and draw in potential consumers.

To grow a podcast's audience, use other social channels to encourage sharing via Twitter and Facebook. Deliver relevant, helpful content to a niche group of consumers.[86] A podcast does not need a large subscriber base to be successful; it just needs the right subscribers—a relevant target audience. One way to ensure the podcast delivers relevant, engaging content is to review the main question-and-answer social channels to see what questions users are asking in an organization's category. Native advertising also applies to podcasting. Many top podcasters sell sponsored ads inside the shows, which are read by the show host. These can be highly influential because they can be seen as endorsements.

The key advantage of iTunes and podcasts is their ability to be taken anywhere to listen anytime. In that respect, podcasts were an early innovator in mobile use. Key performance indicators for iTunes podcasts could be downloads, subscriptions, ratings, reviews, and sentiment of reviews.

Podcast Considerations

Despite George Carlin's quote, people like to hear others talk and accept their answers. In fact, comedians now use podcasting as a marketing tool. Podcasting is growing and could be an important part of an organization's social media strategy. Take a look again at target audience, objectives, and social media big idea. Could podcasting be the ideal channel to implement the social strategy for the business, product, or service?

Feeling Overwhelmed Is Natural

As we conclude the social channel section of this book (part III), many may feel overwhelmed. That is okay and not cause for worry. The amount of social channels covered in this section may have been eye-opening. Don't let the sheer number of options cause a paralysis of analysis. Social media marketing is not complicated when following a strategic planning process. The key to success is realizing that a brand or organization does not have to be in every social media channel to see real results—just the right ones.

Keep focused on the strategic framework developed in part II and select a few choice channels to deliver that strategy based on business objectives, target audience, insight, and big idea. Start small or optimize the social presence the organization already has and then add promising channels one at a time that support existing activity.

Yet remember that social media goes beyond marketing communications to impact many other areas of business operation. Social media has significantly changed the practice of product development, customer service, human resources, and more. Part IV of this book takes a deeper look at how marketing can take the lead in other important areas of business function.[87]

SOCIAL PLAN PART 10

Buzz Building and Knowledge Sharing

People love to share knowledge. Look at the major social bookmarking and social-knowledge channels. What valuable information or partnerships can the brand form? What questions can the organization answer? How does knowledge-sharing fit with the social media insight and big idea? Which users of social-bookmarking and knowledge channels match most closely with the target audience? Also take an in-depth look at podcasts. Is there an opportunity to start a brand podcast or partner with an existing program? Is the target audience actively listening to podcasts and looking for the type of insight and information the brand can deliver? Report all findings and ideas in these areas:

1. Identify the major social-bookmarking and knowledge-sharing sites where the target audience is active.
2. Describe the type of activity and content that is popular on each, and list the type of content the brand could provide that matches the social media plan's big idea.
3. Find the top podcasts to which the target audience is listening, and on which platform they are most active.
4. List and explain possible new podcast shows the brand could create or current shows the brand could contribute to and sponsor.

QUESTIONS FOR DISCUSSION

1. Go onto one of the social-bookmarking sites such as Reddit, StumbleUpon, or Digg. Find an example of a brand that is "doing it right" and an example of a brand that is "doing it wrong."
2. Find a story that has gone viral on one of the social bookmarking sites. Analyze characteristics such as topic, timing, copy, pictures, and headline. Try to determine what made the story go viral versus other stories.
3. Question-and-answer sites are all about delivering value to others by answering their questions. Which of the Q&A social websites are most appropriate for your brand and target audience?
4. Revisit the Behr Paints case study. Now that the first campaign is over, what could Behr do to keep the campaign going and successful?

ADDITIONAL EXERCISES

1. Social bookmarking is all about contributing and building into a community before taking out. The goal of this exercise is to join and explore the three social-bookmarking sites and then meaningfully contribute to one and earn a reputation as a value creator. This will pay off down the road, when you start sharing your own more promotion-oriented content. What

happens if you don't invest the time up front? You could get banned from the community for sharing too many promotional links. In which social-bookmarking community do you see the most potential? Become a valued member and it could provide an enormous amount of traffic and awareness.

2. You may not have checked out a podcast in a long time. Now is the time. In this exercise go to iTunes and explore all the podcasts. Don't just look at the top overall shows. Explore the different topic categories such as marketing and management, society and culture, and technology. It there a show that is related to your brand and targets your customers? Can you envision starting a new show for a brand or organization? Be sure to explore both audio and video podcasts. Some marketers are now even creating limited podcast series for new product or service introductions. Whether you see a place for podcasts in your strategy or not, you may find some useful podcasts that will help optimize your time and keep you up to date on the latest developments in the industry.

Notes

1. "Organizing," BrainyQuote.com, accessed February 18, 2015, http://www.brainyquote.com/quotes/keywords/organizing.html.

2. Pierre Bourdieu and Loic J. D. Wacquant, *An Invitation to Reflexive Sociology*. Chicago: University of Chicago Press (1992), 14.

3. Nicole B. Ellison, Charles Steinfield, and Cliff Lampe, "The Benefits of Facebook 'Friends': Social Capital and College Students' Use of Online Social Network Sites," *Journal of Computer Mediated Communication* 12, no. 4 (2007): 1,143–1,168.

4. John A. Bargh and Katelyn Y. A. McKenna, "The Internet and Social Life," *Annual Review of Psychology* 55, no. 1 (2004): 573–590.

5. John D. Sutter, "How Many Pages Are on the Internet?" CNN.com, September 12, 2011, http://www.cnn.com/2011/TECH/web/09/12/web.index.

6. "Social Bookmarking," Wikipedia, last modified February 16, 2015, http://en.wikipedia.org/wiki/Social_bookmarking.

7. "Social Bookmarking," Wikipedia.

8. "Has Social Media Fundraising Finally Arrived?" Community Organizer 2.0, August 19, 2011, http://communityorganizer20.com/2011/08/19/has-social-media-fundraising-finally-arrived.

9. Lou Dubois, "How to Use Social Bookmarking for Business," Inc.com, September 16, 2010, http://www.inc.com/guides/2010/09/how-to-use-social-bookmarking-for-business.html.

10. "Social Bookmarking," Wikipedia.

11. Dubois, "How to Use Social Bookmarking for Business."

12. "Reddit," Wikipedia, last modified February 16, 2015, http://en.wikipedia.org/wiki/Reddit.

13. "Top 15 Most Popular Social Bookmarking Websites," eBizMBA.com, accessed June 26, 2015, http://www.ebizmba.com/articles/social-bookmarking-websites.

14. "Reddit.com," Alexa.com, accessed October 10, 2014, http://www.alexa.com/siteinfo/reddit.com.

15. Maeve Duggan and Aaron Smith, "6% of Online Adults Are Reddit Users," PewInternet.org, July 3, 2013, http://pewinternet.org/Reports/2013/reddit/Findings.aspx.

16. Jacob O'Gara, "Reddit 101: A Beginner's Guide to the Front Page of the Internet," Digital Trends.com, December 20, 2013, http://www.digitaltrends.com/social-media/reddit-101.

17. "Reddit," Wikipedia.

18. O'Gara, "Reddit 101."

19. "Reddit," Wikipedia.

20. Ben Beck, "6 Ways to Use Reddit to Grow Your Business," SocialMediaExaminer.com, September 20, 2012, http://www.socialmediaexaminer.com/reddit.

21. "sxswdoingredditwrong subreddit," Reddit.com, accessed January 18, 2015, http://www.reddit.com/r/sxswdoingredditwrong.

22. Beck, "6 Ways to Use Reddit to Grow Your Business."

23. "Reddit," Wikipedia.

24. "StumbleUpon," Wikipedia, last modified February 17, 2015, http://en.wikipedia.org/wiki/StumbleUpon.

25. "Top 15 Most Popular Social Bookmarking Websites," eBizMBA.com.

26. "StumbleUpon.com," Alexa.com, accessed October 10, 2014, http://www.alexa.com/siteinfo/stumbleupon.com.

27. Brian Chappell, "2012 Social Network Analysis Report Demographic Geographic and Search Data Revealed," IgniteSocialMedia.com, July 31, 2012, http://www.ignitesocialmedia.com/social-media-stats/2012-social-network-analysis-report/.

28. "StumbleUpon," Wikipedia.

29. "StumbleUpon," Wikipedia.

30. Michael Steltzer, "StumbleUpon Marketing: How to Drive More Traffic to Your Content," SocialMediaExaminer.com, November 22, 2013, http://www.socialmediaexaminer.com/stumbleupon-marketing-with-nick-robinson.

31. Steltzer, "StumbleUpon Marketing."

32. "StumbleUpon," Wikipedia.

33. "Top 15 Most Popular Social Bookmarking Websites," eBizMBA.com.

34. Chappell, "2012 Social Network Analysis Report Demographic Geographic and Search Data Revealed."

35. "Digg," Wikipedia, last modified February 12, 2015, http://en.wikipedia.org/wiki/Digg.

36. "Frequently Asked Questions," Digg.com, accessed February 18, 2015, http://digg.com/faq.

37. "Digg Homepage," Digg.com, accessed January 18, 2015, http://digg.com.

38. Om Malik, "Will the Digg Effect Make a Comeback?," Gigaom.com, August 18, 2013, http://gigaom.com/2013/08/18/will-the-digg-effect-make-a-comeback.

39. Don Gilbert, "Using Digg to Build Traffic and Links," MastersOfSEO.com, accessed October 10, 2014, http://www.mastersofseo.com/using-digg-and-putting-up-a-digg-this-button.

40. "Digg," Wikipedia.

41. Gilbert, "Using Digg to Build Traffic and Links."

42. "Digg," Wikipedia.

43. "Collaboration," BrainyQuote.com, accessed February 18, 2015, http://www.brainyquote.com/quotes/keywords/collaboration.html.

44. "Brian Eno," Wikipedia, last modified February 10, 2015, http://en.wikipedia.org/wiki/Brian_Eno.

45. "wiki," Merriam-Webster.com, accessed February 18, 2015, http://www.merriam-webster.com/dictionary/wiki.

46. Dan Misener, "Why You Should Set Up a Company Wiki," TheGlobeAndMail.com, February 20, 2012, http://www.theglobeandmail.com/report-on-business/small-business/sb-digital/web-strategy/why-you-should-set-up-a-company-wiki/article547626.

47. Rebecca Shakespeare, "Wikis for Innovative Work," Innovation Series, December 12, 2012, http://www.innovation-series.com/2012/12/17/wikis-for-innovative-work.

48. Misener, "Why You Should Set Up a Company Wiki."

49. "Wikipedia," Wikipedia, last modified June 26, 2015, http://en.wikipedia.org/wiki/Wikipedia.

50. Nicole Harrison, "Wikipedia: Is it a 'Go' or 'No Go' for Your Business?" Socialnicole.com, accessed February 18, 2015, http://socialnicole.com/wikipedia-for-business.

51. Harrison, "Wikipedia: Is it a 'Go' or 'No Go' for Your Business?"

52. "Talk: IBM," Wikipedia, accessed January 18, 2015, http://en.wikipedia.org/wiki/Talk:IBM.

53. Harrison, "Wikipedia: Is it a 'Go' or 'No Go' for Your Business?"

54. "Yahoo! Answers," Wikipedia, last modified January 28, 2015, http://en.wikipedia.org/wiki/Yahoo!_Answers.

55. "About Yahoo! Answers," Yahoo! Answers, accessed February 18, 2015, https://in.answers.yahoo.com/info/about.

56. "About Yahoo! Answers," Yahoo! Answers.

57. "Yahoo! Answers," Wikipedia.

58. "Introducing the New Yahoo Answers!" Yahoo! Answers Tumblr, September 12, 2013, http://yahooanswers.tumblr.com/post/61040172053/introducing-the-new-yahoo-answers.

59. Helen Vozna, "How to Get Traffic to Your Website with the Help of Q&A Sites," Webceo.com (blog), October 29, 2013, http://www.webceo.com/blog/how-to-get-traffic-to-your-website-with-the-help-of-qa-sites.

60. Vozna, "How to Get Traffic to Your Website with the Help of Q&A Sites."

61. Vozna, "How to Get Traffic to Your Website with the Help of Q&A Sites."

62. "Quora," Wikipedia, last modified January 30, 2015, http://en.wikipedia.org/wiki/Quora.

63. "Social Media Active Users by Network [INFOGRAPHIC]," TheSocialMediaHat.com (blog), May 26, 2015, http://www.thesocialmediahat.com/active-users.

64. "Quora," Wikipedia.

65. Chappell, "2012 Social Network Analysis Report Demographic Geographic and Search Data Revealed."

66. "Quora," Wikipedia.

67. Constine, "Quora Signals It's Favoring Search Ads for Eventual Monetization, Launches Author Stats Tool."

68. "Quora," Wikipedia.

69. Lisa B. Marshall, "How to Use Quora to Build Your Brand (Part 1)," QuickAndDirtyTips.com, June 13, 2013, http://www.quickanddirtytips.com/business-career/public-speaking/how-to-use-quora-to-build-your-brand-part-1.

70. Marshall, "How to Use Quora to Build Your Brand (Part 1)."

71. Krista Bunskoek, "Blog Traffic: How to Use Q&A Sites and Niche Forums to Increase Blog Visitors," Wishpond.com, accessed February 18, 2015, http://blog.wishpond.com/post/65245501112/blog-traffic-how-to-use-q-a-sites-and-niche-forums-to.

72. "Quora," Wikipedia.

73. "Talk," BrainyQuote.com, accessed February 18, 2015, http://www.brainyquote.com/quotes/keywords/talk.html.

74. "Podcast," Wikipedia, last modified February 13, 2015, http://en.wikipedia.org/wiki/Podcast.

75. "Podcast," Merriam-Webster.com, accessed February 18, 2015, http://www.merriam-webster.com/dictionary/podcast.

76. "Podcast," Wikipedia.

77. Jefferson Graham, "Remember Podcasting? It's Back—and Booming," USAToday.com, August 15, 2013, http://www.usatoday.com/story/tech/columnist/talkingtech/2013/08/15/podcast-explosion/2647963.

78. "Business & Finance," iHeartRadio.com accessed October 10, 2014, http://www.iheart.com/talk/category/Business-Finance-2.

79. "RSS," Wikipedia, last modified February 16, 2015, http://en.wikipedia.org/wiki/RSS.

80. "RSS," Wikipedia.

81. Jason Parker and Jaymar Cabebe, "Google Reader Is Done; Here Are Five Alternatives," CNET.com, June 28, 2013, http://reviews.cnet.com/8301-19512_7-57574201-233/google-reader-is-done-here-are-five-alternatives.

82. Nina Ulloa, "iTunes Has 800 Million Accounts. . . . And 800 Million Credit Card Numbers," DigitalMusicNews.com (blog), April 24, 2015, http://www.digitalmusicnews.com/permalink/2014/04/24/itunes800m.

83. Dan Graziano, "Apple Now Adding Half a Million New iTunes Accounts Each Day," BGR.com, June 14, 2013, http://bgr.com/2013/06/14/apple-itunes-accounts.

84. "iTunes," Wikipedia.

85. Tom Webster, "The Podcast Consumer 2012," Edison Research, May 29, 2012, http://www.edisonresearch.com/home/archives/2012/05/the-podcast-consumer-2012.php.

86. John Lee Dumas, "How to Start a Business Podcast," SocialMediaExaminer.com, July 10, 2013, http://www.socialmediaexaminer.com/how-to-start-a-business-podcast.

87. Keith A. Quesenberry and Michael K. Coolsen, "How to Integrate Social Media into Your Marketing Strategy: Best Practices for Social Media Management," *Ad Age* Research Reports, May 20, 2013, http://adage.com/trend-reports/report.php?id=74.

PART

IV

**Integrating Social
Media across
Organizations**

Crowdsourcing Social Media Research

Money won't buy happiness, but it will pay the salaries of a large research staff to study the problem.[1]

—Bill Vaughan

PREVIEW

Ralph Hertwig tells us in *Science* magazine that since the late nineteenth century, psychology research has associated the group or crowd with either inferior decision-making and disastrous outcomes, or unparalleled wisdom and magical creativity. However, Hertwig says, "the key to benefiting from other minds is to know when to rely on the group and when to walk alone."[2] Leveraging the wisdom of the crowd has been the focus of research for many years.

As early as 1907 researcher Francis Galton published "Vox Populi (The Wisdom of Crowds)" in the magazine *Nature*. Galton found evidence that the median estimate of a group can be more accurate than estimates of experts.[3] This wisdom-of-crowd effect has been more recently supported in experiments involving areas from stock markets and political elections to quiz shows.

Yet, researchers Jan Lorenz, Heiko Rauhut, Frank Schweitzer, and Dirk Helbing found that social influence can undermine the wisdom of crowd. In their experiment, subjects reconsidered responses to factual questions after receiving the average or full information of the responses of others. Groups were initially "wise," but knowledge about estimates of others narrowed the diversity of opinions, creating a "social influence effect."[4] Other studies indicate that the accuracy of the wisdom of a crowd can diminish when more confident members in a group dominate decisions.[5] These findings should be kept in mind when exploring social research and crowd-sourcing as sources of market intelligence.

Real-Time Intelligence

Bill Vaughan was an American columnist and author known for his folksy approach and no-nonsense opinions. His quote at the beginning of this chapter is especially germane for those in marketing who have ever had to pay for a research study. Traditional research is expensive. Fortunately, today marketers have a vibrant research tool that is inexpensive, more efficient, and a more-responsive way to collect business insights for large corporations, startups, and small businesses alike. Traditional research can also be slow. It can take three to six months to develop, field, and obtain results. On the other hand, social media listening can capture real-time consumer insight for continuous brand, product, and service optimization. This is not to say that organizations should eliminate traditional research altogether. It is a valuable tool and provides much information and accuracy that social research cannot.

Despite all the hype over social media, social media research has not been a serious part of most companies' research efforts. A 2009 study of forty global companies found that nearly 90 percent still used more-traditional research approaches, such as focus groups and telephone surveys.[6] By 2012, Wharton Customer Analytics was still reporting a social media research imbalance. US companies spend more than $10 billion a year on consumer research, yet are using traditional methods that are more than three decades old. Most organizations still rely predominantly on focus groups and customer surveys, despite declining customer participation and long turnaround times.[7]

Traditional market research involves face-to-face or traditional media methods, such as focus groups, in-depth interviews, shop-alongs, ethnographic observation, intercepts, and telephone and mail surveys. **Digital market research** involves using new media to collect results through methods such as online surveys, online focus groups, online communities, bulletin boards, and social media sites.[8] Many marketers today are benefiting from adding new digital market-research methods to their more-traditional research.

Think about all the information that is generated online every day about brands, products, services, competitors, and industry. Research today is about leveraging the constant flow of real-time data generated from website analytics, individual-level customer data, and social media conversations. Consumer data can come in many forms, such as polls on organization websites, questions on Facebook pages, or tests of advertising and product ideas on corporate blogs. The idea is to use any digital tool available to leverage research insight from the enormous amount of big data.

A simple example is when Barclays bank launched the first person-to-person mobile payments app in the UK, called Pingit. A traditional new product development approach would follow a process of creating prototypes, conducting a series of focus groups, and then fielding test markets before fully introducing the new product into the market. This process can take up to eighteen months, which is an eternity when trying to launch a new, competitive tech product, service, or feature.

Instead, Barclays released the app sooner and then used real-time social media analysis to significantly improve the product. Through sentiment analysis, they saw the app was received well, but there was still a small percentage of negative mentions. Zeroing in on those comments led to an insight that teens and their parents were upset that the new money-transfer app did not give access to account owners under eighteen.

For example, one tweet said, "Pingit disappointment—sent money to both kids, but it didn't work because they are under 18 (even though they are both Barclays customers)." Barclays was responsive, adjusting access requirements quickly. This helped PR efforts by avoiding news stories picking up the negative feature and making it a significant part of the earned media coverage of the launch.[9] Today the app is a success, receiving more than 11,000 reviews in the Android Apps store and with an average rating of four out of five stars (see figure 11.1).[10]

As seen in the Barclays example, the real power of this research is that it occurs in real time. Data can be collected by monitoring social channels for product issues or brand perception, or can be collected in closed brand communities. Getting this close to the consumer experience provides rich insight. Companies such as SurveyMonkey make this social research easy by offering a free app to embed polls, surveys, and questionnaires into Facebook.

Marketers can leverage a large group of Facebook fans to improve marketing efforts, product features, and service delivery. This is an attractive tool versus email surveys, considering the difficulty of obtaining email lists and the potential of a network of friends or fans sharing the survey on their respective networks for more and faster response.[11]

What kind of response can Facebook research obtain for a marketer? Instead of simply monitoring for positive and negative comments like Barclays, the marketers at Nabisco

Figure 11.1. Monitoring negative comments enabled Barclays to quickly update a new product for long-term success.

Source: "Barclays Pingit," Google play Android Apps, accessed January 18, 2015, https://play.google.com/store/apps/details?id=com.barclays.apps.pingit&hl=en. © Barclays.

Social Media Research Process

Social media research should not just be a series of random questions or polls. To achieve optimum result, conduct a social search with the same formal conventions and process as traditional consumer marketing research. Yean Cheong, head of digital at Mediabrands, suggests the using these steps:[a]

- Identify the target audience.
- Post open-ended information-gathering questions.
- Engage in social conversations.
- Categorize and analyze threads.
- Determine feedback patterns.
- Connect trends to develop insights.

_____

[a] "Insight: Media Debate-planning—Social Media's Role in Real-Time Research," *Campaign Asia-Pacific* 56 (2012).

took a more direct approach. The Oreo brand engaged its Facebook fans by asking, "How would you describe Oreo cookies to someone who never tasted them?" In response the brand page received more than 3,600 replies in just six days.[12] Powerful insight was obtained quickly from loyal consumers. In just a few days the marketers and advertisers at Oreo had valuable outside perspective from their target audience into the most important aspects of its product and brand.

No matter what process marketers use to conduct social media research, be sure to collect data beyond the narrow scope of the company or organization. Also gather information about competitors and the overall industry. Looking at the broader context adds valuable background and perspective that can make the difference in real insight. Yet no matter how powerful, social media research cannot and should not completely replace traditional research. Traditional research methods are still valid and provide valuable information social media research cannot collect. View social research as a way to augment traditional research data and methodologies.

How else can social data be used? Another example involves the hotel industry. The Synthesis agency set up global, regional, and hotel-specific dashboards for Accor hotels to monitor its properties and key competitors. Measurement was based on many factors, from open-ended comments in social media to rating scores on ratings and reviews sites such as TripAdvisor. The system allowed Accor to identify underperforming locations in real time and act on negative comments quickly. Traditional research may take months or up to a year to report these findings and could result in a large amount of lost bookings. Accor management said that the social-media-monitoring research system resulted in a rise in brand equity, satisfaction, and bookings.[13]

These examples demonstrate that social research is good for business-to-consumer (B2C), but is social media research also effective for business-to-business (B2B) organizations? Research does indicate that there are enough social conversations about business-to-business firms to monitor for brand, product, and service optimization. A study in the *World Journal of Social Sciences* reported robust social conversation about two B2B manufacturing companies in Europe. Using social-media-monitoring software, these B2B manufacturers found they generated more than sixty mentions a day. This was a large and significant number in terms of total buzz for the industry sector.[14] Conducting social research for organization-to-organization selling also provides valuable insight that can help meet business objectives.

Once an organization has implemented a continuous monitoring program, consider expanding what is being tracked. In addition to following opinions, complaints, and questions that could influence product design, customer service, marketing messaging, and social media outreach, use trend analysis to track perception and sentiment over time. Look for rises in positive or negative comments to learn what should be repeated or avoided.[15] Real-time social media research can improve lead generation, improve new products and new product launches, and provide insight into potential customers and their decision processes.

Leveraging the Wisdom of the Crowd

Elvis Presley said, "A live concert to me is exciting because of all the electricity that is generated in the crowd and on stage. It's my favorite part of the business, live concerts."[16] Marketers and advertisers may not consider themselves to be rock stars, but there is something that can be learned from Elvis's observation. Except for personal sales, much of business and marketing happens away from the action and results are delayed. Think of a musician spending weeks in a recording studio and waiting months to release a record before getting fan feedback and interaction. Social media can bring a level of real-time crowd interaction to a marketer like a live concert to a musician. Interacting with an organization's target audience at this level of engagement is called crowdsourcing.

Crowdsourcing takes a job normally performed by a professional, such as an employee, and outsources it to a large group of people through an "open call."[17] What makes crowdsourcing so powerful today is that it is empowered through social media—especially in the areas of product development or improvement. It can make these business functions more efficient and effective. Crowdsourcing has also been used in other areas, such as developing taglines and logos and even advertising materials such as television commercials.

Carl Esposti, founder of Crowdsourcing.org, says the benefit of crowdsourcing is that it enables companies to bypass restrictions, such as limited resources. This is an especially useful tool for startups and small businesses to obtain low-cost feedback. For larger corporations, crowdsourcing jumpstarts thinking outside the box of a confining corporate structure or culture. It can drive innovation and gratifies a consumer's desire to be heard.[18] Instead of fighting negative social media comments, brands can leverage them to make a better product or service. Better product service delivery, in turn, creates more positive social media buzz. *Marketing Week* called this a move from fire-fighting to co-creation, where an organization leverages the crowd for everything from consumer-goods ideas to advertising concepts and executions.[19]

Crowdsourcing can also be much more cost effective. Innovation can occur at a lower cost than traditional research or development process methods. Research by Thomas Malone, Robert Laubacher, and Tammy Johns found that design competitions run by TopCoder often provided clients with development work previously obtained by traditional means for as little as 25 percent of the cost.[20] Not only can crowdsourcing deliver lower costs, but it often provides a unique outside perspective that is hard to maintain working from within an organization.

Crowdsourcing has been used to design everything from cars to gaming tablets. Fiat engaged the crowd beyond its team of designers and engineers to crowdsource the design of the Fiat Mio. Fiat received more than seventeen thousand suggestions via Twitter and Facebook from people in more than 160 countries to help create a concept car that was met with rave reviews.[21] The company continues crowdsourcing efforts to this day.

In another crowdsourcing example, two hundred artists (editors, artists, DJs, musicians, and audiophiles) designed the V–Moda Crossfade M-100 headphones, and then more than ten thousand music fans voted on the final design. Razer designed the "Razer Edge" Windows 8 gaming tablet by asking gamers to tweet or post on Facebook specs they would want in a gaming tablet. Again, more than ten thousand responded with suggestions on options such as the game chipset, weight, thickness, and price they would be willing to pay.[22]

Yet crowdsourcing is not only for consumer crowds and consumer products. Mobile tech firm Psion has created an online forum called IngenuityWorking. This community of more than fifteen thousand customers, partners, employers, and resellers visit the site more

MINI CASE

Fiat Mio

In 2009 Fiat Brazil wanted to create a new product and engage consumers. Their idea was to co-create a car with Internet users. To emphasize that the product belonged to consumers, they named it *Fiat Mio* or "My Fiat." Designing an entire car is complicated and takes expertise, so this crowdsourcing project was not created as a competition to find the best idea and award a winner. Instead, consumers were invited to share their firsthand experience with cars to bring novel ideas that may never have occurred to design and production experts.[a]

In twelve months, Fiat's online platform received suggestions from more than seventeen thousand people across 160 countries. Suggestions covered various areas including internal and external design, gadget integration, electronic security, and economy. Ideas were screened by the Fiat design team and then decisions were communicated through the online platform. The result was the world's first crowdsourced car, launched at the Sao Paulo Automotive Show. The company achieved strong brand engagement.[b] Today the company continues to include its consumer by soliciting ideas for new features on all its cars via its website and social media.

[a] Fabio Prado Saldanha, Patrick Cohendet, and Marlei Pozzebon, "Challenging the Stage-Gate Model in Crowdsourcing: The Case of Fiat Mio in Brazil," *Technological Innovation Management Review*, September 2014, http://timreview.ca/article/829.

[b] "Creation of the Fiat Mio Concept Car," Aegis Group, accessed January 18, 2015, http://files.investis .com/aegis/annualreport2010/business_review/case_studies/case_study_01.html.

than six thousand times a month to exchange ideas, support each other, design product and feature solutions, and evaluate choices.[23] Imagine the value of getting everyone in the supply chain offering suggestions for improvement in a continuous feedback cycle.

Cisco held its first online idea competition in 2007 when it collected more than 2,500 ideas from 104 countries for an innovative IT network solution. The winning idea for energy efficiency became a new business unit launched with a $10 million investment.[24] Which industries are most likely to use crowdsourcing? Crowdsourcing.org looks at revenue by section (see figure 11.2) and found Internet services to be the most likely to use crowdsourcing at 29 percent, followed by media and entertainment (20 percent) and technology (18 percent).[25]

Crowdsourcing does not always have to be a formal competition with a winner. Dell turned years of negative social media comments into a product design community called IdeaStorm. Within a year, nine of its laptops and desktops featured innovations generated from consumers in the community.[26] Dell captured more than ten thousand ideas, ultimately implementing more than four hundred of them.[27] This helped Dell greatly improve their product and customers' perception of the company in the marketplace.

Why continue to guess what features and products consumers want when marketers can simply ask? Start working with customers to develop better goods and services to fit their needs. David Bratvold, the founder of Dailycrowdsource.com, sums it up by saying, "Your actual customers are telling you how to sell to them and what they like."

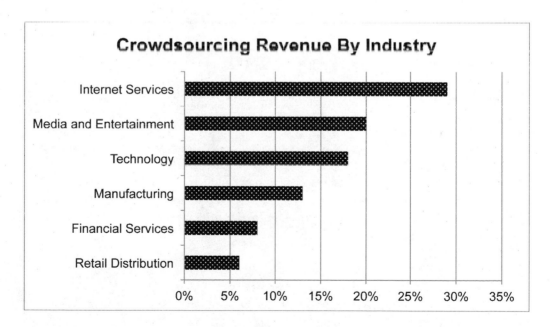

Figure 11.2. Crowdsourcing by Industry Sector

Source: "Enterprise Crowdsourcing Research Report by Massolution: Market, Provider and Working Trends," Crowdsourcing.org, September 2, 2011, http://www.crowdsourcing.org/document/enterprise-crowdsourcing-research-report-by-massolution-market-provider-and-worker-trends/13132.

There are many other uses of crowdsourcing beyond marketing and product development. For example, Facebook faced an enormous challenge of translating its website into seventy languages, so it created a website to mobilize the crowd into helping. The crowd responded by translating Facebook's French site in a day using three hundred thousand volunteers.[28]

Theoretically Speaking: Local Search Constrains R&D

In 1996, Toby Stuart and Joel Podolny looked at the evolutionary changes occurring in corporate research due to technological advances. Research into industry innovation found that "local search" constricts the direction of corporate research and development.[29] Organizations that initiate R&D projects with the technological content and outcomes of their prior searches limit possibilities. For true innovation, organizations need a method to start thinking outside their past knowledge and previous solutions.

Mary Tripsas and Giovanni Gavetti furthered this line of thought in their research indicating that existing technological capabilities, set in routines and procedures, limit adaptive intelligence. In other words, Tripsas and Gavetti say, "A firm's prior history inhibits its future behavior in that learning tends to be premised on local processes of search."[30] When firms need to innovate they can fall into competency traps where core competencies actually become limitations.[31] This theory applies nicely to today's environment of crowdsourcing and social media research. Firms constrained to traditional research may be limiting possibilities when opening up some processes to outsiders could increase innovation.

 SOCIAL PLAN PART 11

Adding Crowdsourcing into a Campaign

Take the social media plan beyond marketing promotion and communication to other aspects of the Four Ps or Four Cs. What social intelligence does the organization need or could it benefit from? Are they launching a new product? Perhaps the brand could use insight into existing products or services for improvement. Or maybe the brand could use additional insight from consumers to create advertising or social media content. What specific project could create a crowdsourcing campaign? Report all thoughts, plans, and ideas in these areas:

1. Identify needs traditional research is currently serving at the organization, and list how social media research could support those efforts.
2. Does the brand have an ongoing social-media-monitoring system in place? What formal social research plan could be put in place?
3. List marketing projects, such as product design and advertising creation, currently done in-house.
4. Of the list above, identify the top projects that could benefit from crowdsourcing. Explain how and why.

QUESTIONS FOR DISCUSSION

1. What is your point of view on the concept of the wisdom of the crowd? Is the collective opinion of a crowd always right or better than individual ideas or thoughts? Find examples or research to support your opinion.
2. The real advantage of social media monitoring is real-time insight and intelligence. Find an example of a brand that, through real-time social media monitoring, either took advantage of an opportunity or avoided a PR crisis with quick action.
3. What role does traditional research play, such as focus groups and survey or ethnographic observation? What cannot be accomplished or gained solely through social media research?
4. Mary Tripsas and Giovanni Gavetti say, "A firm's prior history constrains its future behavior." How can crowdsourcing ideas lead to greater innovation and possible competitive advantage for an organization?

ADDITIONAL EXERCISES

1. In this exercise, explore the options for social media service. Besides specific research efforts, organizations should put in place a program of continuous social media monitoring that goes beyond the initial social media audit. This is made easier through numerous social-media-monitoring services. Refer back to chapter 4 on the social media audit and review table 4.3 for a list of the top free and paid social-media-monitoring methods and services. Some services, such as Hootsuite, allow marketers and students to try them out for free. Research these and others and report the best option for your brand and organization.
2. Plan a crowdsourcing effort for your brand. What does the organization need done that is traditionally handled by a small group of people inside the organization? To ensure a successful crowdsourcing effort, James Euchner, of *Research Technology Management*, suggests starting with: a well-defined problem, a large population of experienced problem-solvers, feedback to the crowd for ideas to evolve, a policy for intellectual property, and a person or group to filter ideas.[32] The last action should especially be considered. Some aspects of social media are free, like media costs, but the real cost to an organization is time. Before launching a crowdsourcing content or campaign, allocate dedicated resources for analysis and implementation of hundreds or even thousands of ideas.

Notes

1. "Research," BrainyQuote.com, accessed February 20, 2015, http://www.brainyquote.com/quotes/keywords/research.html.

2. Ralph Hertwig, "Tapping into the Wisdom of the Crowd—with Confidence." *Science* 336, no. 6079 (2012): 303–304.

3. Francis Galton, "Vox Populi (The Wisdom of Crowds)," *Nature* 1949, no. 75 (1907): 450–451.

4. Jan Lorenz, Heiko Rauhut, Frank Schweitzer, and Dirk Helbing, "How Social Influence Can Undermine the Wisdom of the Crowd Effect," *Proceedings of the National Academy of Sciences of the United States of America* 108, no. 22 (2010): 9,020–9,025.

5. Asher Koriat, "When Are Two Heads Better than One and Why?" *Science* 336, no. 6,079 (2012): 360–362.

6. Mary Eagan, Kate Manfred, Ivan Bascle, Emmanuel Huet, and Sharon Marcil, "The Consumer Voice—Can Your Company Hear It?" the Boston Research Group, November 2009, http://www.bcg.com/documents/file35167.pdf.

7. "Listening to the Online Voice of the Consumer," the Wharton Customer Analytics Initiative, accessed February 20, 2015, www.wharton.upenn.edu/wcai/files/Insights_Netzer_WCAI.pdf.

8. "Traditional vs. Digital Market Research Methods. Does 'New' Mean Better?" The Marketing Directors (blog), February 23, 2012, https://themarketingdirectors.wordpress.com/2012/02/23/traditional-vs-digital-market-research-methods-does-new-mean-better.

9. Jeremy Taylor, "How to Use Social Media Monitoring for a Product Launch," OurSocial Times.com, November 1, 2013, http://oursocialtimes.com/how-to-use-social-media-monitoring-for-a-product-launch.

10. "Barclays Pinit," Google Play Android Apps, accessed January 18, 2015, https://play.google.com/store/apps/details?id=com.barclays.apps.pingit&hl=en.

11. "Facebook Surveys: Embed Your Surveys Using Our Facebook App," SurveyMonkey.com, accessed October 15, 2014, https://www.surveymonkey.com/mp/facebook.

12. Ray Poynter, "Chatter Matters: Social Media Research Is Reaching Its Tipping Point," *Marketing Research* 23, no. 3 (2011): 22–28.

13. Poynter, "Chatter Matters."

14. Aarne Tollinen, Joel Jarvinen, and Heikki Karjaluoto, *World Journal of Social Sciences* 2, no. 4 (2012): 65–76.

15. Maria Ogneva, "How Companies Can Use Sentiment Analysis to Improve Their Business," Mashable.com, April 19, 2010, http://mashable.com/2010/04/19/sentiment-analysis.

16. "Talk," BrainyQuote.com, accessed February 20, 2015, http://www.brainyquote.com/quotes/keywords/talk.html.

17. "Crowdsourcing Definition/Examples," Crowdsourcing.org, accessed January 20, 2015, http://www.crowdsourcing.org/document/crowdsourcing-definitionexamples/1363.

18. Mary Brandel, "Crowdsourcing: Are You Ready to Ask the World for Answers?" *Computerworld* 42, no. 10 (2008): 24–26.

19. Michael Nutley, "There's a Lot More to Social Media than Fire-fighting a Wall of Gripes," *Marketing Week* 35, no. 15 (2012): 12.

20. Thomas W. Malone, Robert Lauhacher, and Tammy Johns, "The Age of Hyperspecialization," *Harvard Business Review,* July 2011, https://hbr.org/2011/07/the-big-idea-the-age-of-hyperspecialization/ar/1.

21. Eric Markowitz, "The Case for Letting Your Customers Design Your Products," Inc.com, September 20, 2011, http://www.inc.com/guides/201109/how-to-crowdsource-your-resarch-and-development.html.

22. Julie Bort, "6 Great Products Designed by the Internet: Crowdsourced Product Design," SAP Business Innovation (blog), March 1, 2013, http://blogs.sap.com/innovation/innovation/crowdsourced-product-design-027607.

23. Maeve Hosea, "Why Social Brands Follow the Crowd," *Marketing Week* 35, no. 17 (2012): 27.

24. Fiona Maria Schweitzer, Walter Buchinger, Oliver Gassmann, and Marianna Obrist, "Crowdsourcing," *Research Technology Management* 55, no. 3 (2012): 32–38.

25. "Enterprise Crowdsourcing Research Report by Massolution: Market, Provider and Working Trends," Crowdsourcing.org, September 2, 2011, http://www.crowdsourcing.org/document/enterprise-crowdsourcing-research-report-by-massolution-market-provider-and-worker-trends/13132.

26. Anthony Malakian, "Harnessing the Power of the Crowd," *Bank Technology News* 21, no. 12 (2008): 20.

27. Laurence Ang, "Community Relationship Management and Social Media," *Journal of Database Marketing & Customer Strategy Management* 18, no. 1 (2011): 31–38.

28. Hosea, "Why Social Brands Follow the Crowd."

29. Toby E. Stuart and Joel M. Podolny, "Local Search and the Evolution of Technological Capabilities," *Strategic Management Journal* 17 (1996): 21–38.

30. Mary Tripsas and Giovanni Gavetti, "Capabilities, Cognitions, and Inertia: Evidence from Digital Imaging," *Strategic Management Journal* 21, no. 10/11 (2000): 1,147.

31. Dorothy Leonard-Barton, "Core Capabilities and Core Rigidities: A Paradox in Managing New Product Development," *Strategic Management Journal* 13 (1992): 111–126.

32. James A. Euchner, "The Limits of the Crowds," *Research Technology Management* 53, no. 5 (2010): 7–8.

Branded Content and Customer Evangelism

Engaging with the audience lets them know I'm approachable.[1]

—Sheila E.

PREVIEW

In 2013 Abigail Posner, head of Google's Agency Strategic Planning team, started the Engagement Project to find meaning in memes. **Memes** are ideas expressed as visuals, words, and/or videos that spread on the Internet from person to person. To study memes and how they spread, Posner partnered with cultural anthropologists, psychologists, and creators of digital content to determine what motivates creating, curating, and connecting across the web. What makes one particular idea or concept more likely to be picked up and shared on a mass scales versus other pieces of content?

People are attracted to the fascinating familiar. On the web, everyday moments that are framed in a different way or juxtaposed for a new perspective elevate those regular moments by tapping into imagination and discovery. Our brains love synaptic play. We also love the freedom of the visual web where different, unrelated images and clips can come together in a childlike way. Online, cats play keyboards and babies ride roller skates easily, connecting random components in our brains to form synapses. This is the basis of creative joy. We love the energy of exchange with other humans. Sharing is caring, but also amplifies our own pleasure. Sharing a picture or video on the web is really about sharing the emotional response to the object. The sharing of the object becomes a gift or movement of pleasure that bonds us together.[2]

Facebook has also conducted research into memes. Their data scientists found that adding the words "please post this" or "copy and paste" make a meme twice as likely to go viral. In addition, researchers found phrases that are easy to agree or identify with, like "if you love your . . ." or "share if you agree," drive content sharing. Brands that understand these factors can increase their chances for social-media-marketing success.[3]

Creating a New Level of Engagement

Sheila E. is a Grammy-nominated singer and drummer with a long, successful music career on her own and in collaboration with other famous artists such as Lionel Richie, Prince, Jennifer Lopez, Beyonce, and Kanye West. Sheila E. and many other artists know that one secret to success is engaging with their audience. Marketers must ask themselves if their organization is engaging their target audience. Traditional paid advertising and promotional sales messages are not engaging. Remember that in social media, the audience has to choose to spend time with the brand; the brand cannot buy their attention.

How can marketers gain the attention of their audience in social media? Create valuable content that the target audience will find entertaining or useful. The Content Marketing Institute defines **content marketing** as "a marketing technique where brands create and distribute valuable, relevant and consistent content to attract and acquire a clearly defined audience—with the objective of driving profitable customer action."[4]

Quality brand-sponsored content will draw consumers to an organization. BMW was an early innovator in content marketing. In 2001, they took $25 million normally spent on Super Bowl commercials and produced online short films with Hollywood directors, actors, and actresses. The films were excellent stories in and of themselves that just happened to take place around the brand's cars. The car manufacturer's busy target audience no longer had time or interest for traditional media. Within a year more than 21 million people downloaded the first film, and the effort delivered the most successful sales year in BMW's history. In 2002 three more films were added with a download total of 100 million. One million customers even bought a DVD of all eight of the BMW marketing films.[5]

Today, we call this type of strategy branded content or content marketing. A more recent star in content marketing has been Red Bull (see figure 12.1).[6] Red Bull was the original energy drink, but has managed to maintain its dominance despite many competitors entering the market. Red Bull is still the top brand, controlling 43 percent of market share.[7] Red Bull has done little traditional advertising over the years. Instead they created Red Bull Media House (RBMH) with more than 135 employees, which produces extreme-lifestyle content in print, online, on TV, and in feature films.

Red Bull's sports magazine *Red Bulletin* has a circulation equal to *Sports Illustrated*. Red Bull distributes its more than five thousand videos and fifty thousand photos free of charge, and they show up in the news on MSNBC and ESPN and in a weekly show on Halogen TV. Rebecca Lieb, analyst at Altimeter Group, observes, "Nobody is going to go to a website and spend 45 minutes looking at video about a drink. But Red Bull has

Figure 12.1. Red Bull Media House is a content-marketing powerhouse.

aligned its brand . . . with extreme sports and action." It is working. They are selling nearly five billion cans a year doing it.[8]

Content marketing is powerful, even in the business-to-business (B2B) context. Research by the Content Marketing Institute reports that 58 percent of B2B marketers planned on increasing their content marketing budget in 2014.[9] Why are they moving money from traditional advertising? B2B marketers indicate that content marketing improves engagement with important audiences; enhances trust; delivers faster, more relevant touch points; and improves search engine optimization (SEO).[10] Showcasing expertise and improving trust can go a long way toward building a B2B sale.

In the travel industry, Google research found that 84 percent of travelers use the Internet as a planning resource and visit an average of twenty-two websites before booking. The more branded content a company publishes across social media channels, the more likely it is that people planning trips will come across it. Active content on Facebook, Twitter, YouTube, and Flickr using SEO tags can deliver multiple hits per search, versus a single hit for a brand website.[11] Creating content around a related subject ultimately can help drive more customers to an organization's website.

On mobile devices, content marketing is even more effective because of small screens that limit traditional display advertising. Pulse publishes mobile content for marketers by distributing messages that "don't feel like advertising." Content such as this is sometimes referred to as producing native content or native advertising when it appears on media sites. Amazingly, users of the Pulse mobile reading app are 25 percent more likely to share the branded stories than they are to share actual news articles. This success is attracting big brands, such as Microsoft, T. Rowe Price, Disney, Lexus, and Forbes.[12] Even readers of the *New York Times* are spending just as much time with paid articles as editorial.[13] Remember that native advertising is different from content marketing in that it is paid media. However sponsored posts or articles on sites like *Forbes*, Buzzfeed, and the Huffington Post are growing in popularity as a way to reach a larger audience more quickly. Another option for native advertising is to boost reach of content through content recommendation engines that appear at the ends of articles such as "From the Web" listings on media sites like Fast Company.

Another content marketing strategy is to hire an in-house department full of former journalists. That is what Nick Panayi of Computer Sciences Corporation did. Besides website and social media content, his company publishes Infographic Central to showcase the latest industry research, Success Story Briefing Center to highlight case studies, and Ingenious Minds for employees to help them solve important IT problems.[14] He is creating valuable content that keeps current customers happy and attracts new customers looking for another provider.

 MINI CASE

Dove Real Beauty Sketches

Dove originally launched the Campaign for Real Beauty in 2004 in reaction to a study that found the definition of beauty had become limiting and unattainable, with overly thin models setting an impossible standard. Dove released the short film *Evolution* on YouTube in 2006, and it became a viral success. Thus, Dove films started a global conversation.[a]

Nearly ten years after the campaign began, the brand kept it fresh with *Dove Real Beauty Sketches*. This short film documented a social experiment where an FBI-trained sketch artist drew women's portraits according to their own self-description and one according to a stranger's description of her. The contrast struck an emotional chord, resulting in the most viewed online video ad of all time with more than 163 million global views. Additionally, the campaign generated more than 4.6 billion PR and blogger media impressions and more than one million likes on the Dove Facebook page, reaching one out of every ten Facebook users. The campaign was awarded a Titanium Grand Prix at the Cannes Lions Festival.[b]

[a] Kiley Skene, "A PR Case Study: Dove Real Beauty Campaign," Tuning In (blog), April 11, 2014, http://www .newsgeneration.com/2014/04/11/pr-case-study-dove-real-beauty.

[b] "Real Beauty Shines Through: Dove Wins Titanium Grand Prix, 163 Million Views on YouTube" (2013, June). Google Think Newsletter, June 2013, https://www.thinkwithgoogle.com/case-studies/dove-real -beauty-sketches.html.

Unfortunately, some organizations get into content marketing as a result of high-profile failures. In 2007, an *MSN Money* journalist wrote a column criticizing the Home Depot for horrible customer service. More than seven thousand people agreed and posted mostly negative comments. Boldly, Frank Blake, Home Depot's CEO, responded with his own comment to the blog post offering an apology and a promise to change. Social media became a key component in that change. Today, Home Depot uses store associates to produce valuable social media content with how-to videos on a branded YouTube channel. Store associates also provide home improvement advice and tips on Home Depot's Facebook and Twitter accounts.[15]

How do brands create content? In *EContent*, Ahava Leibtag suggests marketers first consider the format.[16] The most popular social channels for business-to-business (B2B) are Facebook, Twitter, LinkedIn, YouTube, Google+, and SlideShare, but don't rule out apps and games. For business-to-consumer (B2C), an organization should study the target audience's social media patterns and create content to engage consumers where they are talking about the brand, product, or service. Are they asking questions? Create articles, videos, and tips that answer them.

In content marketing, treat the customer or potential customer as a friend rather than a target. Magazines and newspaper publications have readers, not target audiences. They deliver valuable information to a community of shared interest. In content marketing, marketers and advertisers must do the same to succeed. Joe Pulizzi, founder of the Content Marketing Institute, says, "Marketers need to take off their sales hats and put on publisher hats."[17] Like Sheila E. says, being approachable is the only way to be engaging. Look for collaboration opportunities with content providers and consumers or start a new brand or organization content delivery vehicle.

Supercharge Word-of-Mouth

Facebook founder Mark Zuckerberg said, "But it's really all about how people are spreading Facebook around the world in all these different countries. And that's what's so amazing about the scale that it's at today."[18] Mark Zuckerberg may have built a new and unique online network, but the really amazing part is how Facebook simply spread via people to more than one billion users around the world. That is the power of Web 2.0 customer evangelism. This process doesn't have to happen all on its own. Organizations can deliberately recruit and equip loyal fans to be word-of-mouth brand ambassadors. **Evangelism marketing** is a form of word-of-mouth marketing in which marketers develop relationships with customers who strongly believe in a product or service and who voluntarily advocate for the brand.[19]

Social media, such as Facebook, turns fans into media vehicles for companies, especially considering the average Facebook user has 224 friends.[20] In addition, research reports that consumers trust other people more than advertising. So brand evangelists have enormous potential to greatly impact the demand and perception of a product or service.[21] Knowing how to tap into these consumers presents an opportunity to tap into enormous marketing potential.

Procter and Gamble (P&G) knows how to supercharge word-of-mouth. They set up a website community called Vocalpoint for influential mothers. These mothers share their experiences with new P&G products, and they often reach out to social networks outside of Vocalpoint with remarkable results. P&G found markets with active Vocalpoint online community influencers produced revenue twice the amount in markets without Vocalpoint.[22] Word-of-mouth supercharged P&G's traditional advertising and marketing efforts.

Yet a business doesn't have to be a big corporation to benefit from social media evangelism. For example, Kurt Walchle launched Survival Straps through social media. In six years of business, his company found that nearly 50 percent of its sales came from word-of-mouth social media efforts. This helped him grow from a home-based business into a thriving company with more than fifty employees.[23]

In *The Tipping Point*, Malcolm Gladwell advises that marketers should find "Connectors"—the people who seem to know everyone and have the ability to reach and influence a variety of consumers. When influenced by a "Market Maven," someone Gladwell depicts as knowing a lot about products, a Connector follows trends in specific areas and shares this information with others, joining consumers and brands together.[24] Figure 12.2 shows how this small group of mass influencers is responsible for 80 percent of the more than 500 billion online impressions made about products and services every year.[25]

Is there a way to measure how influential potential ambassadors will be? In *Return on Influence*, Mark Schaefer explains that influence has become the new currency of the social media age, and there are tools to measure this influence and calculate return. Services such as Klout use algorithms to measure online power and influence, taking into account

---

 How to Find a Brand Evangelist

In the book *Evangelist Marketing*, Alex Goldfayn suggests finding the average consumer who is a "hyper-repeat customer."[a] In order to turn these customers into evangelists, marketers and advertisers have to leverage the organization's strengths. The blog Scripted explains how to find brand evangelists through these five steps:[b]

1. *Excel at service.* When someone has a great experience they want to tell everyone about it.
2. *Show appreciation for repeating customers.* Give them special deals or offers.
3. *Listen and respond to complaints.* Admitting a mistake and fixing it also gives customers something to talk about.
4. *Leverage employees.* Train and reward employees who spread the brand message.
5. *Focus on quality, not quantity.* Relationships take time, so concentrate efforts on a smaller group of influential customers or clients to make the effort more manageable.

---

[a] Alan K. "How to Find Evangelists in Your Audience," Scripted (blog), November 18, 2013, http://scripted.com/content-marketing-2/how-to-find-evangelists.

[b] Malcolm Gladwell, *The Tipping Point: How Little Things Can Make a Big Difference*, Boston: Little, Brown (2000).

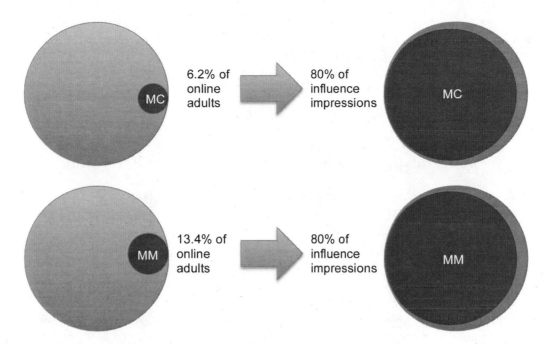

Figure 12.2. Mass influencers such as Mass Connectors (MC) and Mass Mavens (MM) create 80 percent of the product and service impressions each year.

Source: Josh Bernoff, "Spotting the Creators of Peer Influence," AdAge.com, April 20, 2010, http://adage.com/article/digitalnext/marketing-spotting-creators-peer-influence/143372.

various online and offline factors. With these tools, marketers can identify and quantify social media influencers who can drive demand for products and services.[26]

Betsy Weber is chief evangelist of the software development company TechSmith. She creates and cultivates relationships with key customers through roughly four hundred chats per month via email, instant messaging, phone, private forums, and in-person meetings. Weber keeps brand evangelists happy by replying to every email, forwarding problems or complaints to product specialists, and inviting brand advocates to join beta-testing groups. She also sends occasional free products and promotional items.[27]

A much larger brand-advocated effort was Coca-Cola's Expedition 206. This campaign sent three Open Happiness Ambassadors to visit all 206 countries where Coca-Cola is sold. The ambassadors were sent to blog, post video, and tweet their experiences. Ambassadors were recruited by identifying sixty social media users from Coca-Cola's fan base, which was narrowed down to eighteen, who were then interviewed in person. The nine remaining candidates were divided into three teams who promoted themselves via Twitter and Facebook to be voted as the winning ambassadors.[28] The campaign ended up generating 650 million media impressions and engaging billions of individuals both on and offline.[29]

Another example of a consumer evangelist program built around passionate product enthusiasts is Lego Ambassadors. Lego drives word-of-mouth by placing the company's most enthusiastic adult fans into an exclusive club. Members get previews about upcoming products, which they in turn share with their personal networks. Not everyone gets in. Enthusiasts must vie with one another to be chosen. The competition for limited membership energizes fans to become brand spokespeople.[30] Think of ways an organization can motivate and excite its most active fans, perhaps even on an amazing scale such as Mark Zuckerberg described.[31] That is the unlimited power of viral marketing.

Theoretically Speaking: Consumer-Brand Relationships

Can a person have a relationship with a product? This is a question researchers have been asking themselves for decades. As early as 1959, Sidney Levy proposed that products and brands can go beyond their utilitarian value and can be used as symbols with social meaning.[32] When a consumer displays or uses a product, the brand meaning is transferred to the consumer.[33] Branded products contribute to and communicate a consumer's self-image and personality, thus creating product attachment. A close relationship with the brand is formed because repeated usage satisfies the consumer's needs.

Kurt Matzler, Elisabeth Pichler, Johann Füller, and Todd Mooradian took this theory one step further to brand communities. Consumers identify with other consumers who use the same products and brands. In their study they found that both attachment to the product and ties to a brand community led to greater brand trust and loyalty.[34] Other researchers, Hyejune Park and Young-Kyung Kim, proved this theory with a study on Facebook published in the *Journal of Retailing & Consumer Services*. They found support for a brand's social network to positively influence a consumer's perception of the relationship investment made by the brand. This contributed to both brand relationship quality and the willingness to spread good words about the brand's social network, strengthening the quality of the consumer–brand relationship.[35] Investing in social media strengthens a consumer attachment to a product and builds stronger ties with the brand community, leading to the consumer sharing brand social content and increasing brand trust and loyalty.

SOCIAL PLAN PART 12

Creating Branded Content and Motivating Brand Evangelists

Take the social media strategy, consumer insight, and big idea to the next level with branded content and brand evangelism. What content is the target audience looking for? What type of content do they tend to view and share? Develop ideas for educational as well as entertaining text, photo, and video content. Will the content be brand-generated or co-created? Where will it be distributed? Also, devise a strategy and policy to engage and reward brand evangelists. What information, products, promotional trips, or events can the organization offer the most loyal and outspoken fans? Set guidelines in terms of scale and scope for the evangelists and the reward program. Report all thoughts, plans, and ideas in these areas:

1. Identify the information and entertainment needs of the target audience. List the main types of content they view and share.
2. Explain the types of content the brand can create to match target audience interests. Plan content to be brand-generated, consumer-generated, or co-created.
3. Research and identify the organization's most active customers in social media.
4. Create a brand evangelist program to both engage and reward the brand advocates. Spell out specific policies, promotions, and events.

QUESTIONS FOR DISCUSSION

1. What is the difference between content marketing and journalism? Research both editorial and advertorial content. List guidelines for writing each.
2. Is all branded content or native advertising ethical? Find an example of branded content that you feel may cross ethical or legal constraints on commercial speech. Support your opinion with research.
3. Mark Schaefer's book on Klout, *Return on Investment*, describes how far some brands will go to engage social media influences. Find an outlandish example of your own. How much will a brand give to a social media maven with a high Klout score and hundreds of thousands of followers?
4. The Dove Real Beauty Campaign is now more than ten years old. What could the brand do next to sustain attention and drive further viral success?

ADDITIONAL EXERCISES

1. For this exercise, remove your marketing hat and put on your publisher hat. Make a list of possible content you could create for your brand's customers, potential customers, or influencers. What common problems does your customer face? Can you provide tips, advice, or solutions? Do you have existing content somewhere that is not being accessed or used to its full potential? Also consider delivering value in other ways. An entertaining video or story can be just as engaging to a consumer audience. After you generate a list of ideas, go back and look for real opportunity to generate real value for your customers while meeting social-media-strategy objectives.
2. For this exercise, think about ways you can energize your brand evangelists. Customer evangelism doesn't always require big programs. Tap the power of evangelists simply by creating opportunities for customers to participate in the brand. Think about creating experiences they will in turn share with their social networks. Parties, openings, product launches, and cause-related events are ways to include brand enthusiasts and generate sharable content including videos, pictures, blog posts, and e-vites. Sponsoring an event or cause that a target audience cares about can really motivate evangelists to participate and spread the word. What is possible with your product or service?

Notes

1. "Engaging," BrainyQuote.com, accessed February 20, 2015, http://www.brainyquote.com/quotes/keywords/engaging_3.html.

2. Abigail Posner, "The Engagement Project: Finding the Meaning in Memes," *Google Think Newsletter,* June 2013, https://www.thinkwithgoogle.com/articles/memes-with-meaning.html.

3. Lada Adamic, Thomas Lento, Eytan Adar, and Pauline Ng, "The Evolution of Memes on Facebook," Facebook.com, January 8, 2014, https://www.facebook.com/notes/facebook-data-science/the-evolution-of-memes-on-facebook/10151988334203859.

4. "What Is Content Marketing?" Content Marketing Institute, accessed February 20, 2015, http://contentmarketinginstitute.com/what-is-content-marketing.

5. Gail Edmondson, "The Secret of BMW's Success," *Bloomberg Businessweek,* October 16, 2006, http://www.businessweek.com/magazine/content/06_42/b4005078.htm.

6. Red Bull, "Red Bull Media House Homepage," accessed February 20, 2015, http://www.redbullmediahouse.com.

7. "Top Selling Energy Drink Brands," CaffeineInformer.com, last modified May 13, 2015, http://www.caffeineinformer.com/the-15-top-energy-drink-brands.

8. James O'Brian, "How Red Bull Takes Content Marketing to the Extreme," Mashable.com, December 19, 2012, http://mashable.com/2012/12/19/red-bull-content-marketing.

9. Joe Pulizzi, "2014 B2B Content Marketing Research: Strategy Is Key to Effectiveness," Content Marketing Institute, October 1, 2013, http://contentmarketinginstitute.com/2013/10/2014-b2b-content-marketing-research/.

10. Christopher Hosford, "Content Marketing Comes of Age." *B To B* 97, no. 8 (2012): 1.

11. Breffni M. Noone, Kelly A. McGuire, and Kristin V. Rohlfs, "Social Media Meets Hotel Revenue Management: Opportunities, Issues and Unanswered Questions," *Journal of Revenue & Pricing Management* 10, no. 4 (2011): 293-305.

12. Jeff Bercovici, "Ads That Get More Love Than the Stories Around Them? Pulse Has Them," Forbes.com, November 14, 2012, http://www.forbes.com/sites/jeffbercovici/2012/11/14/ads-that-get-more-love-than-the-stories-around-them-pulse-has-them.

13. Nathalie Tadena, "NYT Readers Spend Same Amount of Time on Paid Posts as News Stories," the *Wall Street Journal* (blog), May 14, 2014, http://blogs.wsj.com/cmo/2014/05/14/nyt-readers-spend-same-amount-of-time-on-paid-posts-as-news-stories.

14. Hosford, "Content Marketing Comes of Age."

15. Charlene Li and Josh Bernoff, *Groundswell, Expanded and Revised Edition: Winning in a World Transformed by Social Technologies,* Boston: Harvard Business Review Press (2011).

16. Ahava Leibtag, "Is a Mobile-First Mentality Right for Your Organization?" *EContent* 35, no. 8 (2012): 12.

17. Nancy Davis Kho, "Content Connects People with Products," *EContent* 33, no. 6 (2010): 30-34.

18. "Spreading," BrainyQuote.com, accessed February 20, 2015, http://www.brainyquote.com/quotes/keywords/spreading.html.

19. "Evangelism Marketing," Wikipedia, last modified January 28, 2014, http://en.wikipedia.org/wiki/Evangelism_marketing.

20. Sara Goo, "Facebook: A Profile of its 'Friends,'" PewResearch.org, May 16, 2012, http://pewresearch.org/pubs/2262/facebook-ipo-friends-profile-social-networking-habits-privacy-online-behavior.

21. "Global Advertising: Consumers Trust Real Friends and Virtual Strangers the Most," Nielsenwire (blog), July 2009, http://blog.nielsen.com/nielsenwire/consumer/global-advertising-consumers-trust-real-friends-and-virtual-strangers-the-most.

22. Lawrence Ang, "Community Relationship Management and Social Media," *Journal of Database Marketing & Customer Strategy Management* 18, no. 1 (2011): 31–38.

23. Karen Russo, "Debate: Does Social Media Deliver Results for Small Business?" the *Wall Street Journal*, February 12, 2012, http://online.wsj.com/article/SB100014240529702048833045772 21664033429788.html?mod=googlenews_wsj.

24. Alex Goldfayn, *Evangelist Marketing: What Apple, Amazon, and Netflix Understand About Their Customers (That Your Company Probably Doesn't)*, Dallas, TX: BenBella Books (2012).

25. Josh Bernoff, "Spotting the Creators of Peer Influence," AdAge.com, April 20, 2010, http://adage.com/article/digitalnext/marketing-spotting-creators-peer-influence/143372.

26. Mark Schaefer, *Return on Influence: The Revolutionary Power of Klout, Social Scoring, and Influence Marketing*, New York: McGraw-Hill (2012).

27. James Pethokoukis, "Spreading the Word: Corporate Evangelists Recruit Customers Who Love to Create Buzz about a Product," *U.S. News & World Report*, November 27, 2005, http://www.usnews.com/usnews/biztech/articles/051205/5eeevangelist.htm.

28. Natalie Zmuda, "Digital: Behind Coca-Cola's Biggest Social-Media Push Yet," AdAge.com, November 17, 2009, http://adage.com/article/digital/digital-coca-cola-s-biggest-social-media-push/140591.

29. Nikola Banchfischer, "Expedition 206: First Results of Coca Cola's biggest Social Media Project," Aquarius Digital Potential (blog), January 10, 2011, http://www.aquarius.biz/en/2011/01/10/expedition-206-first-results-of-coca-cola's-biggest-social-media-project.

30. Li and Bernoff, *Groundswell*.

31. Dave Evans, *Social Media Marketing an Hour a Day, 2nd Ed.*, Indianapolis, IN: John Wiley & Sons (2012).

32. Sidney J. Levy, "Symbols for Sale," *Harvard Business Review* 37 (1959): 117–124.

33. Kelly Tepper Tian, William O. Bearden, and Gary L. Hunter, "Consumers' Need for Uniqueness: Scale Development and Validation," *Journal of Consumer Research* 28, (2001): 50–66.

34. Kurt Matzler, Elisabeth Pichler, Johann Füller, and Todd A. Mooradian, "Personality, Person-Brand Fit, and Brand Community: An Investigation of Individuals, Brands, and Brand Communities," *Journal of Marketing Management* 27, no. 9/10 (2011): 874–890.

35. Hyejune Park and Young-Kyung Kim, "The Role of Social Network Websites in the Consumer–Brand Relationship," *Journal of Retailing & Consumer Services* 21, no. 4 (2014): 460–467.

Customer Service

The Art of Turning Complaints into Compliments

Right or wrong, the customer is always right.[1]

Marshall Field

PREVIEW

A **customer service system** is a configuration of technology and organization networks designed to provide services that satisfy customers.[2] This term is used in and by service management, operations, marketing, engineering, and design. Service systems provide value that can improve customer service and create competitive advantage, especially within industries where there is much parity in products. How did we get to today's current state of customer service operations?

In the beginning, customer service was limited. If a person had a problem with a product they either fixed it themselves or physically returned it to the store owner. With the invention of the telephone in the late 1800s came direct ways to contact stores and companies from the home or office. However, early telephone switchboards and rotary-dial technology still made it challenging to contact companies and limited customer complaints. As technology improved through touch-tone dialing and the introduction of the 1-800 number, more customers began to call companies. This increase in demand led to the creation of the call center, and call centers evolved into customer-service departments.

In the 1970s and '80s, customer support departments began using interactive voice response technology to improve efficiency and created automated responses that led customers through complex phone trees. At the end of the 1980s, formal customer-service strategies emerged, and outsourcing customer service functions to other countries became a main strategy to help meet increased demand from customers in more cost-effective ways.[3]

In the 1990s and early 2000s, customer service changed dramatically with the introduction of the Internet as a new channel of contact, leading to the development of customer service email, instant messaging, and live chat as well as integrated customer-service management systems. Thus the story of customer service is tied directly to the development of technology. Now we are faced with the new communication technology of social media. As we have seen from history, when a new avenue opens to contact companies, customers will use it, customer-service expectations will change, and customer-service systems must evolve to follow suit.

The Customer Is Always Right

Marshall Field of Chicago department store fame is credited with the saying, "The customer is always right." If this saying applied in the 1800s before digital media, it most certainly applies even more today. Now even wrong customers, with the power of social media, can turn a single complaint into a movement against a company.

Just one example came with Molly Katchpole, whom we first saw in chapter 2. Through a social media campaign using Facebook, Twitter, and Change.org, she was able to get Bank of America to revoke a $5 debit-card fee.[4] In chapter 4, Dave Carroll demonstrated how he indirectly used his voice, YouTube, and Twitter to cause United Airlines stock to drop 10 percent.[5] The consumer voice is more powerful today than it has ever been, and customer demands on customer-service quality and delivery are increasing.

Whether an organization is big or small, business customer service is at the heart of keeping current customers happy and attracting new ones. Business is built on reputation and relationships through care, honesty, and trust that can be nurtured through social media.[6] In 2008, Frank Eliason of Comcast figured this out and went on to become the most famous customer-service manager in the US. Eliason grew tired of all the negative talk that was occurring on social media about his cable company. Instead of sitting back and letting it occur, Eliason got the idea to use Twitter to interact with those Comcast cable customers. Instead of making the customer come to him, he decided to engage the customers where they were having the conversations.

Eliason's idea was so effective that today Comcast provides real-time customer service on Twitter and Facebook with a full-time dedicated social media staff. Cable customers love the immediate online results, compared to fruitless hours spent on the phone.[7] Comcast's Social Care team has worked. As a result, Comcast Cable's J. D. Power Overall Satisfaction score has improved.[8] The beginning of this improvement was based on the simple idea of delivering service on the customer's terms, not the corporation's.

Despite its social media customer service success, Comcast is still working on improving customer service delivered over the phone. This lack of progress was evidenced by a recent recorded service call that went viral in social media. After mass media attention, the company was forced to apologize for a customer service representative who held a customer captive on the phone for nearly twenty minutes despite the customer's simple request. The phone representative was aggressive and rude, refusing to cancel the customer's service because he was moving. The customer recorded the call and put it on Sound-Cloud, where it was listened to millions of times and picked up by major media such as *Time* magazine, NPR, and *Good Morning America*.[9] Even companies that deliver social media customer service well may be forced through the power of social media to make improvements in their older, more-traditional service delivery channels.

A survey by *CRM* magazine reports that 31 percent of all customer interactions today are conducted via the web, with an additional 9 percent conducted via mobile devices. Only 46 percent of all interactions are conducted via phone.[10] An additional survey of worldwide companies also reports that the second-most-used social media activity behind marketing is customer service.[11] As customer-service activity moves to social media, companies must be prepared. To be effective, marketing must work with customer service. The customer doesn't distinguish between company departments and will seek engagement with both in the same channel. See figure 13.1 for a breakdown of the percentage of business now conducted via social media, by type of business activity.

Today, smart organizations are using social media to manage customer relationships. Social media can help increase customer retention by finding complaints early and making the service personal. Social media customer relationship management can also reduce operational costs because providing online customer service is generally less expensive than service over the phone.[12] In *Groundswell*, Charlene Li and Josh Bernoff estimate that the average call to a company's call center costs $6 or $7 and technical support calls can cost as much as $10 to $20.[13] Social media support can cost a lot less as representatives are

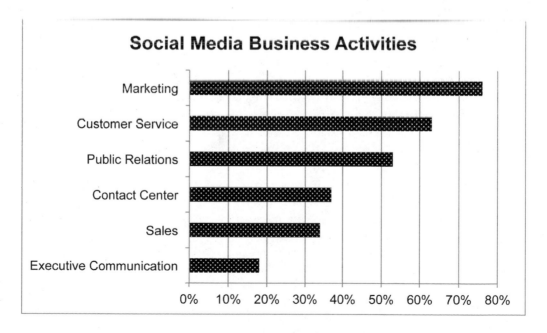

Figure 13.1. Customer service is the second-most-used social media activity.

Source: Donna Fluss, "Using Social Media for Customer Service," *CRM* magazine 16, no. 4 (2012): 10.

able to handle several customers at once and take advantage of many automated tasks and information. Solving a problem in a real-time stream within public view can stop negative conversation before it spreads to more permanent links like blogs, forums, or an article or even a book.[14] Resolving issues in public view has other advantages as well. Solving one customer's problem or answering a question in the public social media stream enables everyone to benefit from the response.

Fixing customer-service problems or appeasing disgruntled customers in social media is one consideration, but sometimes a negative comment can turn into a big public relations disaster. How should an organization handle a complaint or issue that could quickly get out of control? Marketing specialist Rob Stokes suggests a few rules:[15]

- *Be humble.* Listen before acting. Get an understanding of the scale and scope of the problem and how consumer complaints evolved.

MINI CASE

Hertz 24/7 Social Care

In 2014 Hertz Rent-a-Car announced 24/7 global social customer care. Hertz's director of service excellence, Laura Smith, said the company was shifting from a marketing-oriented view of social media to a customer-oriented view. Prior to this initiative, marketing was the owner of social media and customer complaints. Because of this former structure, customer complaints in social media were filtered through marketing staff, who would in turn email the complaints to customer service agents. The customer service agents would then often take days to respond. The new Hertz 24/7 social care system includes customer service in its social media monitoring for improved efficiency and quicker response. Now the cross-discipline departments work together.[a]

When only Hertz marketing was monitoring social media, service was limited to Monday through Friday. Marketing would forward social media posts, customer service would reply via email, and then marketing would post the responses on social media. For the new system, Hertz partnered with software vendor Conversocial to give customer service a seat at the social-media-monitoring table. The company reports that responding to customer-service issues in real time via social media has influenced other users and is increasing customer loyalty, which contributes to customer lifetime value.[b] The new Hertz cross-departmental social care system has enabled the company to exceed expectations. They are able to respond within seventy-five minutes to more than one thousand unique customers per week.[c]

---

[a] Lloyd Waldo, "Hertz Hands the Social Media Keys over from Marketing, to Customer Care," *Future Care Today*, October 31, 2014, http://futurecare.today/news/hertz-hands-the-social-media-keys-over-from-marketing-to-customer-care.

[b] "Video: How Hertz Provides 24/7 Social Customer Service Globally," WhySatisfy.com, October 10, 2014, http://whysatisfy.com/video-how-hertz-provides-247-social-customer-service-globally.

[c] "Hertz's Cross-Departmental Collaboration Helps it Delight and Retain its Customers," *Future Care Today*, September 24, 2014, http://futurecare.today/downloads/case-studies/hertzs-cross-departmental-collaboration-helps-it-delight-and-retain-its-customers.

- *Act right away.* Responding quickly by acknowledging a wrong and promising to correct it can wipe out a brand attack before it gets started.
- *Keep negative pages out of search engines.* Add positive content and links to drive negative links off the first page of search results.
- *Respond via blogs and industry forums.* This will help to present the organization's side of the story.
- *Care about the customer.* Show them the organization truly cares about their concerns. Treat them with kindness and respect.

Remember that when a business enters social media it must act like an individual. Practice good personal skills, the same that would be used in a face-to-face conversation. Encourage social media employees to think of the customer first and try to treat them the way they would want to be treated. These simple practices can go a long way. No one expects perfection, but they do expect empathy, apology, and corrective action.

Social Care Is No Longer a Choice

Organizations may no longer have a choice on whether or not to provide social media customer service. Customer expectations for service and response in this new medium are rising. A survey of consumers who have complained on Twitter revealed that nearly half of respondents expected a company to read their tweet. Yet only 29 percent of those customers who tried to engage an organization on Twitter received a follow-up from the company.

This gap represents a real opportunity for competitive advantage to the companies who take the time to respond. Some 83 percent of customers who received a response from a company on Twitter said that they loved or liked receiving it.[16] A simple response

---

 Types of Social Information Impacting Customer Service

Customer service provided via social media can deal with multiple issues in many areas. What are those possibilities? According to DMG Consulting, five out of the top six types of information gained from social media engagement directly impact customer service:[a]

1. Positive or negative sentiment
2. Issues with products
3. Complaints or follow-ups for previous customer-service interactions
4. Issues with procedures
5. Crisis identification

---

[a] "Social Media: Guide for Building a Customer Support Strategy," DMG Consulting, July 7, 2010, http://www.dmgconsult.com/publications/whitepapers.asp.

can make a happy customer, who in social media can easily share that happiness to others. Customers have high expectations for engagement online. In the past, businesses have had to make adjustments by offering customer service via telephone service, email, and live chat. Now demand for that customer service is shifting to social media networks, and organizations must follow.

The impact of social media is why companies such as Comcast, Dell, Best Buy, and United Airlines monitor Twitter to find references to their brands and resolve customer issues with social care teams. **Social care** is simply defined as efforts employees make through social media to care for customers.[17] American Airlines now has seventeen employees dedicated to social customer service, with four more focused on brand engagement and one assigned to social media measurement and reporting.[18] They are presenting a uniform cross-discipline social media presence to their customers.

In the definition of social care and the American Airlines example, notice that social care is not limited to traditional contact-center agents working in customer-service departments. Many companies are empowering customer-service representatives, engineers, product managers, and executives to provide positive customer service on social media.[19] A good social-care team requires cross-business unit integration. This is yet another reason to do some silo smashing in an organization.

In a white paper on social care, TELUS International authors Kim Keating and Dave Evans suggest many best practices for forming a successful social-care program. One of the best practices is to start by defining the vision and objectives of the social-care effort. Once vision and objectives are in place, recruit a cross-functional team that includes employees from all departments. It is important to ensure the team is working toward a common goal and that all departments are represented, but it is equally important to be sure that each individual has a defined role. Following a strategic structure from the beginning will more likely lead to a successful social-care program. See table 13.1 for an example of cross-functional social-care team organization and responsibilities.[20]

Table 13.1. Cross-Functional Social-Care Team Organization and Responsibilities

Department	Responsibility
Customer Service	Set up to be the main point of contact for service-related issues
Marketing	Promote social support and provide brand briefing on communication style
Corporate Communication/PR	Develop crisis and stakeholder communication plans
Legal	Define social media policies that govern agent responses
Human Resources	Define hiring profiles and set training standards for social agents

Source: Kim Keating and Dave Evans, "Benchmarking Social Media Customer Service: Uncovering Opportunities & Best Practices for Social Care," TELUS International, accessed February 20, 2015, http://www.telusinternational.com/social_care_study.

Bianca Buckridee, VP of social media operations for JPMorgan Chase, says that an advantage she sees in social customer service is that customers can go to Chase's Twitter page and see the person they are chatting with. This restores some of the intimacy and comfort lost in a phone conversation. She has seen Chase customers returning to social media saying, "Hey, let me know when Theo gets in," or "I want to talk to Danni; she knows exactly where I'm at and what I'm going through." Social media can help bring back that personal connection once found in the small-town marketplace.

The Chase customer service team also crosses lines of business so that customers can tweet one handle and get help for a retail account, credit card, mortgage, auto loan, student loan, or investment.[21] This is an excellent example of the transition in thinking from the Four Ps of product, price, place, and promotion to the Four Cs of consumer, cost, convenience, and communication. Rather than social media being a burden, it simplifies the process for companies and customers alike. It is also a good example of social media tearing down silos and cutting down on phone transfers to other departments that simply waste everyone's time.

The marketing department can and should take the lead in social media monitoring and strive to remove functional silos, but marketing professionals must also remember there is still value in discipline-specific expertise. Jonathan Salem Baskin reminds marketers of this in his *Ad Age* article, "Customer Service Belongs to Operations, Not Marketing: How Apple Turned Problem-Fixing Into a Promotional Tool." He explains that the core capability of fixing customer product or service problems is not a communications solution that marketers can provide.

Marketers cannot reboot routers, install software patches, send replacement parts, or answer billing problems. Providing service belongs to operations. Social monitoring can reveal how bad operations issues may be and how the public is reacting to them, but operations people are the ones who actually need to fix the problems. In fact, when operations provides excellent service, the service can be a driver of the brand and enable marketing.[22] A key component of the Zappos.com brand is its customer service and exceptional employees who deliver that service via traditional and social customer service channels.

Remember that everyone is watching an organization's every tweet, post, and update. Marshall Field understood this on a smaller scale. Field's department store employees were always instructed not to push products on uninterested customers and to know that even when the customer was wrong, they were right. Perhaps marketers and advertisers could benefit from that nineteenth-century personal sales wisdom in this twenty-first century social interaction technology.

Theoretically Speaking: Word-of-Mouth in a Service Context

Most agree that word-of-mouth marketing is powerful, but few have delved deeper into why that is. Researchers focusing on word-of-mouth (WOM) have contended that it is one of the most powerful forms of marketing because consumers rely on personal communication sources in making purchase decisions over organizational sources such as advertising campaigns. The sender of the information generally has nothing to gain from the receiver's actions, so the opinion is seen as unbiased and more credible.[23] WOM in a service context is unique because it offers special solutions to the problem of intangibility of services. Before service consumption, a consumer might seek WOM information from an experienced source.[24] Thus, WOM is also important in shaping expectations of service and becomes especially important within the services purchase decision.[25]

How can marketers improve WOM? Researchers Harvis Bansal and Peter Voyer conducted a study that found marketers should initiate WOM messages that try to focus on ties between the sender and the receiver in their target audience. In other words, company communication should not only emphasize the attributes of the product and service but also suggest consumers seek information from other people in the target audience who they consider "friends." This is called tie-strength. The closer the relationship or the more a person can relate to the person offering the WOM communication, the more impact it has in the decision-making process. Thus marketers should also encourage happy customers in the target audience to share their positive experience through social media WOM so others can discover the company.[26]

 SOCIAL PLAN PART 13

Creating Cross-Functional Social Care

If the organization does not have an active social care program, now is the time to plan it. First investigate and analyze the existing system that is in place. Is there a customer-service department? How do they currently find out about customer needs? What system are they using? Is customer service limited by delivery method or hours? Is the organization conducting social media monitoring? If so, who is doing it? Are other departments involved? Table 13.1 describes a plan for a cross-functional social-care team. Report all thoughts, plans, and ideas in these areas:

1. Identify the current system. Explain what kind of social media monitoring is occurring. Is it 24/7 or intermittent? What systems are being used?
2. Identify the employees responsible for social media monitoring. What department are they from? Is the team cross-functional?
3. Plan a structure for a new cross-functional social-care team that can address all areas of social information efficiently and effectively. What systems are needed?
4. Plan the marketing responsibility in a cross-functional social-care team by explaining how marketing will provide social support. Also provide a briefing on the brand communication style and big idea for the social media plan.

QUESTIONS FOR DISCUSSION

1. Must all organizations, brands, products, services, or industries provide customer service via social media? Can you name a company or industry that does not need to build a social care team? Why or why not?

2. Revisit the Comcast Cable example of the viral audio of a customer-service representative refusing to discontinue a customer's service. Why do you think there is such a disconnect between Comcast Cares social media service and its customer-service via telephone? What can Comcast do to fix the issue?

3. Voice recordings and phone trees helped automate customer service via the phone and helped make it more efficient. What are your thoughts on automation in social media customer service? Can it help? Find an example of social automation working and one example where it is not working.

4. Hertz Rent-a-Car's 24/7 social care response is impressive, but what can a small business or startup do with fewer resources? Is there a software system or employee response that can help? Should expectations be lowered or not given at all?

ADDITIONAL EXERCISES

1. For this exercise, go on Twitter and make comments and requests to the handles or hashtags of several companies. Note how long it takes to get a response, who responds, and how they respond. Compare the different company actions. From what you observe, try to determine what type of social-care plan the organization is running. Do they have a plan? Is one department, such as marketing, obviously running it without the other departments being involved? Or is there truly a cross-functional social-care system in place? Pick one of the companies and ask the same question or try to solve the same issue via another communication channel, such as the telephone or email. Do you notice a difference in response time, quality, and content?

2. For this exercise, think about worst-case scenarios. In social media, brand attacks can spring up instantly for reasons you can't always predict. What should an organization do? Make a list of some of the bad situations in which the organization could find itself. Think of horrible customer-service experiences, product failures and recalls, environmental disasters, scandals, and accidents. How should a company react when social media is lighting up with activity?

Notes

1. "Marshall Field," BrainyQuote.com, accessed February 20, 2015, http://www.brainyquote.com/quotes/quotes/m/marshallfi379060.html.

2. "Service System," Wikipedia, last modified December 18, 2014, http://en.wikipedia.org/wiki/Service_system.

3. Marck Herschberger, "The Complete History of Customer Service Operations," Eventus Contact Center Solutions (blog), March 31, 2014, from http://www.eventusg.com/blog/the-complete-history-of-customer-service-operations.

4. Jeff Howe, "How Hashtags and Social Media Can Bring Megacorporations to Their Knees," TheAtlantic.com, June 8, 2012, http://www.theatlantic.com/business/archive/2012/06/the-rise-of-the-consumerate/258290.

5. Ravi Sawhney, "Broken Guitar Has United Playing the Blues to the Tune of $180 Million," FastCompany.com, July 7, 2009, http://www.fastcompany.com/blog/ravi-sawhney/design-reach/youtube-serves-180-million-heartbreak.

6. John George and Phil Simon, "Connecting with Customers," *Baylor Business Review* 30, no. 1 (2011): 22–25.

7. Donna Fluss, "Using Social Media for Customer Service," *CRM* magazine 16, no. 4 (2012): 10.

8. Bill Gerth, "Lithys 2014: Comcast—Excellence in Customer Satisfaction," Lithium.com (blog), April 1, 2014, http://community.lithium.com/t5/Social-Customer-Excellence/Lithys-2014 -Comcast-Excellence-in-Customer-Satisfaction/idi-p/140812.

9. Susanna Kim, "Comcast Apologizes for 'Unacceptable' Customer Service Call That Won't End," ABCNews.com, July 15, 2014, http://abcnews.go.com/Business/comcast-apologizes -unacceptable-customer-service-call-end/story?id=24567047&singlePage=true.

10. "New Survey Highlights the Growth of Web Self-Service," *CRM* magazine, July 8, 2013, http://www.destinationcrm.com/Articles/CRM-News/Daily-News/New-Survey-Highlights -the-Growth-of-Web-Self-Service-90678.aspx.

11. Fluss, "Using Social Media for Customer Service."

12. Nichole Kelly, "How to Measure Social Media's Impact on Customer Retention," Social-MediaExaminer.com, September 8, 2010, http://www.socialmediaexaminer.com/how-to-measure -social-media%E2%80%99s-impact-on-customer-retention.

13. Charlene Li and Josh Bernoff, *Groundswell, Expanded and Revised Edition: Winning in a World Transformed by Social Technologies*, Boston: Harvard Business Review Press (2011).

14. Dave Evans, *Social Media Marketing an Hour a Day,* 2nd ed. Indianapolis, IN: John Wiley & Sons (2012).

15. Rob Stokes, *eMarketing: The Essential Guide to Online Marketing, v. 1.0.* Irvington, NY: Flatworld Knowledge (2010).

16. "Maritz Research and evolve24 Twitter Study," MaritzResearch.com, September 2011, http://www.maritzresearch.com/shared-content/Press-Releases/2011/Are-you-listening -Twitter-users-want-complaints-read-addressed.

17. "Why Social Media Is Important Customer Service Channel?" TELUS International (blog), accessed January 20, 2015, http://telusinternational-europe.com/why-social-care-is-important -customer-service-channel.

18. "The Ignored Side of Social Media: Customer Service," Knowledge@Wharton, January 2, 2014, http://knowledge.wharton.upenn.edu/article/ignored-side-social-media-customer-service.

19. "Why Social Media Is Important Customer Service Channel?" TELUS International.

20. Kim Keating and Dave Evans, "Benchmarking Social Media Customer Service: Uncovering Opportunities & Best Practices for Social Care," TELUS International, accessed February 20, 2015, http://www.telusinternational.com/social_care_study.

21. "The Ignored Side of Social Media: Customer Service," Knowledge@Wharton.

22. Jonathan Salem Baskin, "Customer Service Belongs to Operations, Not Marketing: How Apple Turned Problem-Fixing Into a Promotional Tool," AdAge.com, June 27, 2011, http://adage .com/article/cmo-strategy/customer-service-belongs-operations-marketing/228447.

23. Leon G. Schiffman and Leslie Lazar Kanuk, *Consumer Behavior,* 6th ed. Upper Saddle River, NJ: Prentice Hall (1997).

24. Julia M. Bristor, "Enhanced Explanations of Word of Mouth Communications: The Power of Relationships," *Research in Consumer Behavior* 4 (1990): 51–83.

25. Valarie A. Zeithaml and Mary Jo Bitner, *Services Marketing.* New York: McGraw-Hill (1996).

26. Harvir S. Bansal and Peter A. Voyer, "Word-of-Mouth Processes Within a Services Purchase Decision Context," *Journal of Service Research* 3, no. 2 (2000): 166.

PART

V

**Pulling It
All Together**

Write Your Plan, Plan Your Sell

Even when you have gone as far as you can, and everything hurts, and you are staring at the specter of self-doubt, you can find a bit more strength deep inside you, if you look closely enough.[1]

—Hal Higdon

PREVIEW

"Being unable to see the forest for the trees" is a phrase familiar to many. This is an idiom that was seen as early as John Heywood's 1546 collection of proverbs. It means getting so caught up in the small details that a person fails to understand the bigger picture. The ability to discern an overall pattern from a mass of details is a valuable skill.[2] This skill is at the heart of strategies that plan and marshal organizational resources to meet and exceed business goals. This ability is seen as very valuable.

In 2013, Management Research Group (MRG) conducted a global study of more than sixty thousand managers that accessed more than twenty leadership practices and twenty measures of effectiveness. Practices included innovation, persuasion, communication, and results orientation, while effectiveness measures included future potential, credibility, business aptitude, and people skills. Results of the study found that having a strategic approach was ten times more important to effectiveness than other leadership behaviors, and almost fifty times more important than tactical behaviors. In a follow-up study, ten thousand senior executives were asked to select the leadership behaviors most critical to an organization's success. "Strategic" was chosen 97 percent of the time.[3]

Strategic thinking means taking a broad, long-range approach and thinking systematically. Most people may agree that this skill is very important, yet thinking strategically is not easy. Strategic thinking is especially hard when immediate demands are often rewarded over long-term vision and planning. When faced with more than eight hundred social media sites, apps, and services, being able to focus on a long-term approach and systematic thinking is necessary for action. Seeing the forest for the trees is more than a mindset. It is a leadership quality that is necessity for success.[4]

Slow and Steady Wins the Race

Hal Higdon is a famous marathon runner, the longest contributing writer to *Runner's World* magazine (more than forty years), and has written more than thirty marathon-training books. Yet what he says about training for a marathon can easily apply directly to social media marketing. Training for a marathon is long. Most marathon-training programs last four months and only begin after months of setting a solid base of twenty to thirty miles a week.[5]

The marathon itself is long. The beginning is exciting with the crowd, the newness, the scenery. Then somewhere after the halfway point, away from the crowds, the novelty wears off. The excitement is gone and is simply replaced with grueling mile after mile. This is when doubt sets in for many runners. "Why am I doing this?" "I can't do this!" "What was I thinking?" Then around mile twenty, runners hit "the wall." At the wall all energy is used up and it feels as if one cannot continue.

Yet if they pop some energy gels and will themselves to the end, most runners discover running the marathon is more than worth it. The *Baltimore Sun* captured that feeling appropriately in an article following the Baltimore Marathon. The article described a runner who crossed the marathon finish line, vomited, and then said, "That was the best time of my life!"

Social media can be like this. Not necessarily the vomiting part, but more the day-to-day posting, monitoring, content generation, and curation. The grueling post after post and comment after comment can be draining. Despite all the talk about ROI and immediate measurement, the majority of social media marketing doesn't give immediate significant return like a new TV campaign that can spike retail sales the weekend a marketer or advertiser runs it. Viral hits are the exception, and these overnight successes are rare. Many marketers, advertisers, public relations professionals, and entrepreneurs are jumping into the social media race, but they must be in for the long haul to see real results.[6] Take a step back to see the forest of eight hundred social media trees.

Jay Baer captured this mindset well in his blog post, "Are You Slow Enough to Succeed in Social Media?" He observes that social media adoption is quick, but interacting and engaging with customers and prospects happens on a one-to-one or one-to-few basis, and that takes time. Social media is also built on trust, and building trust is a longer process. Baer likens this process to recruiting a volunteer marketing army one soldier at a time. This is something that doesn't happen overnight.[7] If marketers are used to buying mass audience attention through traditional methods, the slow burn of social media could require some adjustment time. It also could require explanation to organization management to set up realistic expectations.

Reading the trade press, case studies, and white papers on social media efforts can be deceiving. From these accounts, marketers and advertisers may think social growth and success does happen overnight if they simply hit the right formula. We read about many social media stars, but many of those articles tend to skip over the backstory and the years of groundwork. The Dove Real Beauty campaign is one example. Before Dove turned to social media with its online films, the campaign started as a traditional advertising campaign. They proved success in small steps at first, and built trust with company management before the campaign became the viral-success case study we see now. This type of example happens in the music industry all the time. A band will be positioned in the press as an overnight success, but upon further inspection readers may find that the band is actually on its fifth or sixth album release and has been playing small venues for a decade.

Seth Godin is a great example of this long-term thinking. He has been publishing a blog post every day since 2002. For well over ten years, he has faithfully put out daily social media content. Highly successful now, his blog did not always have a mass audience. Godin's first post "Death of a Myth?" to this day only has one tweet and four likes. Yet a more recent post, "Trading Favors," received 1,162 tweets and 568 likes.[8] Marketers and advertisers should keep this long-term perspective in mind as they complete a social media strategy and start to execute the plan. Success may not take twelve years, but it also may not happen in twelve days. Once the social media plan is finished, the real race and real work have just begun.

Content Creation Takes Time and Focus

A survey of social media professionals investigated in which areas they spent most of their time. The results revealed that only 12 percent of social media staff's time was spent on strategy development, and the majority of their time (60 percent) was devoted to content creation. In social media, content development takes up nearly six times the amount of time as strategy development, posting content, listening and monitoring, measuring, responding to fans and followers, and reporting results to leadership (See figure 14.1).[9] After putting the social media plan together and completing the social media strategy process, be prepared to spend the majority of time on content development.

Yet for those who have patience and daily persistence, social media does deliver results. As stated before, it may not take twelve years, but it may take longer than some expect. NASCAR is a good example of social media strategic thinking on the right time scale. David Higdon is NASCAR's IMC managing director. At an integrated marketing communications conference he spoke about the brand's remarkable overhaul that came from a focus on a younger audience and a commitment to reach them in the social channels where they participate.

Today NASCAR's social media effort can be seen as successful. Sponsorship deals have risen 8 percent since 2008—higher than before the recession. Also, 23 percent of Fortune 500 brands are now part of NASCAR, which is an increase of 20 percent from

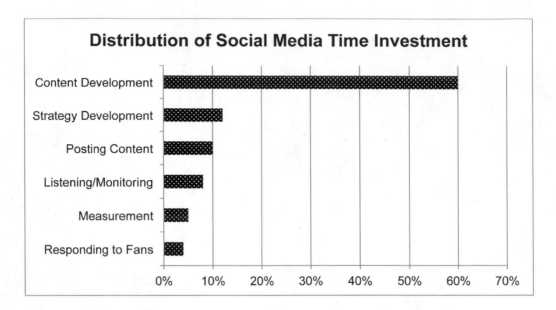

Figure 14.1. Social Media Areas That Require the Biggest Investment of Time

Source: "Social Media Marketing's Main Expense is Staff. How Do They Spend Their Time?" MarketingCharts .com, May, 2014, http://www.marketingcharts.com/online/social-media-marketings-main-expense-is-staff-how -do-they-spend-their-time-42651/attachment/smmu-top-areas-social-media-time-investment-may2014.

2012.[10] In addition, a survey has found that 61 percent of eighteen- to thirty-four-year-old avid fans are more interested today in NASCAR than the previous year, and 65 percent of those have been fans for fewer than five years. This increase in fan interest is attributed to NASCAR's new social media engagement efforts.[11] However, the real insight into NASCAR's success is that these results came after an eighteen-month review and then a three- to five-year integrated marketing communications plan to achieve those successful results.

How does a three- to five-year timeline work in a business culture where the average CMO is ousted every two to three years? Culture simply must change. Trying to apply old strategies and expectations in this new social media–empowered consumer environment does not work. Social media marketing is a different game with different rules. Push marketing and all its perceptions and expectations do not apply.[12] Perhaps David Higdon of NASCAR learned the new rules from his father Hal Higdon of marathon fame. Did his father's marathon strategy influence the son's social media strategy? Short-sighted sales results are slowly giving way to lifetime value, and the increasing importance of social media consumer engagement may be helping to drive that change.

Tom Martin from Converse Digital polled digital marketers and asked how long it takes to see results from social media marketing. Most respondents felt six months was a fair average if you were doing it right. Others thought time frames of nine to eighteen months were more appropriate.[13] Why do social media results take so long? Some answer that question with another question. How long does it take to create a loyal following? Social media is about engagement, relationships, and listening. It can take months to curate a community by targeting them with articles, pictures, videos, and other content to foster engagement.[14]

Content creation also takes a laser focus on the customer and their changing needs. As you move into the content development stage, practice a customer-centric approach. When creating content, flip from a brand-first to customer-first approach. A marketer's or advertiser's target audience will seek different information depending on which stage of the buying cycle they're in. Recognizing this and customizing content to the target audience's changing needs will increase engagement. Consumers' needs and behaviors are different when they're not in the market to buy, when they become engaged in buying, and when they become customers. Consider developing different messages and content for the prepurchase, purchase, and postpurchase consumer.[15]

Rosalia Cefalu of HubSpot believes different employees are best suited for communicating with customers in different stages of the buying cycle. These employees can come from various departments throughout your company or organization. Distributing social responsibilities across departments to the most relevant people makes communication more effective and efficient. It also spreads the workload so that one-on-one social media engagement becomes more scalable. Setting up a multi-department social-care team can help generate customer engagement throughout the buying cycle to gain new customers, repeat purchases, loyalty, and brand advocates.[16]

For the prepurchase stage of the buying cycle, monitor social media for consumers who are in the market to buy, but have not purchased. Look for people using the right keywords, such as mentions of your company, competitors, industry, or specific products and services. Here marketing and advertising departments can create relevant messages and content to grow fans and followers and monitor conversations to engage with those responding. The public relations or corporate communications department in a company may play a role looking for larger industry or corporate issues and identifying journalists or bloggers for media outreach.

In the purchase stage, monitor social media for consumers actively seeking purchase information. With these customers the marketing or advertising team can help them along with their purchases. However, sales representatives may be best suited to deliver more relevant engagement. In a B2C context, the sales team could interact with customers on social media to facilitate the sale. In a B2B company, sales representatives could address the needs of qualified leads helping them to conversion.

The postpurchase stage is about keeping current customers happy. Monitor social media for current customers seeking help. Marketing and advertising can play a role, but resolving issues and getting customers the answers they need is probably best served by customer-service representatives. The customer-service department is ideal for providing the type of service that they already provide via phone, email, or online chat. To fully address the needs of consumers through all the stages of the buying cycle, consider building a multi-discipline social care team to help meet marketing and organizational goals.[17]

Theoretically Speaking: Uses and Gratification

What do people find valuable about media? Uses and gratifications has been a core theory in communications since the early 1970s. This theory was first developed by researchers such as Jay Blumler, Elihu Katz, Michael Gurevitch, and Alan Rubin. To them this theory represented a dramatic shift from previous mass-communication research. It flipped the perspective from studying what mass media does to people to what people do to mass media.[18] **Uses and gratifications theory** proposes that audiences are active in media consumption and that they consciously select media content to satisfy their various needs. This theory also shifted perspective in another way by suspending judgments about the cultural value of content. Uses and gratifications assume all content has a potential functional value.[19] Today this would even apply to funny cat videos or any meme. Some people value them simply for the entertainment.

With the current increased use of interactive and social media, uses and gratifications theory has taken on new dimensions. Shyam Sundar and Anthony Limperos write about this transition in "Uses and Grats 2.0: New Gratifications for New Media." The authors argue that with the development of interactive, two-way media more and different gratifications are being sought and obtained from media. Understanding how consumers use various media and the different gratifications they seek can help marketers tailor traditional and social media content to be more effective. See table 14.1 for the proposed new gratifications sought by consumers from media technology. Marketing and advertising professionals can look at these gratifications and consider how knowing the gratification sought by a target audience could influence the content produced in a social media marketing campaign.[20]

Leap of Faith?

It is one thing to create a smart social media strategy; it is another to sell it to management and implement it in the real world. *The Guardian* looked at this issue recently when reporting results of a poll of global senior marketers. The survey found that only half of all boardrooms are convinced about social media's value.[21] Why don't executives believe in the business power of social media? It's hard to see the value of social media if a person is

Table 14.1. Proposed New Gratifications from Media Technology

Modality	Agency	Interactivity	Navigability
Realism	Agency-Enhancement	Interaction	Browsing/Variety-Seeking
Coolness	Community Building	Activity	Scaffolds/Navigation Aid
Novelty	Bandwagon	Responsiveness	Play/Fun
Being There	Filtering/Tailoring	Dynamic Control	
	Ownness		

Source: Shyam S. Sundar and Anthony M. Limperos, "Uses and Grats 2.0: New Gratifications for New Media," *Journal of Broadcasting & Electronic Media* 57, no. 4 (2013): 504–525.

MINI CASE

C   Saucony Find Your Strong

Saucony is a brand of shoes and apparel that focuses on the sport of running. The company is unique from other brands that manufacture products for multiple sports. To emphasize this difference, the brand wanted to create a campaign that really connected with their exclusive target audience of runners.

The result was the Find Your Strong Project. Find Your Strong is described on the Saucony microsite as thus: "This Site Is Dedicated to You, The Runner. You are our inspiration and the reason we do what we do. Rather than tell you how we feel about running, we'd rather hear from you." Emphasizing interactivity and leveraging two-way social media, the campaign is based on an ever-changing Running Manifesto of user-generated social media content. Visit the site (http://community.saucony.com/findyourstrongproject) to see live aggregated content of sayings and photos from real runners sharing their passion for running and the brand. Content is shared on Twitter sent to @Saucony or posted with #findyourstrong.[a]

The campaign includes and integrates traditional media such as print and banner ads in running publications such as *Runner's World*, but most of the effort is delivered through social media such as Twitter, Facebook, blogs, and YouTube videos.

Since the original launch the brand has increased social media followers from ten thousand in 2011 to one million in 2014. Chris Lindner, CMO of Saucony, said, "The message was whether you run to get physically stronger or for other reasons, people were finding strength from running . . . We didn't say, 'Be like Saucony.' We said, 'Find your strong.' People really internalized that and shared their stories with us."[b] In three short years the Find Your Strong campaign has propelled Saucony to become the fastest growing brand in the running channel.[c] The brand found a way to translate product features into customer benefits and express them using social media in a way that invites participation. Saucony also created a campaign that helps lessen the pressure and load of generating all social media content themselves.

[a] "The Find Your Strong Project," Saucony.com, accessed January 20, 2015, http://community.saucony.com/findyourstrongproject/.

[b] Amy Gesenhues, "Get to Know: CMO & SVP of Business Development for Sperry Top-Sider Chris Linder," MarketingLand.com, July 16, 2014, http://marketingland.com/get-know-cmo-svp-sperry-top-sider-chris-lindner-90798.

[c] Meredith Derby Berg, "Saucony Finishes Strong With Its 'Find Your Strong' Strategy." AdAge.com, January 27, 2014, http://adage.com/article/news/saucony-finishes-strong-find-strong-strategy/291329.

not actively using it themselves. According to another survey, 64 percent of CEOs do not use social media at all, with only 5 percent of all Fortune 500 company CEOs on Twitter. Thus, many marketing, advertising, and public relations professionals may face roadblocks when presenting social media plans and pitches to the executive level.[22]

It is easier to understand the influence of a TV commercial on purchasing decisions when one has the personal experience of watching TV themselves. It is harder to see how

Facebook could influence a purchase decision when one does not personally use the social media network. However, the bottom line is that social media marketing works not because executives are using it, but because the customer is using it for purchasing decision information. And this reality will impact the organization's bottom line as social engagement becomes an increasing purchasing decision factor.

Because of this reality, social media strategists must not only understand social media and how to complete and execute plans; they must also play another role. In addition to being a social media strategist, a social media professional must also be willing to be a social media educator. It is also the social media manager's job to help executives understand that the rest of the world is embracing social media. Explain that customers are making purchasing decisions about consumer products and services and about business-to-business products and services. Show the data that proves more and more consumers are relying on social media to help them determine what products and services to buy.

Be sure to build a solid social media plan, but also plan to build a solid case for social media acceptance. For a social media marketing plan to be successful it must first be approved. Build the case for organizational use of social media and be prepared to combat corporate-suite skepticism of social media. It may be helpful to follow other brand examples, like Dove, which built social media efforts slowly over time. Complete the full plan, but gain approval for smaller-scale efforts that can be added to as success is proven.

SOCIAL PLAN PART 14

Compile the Parts and Sell the Story

For this final part of the plan, collect all other social plan parts, 1 through 13, that have been completed throughout the book. Pull these sections together into one cohesive social media marketing story. Strategically this is a plan to follow, but also a story to sell. Even though most leaders know social media is important and want to do something with it, most are still skeptical of social media methods. This plan will serve as a reference to follow, but also to show and present to organization decision-makers in order to get social media efforts approved and running.

Begin by pulling out the main sections from each part of the plan completed from chapter 1 to chapter 13. Compile the sections into a single report that tells the overall social media story, from research, target audience, and insight to big idea, selected social channels, and content. As you tell the social media plan story, remember to support and quantify everything with outside references and data to build a strong and convincing argument. Don't forget to define social media terms for full context and understanding. Most executives may not be familiar with social media terminology. Also, remember that a picture is worth a thousand words. Use screen grabs and charts and graphs when appropriate to provide a more complete and convincing vision of the proposed effort.

Finally, put the pieces together in an order that makes sense. Start with a big picture of the current situation, objectives, and background leading up to the brilliant-solution big idea and executions in the selected ideal social media channels. Explain why you chose these channels and help people see what the campaign will look like with example content posts. Show at least one "mock up" post per social media channel, visually set in screen grabs of the environment to make each post look as real as possible. Also provide example consumer response through comments and other interactions. While structure of the final plan document and presentation can vary, below is an example social media plan format and order to follow:

1. Provide an overview of the brand, product or service, and current marketing activities.
2. Identify the target audience and describe their social media use.
3. Identify overall business objectives and social media campaign objectives.
4. Include the social media audit results and describe the insights gained.
5. Present the overall social media strategy and big idea.
6. Provide the social media channels and rationale behind their selection.
7. Write and design example content for each social channel to bring the big idea to life.
8. Identify metrics by channel and objective to show how success will be measured.
9. Don't forget an overall introduction and conclusion or executive summary.

Measurement and ROI are important. Be sure to link SMART objectives with big idea content in each social channel and indicate what metrics will be measured. See table 14.2 for an example chart that easily organizes and links social media plan objectives to social channels and metrics or key performance indicators (KPIs). Place social media campaign objectives across the top with objectives such as increasing awareness, increasing engagement, or improving customer service. For more detail, these objectives can be quantified in the chart with the SMART objectives, such as "Increase awareness by 20 percent in six months." Next list the social media channels that have been selected down the left column. For each objective and corresponding social media channel, list the specific metric that will measure each objective.

Table 14.2. Sample Social Media Marketing Campaign Metrics

	Increase Awareness	Increase Engagement	Improve Customer Service
Facebook			
Instagram			
YouTube			
LinkedIn			

For example, awareness could be measured with likes on Facebook and views on YouTube. To take this further, plug in current levels (of likes, views, etc.) and give the new totals that show what activity will meet objectives in each channel. Fill in as much or as little detail as needed, but this format should provide a simple way to sum up and visualize the entire social media effort.

Once the formal written report is complete, create a fifteen- to twenty-minute presentation to sell the plan in person to organization management and decision-makers. Keep slides simple, using them for visual support, and tell the audience the social media story. Show them how to see the forest for the trees to social media success.

QUESTIONS FOR DISCUSSION

1. Why is long-term strategic thinking so valuable to success, yet so undervalued in everyday business operation? What can be done to change this focus?
2. The Saucony Find Your Strong campaign relies heavily on user-generated content. Find another example of a brand that uses fan content as a main component of its social media efforts and explain how they motivate or reward participation.
3. Conduct a brief content analysis of NASCAR's social media presence. What strategy are they following and what kind of content are they producing? Why do you think it has worked so well?
4. Measurement, metrics, and return on investment (ROI) are very important. Do some research and find what experts agree to be the top social media metrics that prove real ROI.

ADDITIONAL EXERCISES

1. For this exercise, go to Seth Godin's blog (sethgodin.typepad.com) and read through some of the thousands of posts he has made over the years. Be sure to cover earlier and later time periods. What do you notice about the posts? Are they all of equal quality? If each is not an earth-shattering insight, then what is consistent that has drawn hundreds of thousands of readers over time? What specifically can you learn from Seth Godin's persistence and consistency that you can apply to your social media strategy? List at least three qualities.
2. For this exercise, go back to the uses and gratifications theory. Look at table 14.1 and the proposed new gratifications consumers seek from media technology. Select the gratifications that most apply to social media. Next, select five different social media categories or channels (i.e. social networks and media sharing or Facebook and YouTube) and list the types of gratifications each social channel or category could possibly satisfy. Finally, brainstorm and explain examples of the type of marketing content that would be created for each type of gratification within each social channel or category.

Notes

1. "Hal Higdon Quotes," GoodReads.com, accessed February 20, 2015, http://www.goodreads.com/author/quotes/69749.Hal_Higdon.

2. Wiktionary, "See the forest for the trees," accessed February 20, 2015, http://en.m .wiktionary.org/wiki/see_the_forest_for_the_trees.

3. Robert Kabacoff, "Develop Strategic Thinkers Throughout Your Organization," *Harvard Business Review*, February 7, 2014, https://hbr.org/2014/02/develop-strategic-thinkers-throughout -your-organization.

4. Craig Smith, "How Many People Use 800+ of the Top Social Media, Apps and Digital Services?" DMR Digital Marketing Ramblings (blog), January 23, 2015, http://expandedramblings .com/index.php/resource-how-many-people-use-the-top-social-media.

5. "Hal Higdon Biography," HalHigdon.com, accessed June 26, 2015, http://www.halhigdon .com/biography.

6. Keith A. Quesenberry, "Social Media Is Like Running a Marathon," PostControlMarketing .com (blog), July 31, 2014, http://www.postcontrolmarketing.com/?p=1938.

7. Jay Baer, "Are You Slow Enough to Succeed in Social Media?" ConvinceandConvert.com, accessed February 20, 2015, http://www.convinceandconvert.com/social-media-strategy/are-you -slow-enough-to-succeed-in-social-media.

8. Seth Godin, "Trading Favors," SethGodin.typepad.com (blog), July 31, 2014, http:// sethgodin.typepad.com/seths_blog/2014/07/trading-favors.html.

9. "Social Media Marketing's Main Expense Is Staff. How Do They Spend Their Time?" Mar ketingCharts.com, May, 2014, http://www.marketingcharts.com/online/social-media-marketings -main-expense-is-staff-how-do-they-spend-their-time-42651/attachment/smmu-top-areas -social-media-time-investment-may2014.

10. Matthew Rocco, "Fortune 500 Brands Ride Shotgun as NASCAR Grows," FoxBusiness .com, July 30, 2013, http://www.foxbusiness.com/industries/2013/07/30/fortune-500-brands -ride-shotgun-as-nascar-grows.

11. Alicia Jessop, "NASCAR's Innovative Social Media Approach Leads to Significant Growth in Fan Base," Forbes.com, November 17, 2012, http://www.forbes.com/sites/aliciajessop/2012/ 11/17/nascars-innovative-social-media-approach-leads-to-significant-growth-in-fan-base.

12. Quesenberry, "Social Media Is Like Running a Marathon."

13. Tom Martin, "How Long Before a Social Media Campaign Shows Results," Converse Digital.com (blog), January 17, 2012, http://www.conversedigital.com/social-media-marketing -strategy/how-long-before-a-social-media-campaign-shows-results.

14. Keith Quesenberry, "FoMO: Why Fear of Missing Out Could Hurt Your Social Media Efforts," SocialMediaToday.com (blog), May 19, 2015, http://www.socialmediatoday.com/social -business/2015-05-19/fomo-why-fear-missing-out-could-hurt-your-social-media-efforts.

15. Keith Quesenberry, "How to Create a Social Media Plan," SocialMediaExaminer.com (blog), May 14, 2015, http://www.socialmediaexaminer.com/how-to-create-a-social-media -marketing-plan.

16. Rosalia Cefalu, "Can a People-Centric Social Media Strategy Scale?" HubSpot.com (blog), May 30, 2013, http://blog.hubspot.com/marketing/can-a-people-centric-social-media-strategy -scale.

17. Quesenberry, "How to Create a Social Media Plan."

18. Elizabeth Perse, "Uses and Gratifications," Oxford Bibliographies, accessed February 20, 2015, http://www.oxfordbibliographies.com/view/document/obo-9780199756841/obo-978 0199756841-0132.xml#obo-9780199756841-0132-bibItem-0007.

19. Elihu Katz, Jay G. Blumler, and Michael Gurevitch, "Uses and Gratifications Research," *Public Opinion Quarterly* 37, no. 4 (1973): 509.

20. Shyam S. Sundar and Anthony M. Limperos, "Uses and Grats 2.0: New Gratifications for New Media," *Journal of Broadcasting & Electronic Media* 57, no. 4 (2013): 504–525.

21. Sharon Flaherty, "Why the C-suite Don't 'Get' Social Media Marketing—And How to Change That," *The Guardian*, August 4, 2014, http://www.theguardian.com/media/2014/aug/04/c-suite-social-media-marketing-adoption-boardroom.

22. TJ McCue, "LinkedIn Is Preferred by Executives," Forbes.com, April 9, 2013, http://www.forbes.com/sites/tjmccue/2013/04/09/linkedin-is-preferred-by-executives.

Appendix A: The Complete Social Plan (Parts 1–14)

Here is the blueprint for an integrated social media marketing plan. This is a collection of all the chapter social plan parts plus important figures and tables presented in each chapter. Complete these sections to develop a cross-disciplinary social media strategy for any brand, product, service, or organization. Work through each of these steps, 1 through 13. Then in part 14 combine all sections into a comprehensive social media marketing plan that can be presented, approved, and activated. For a simplified, quick, five-step version of the social media plan framework, see Appendix B, Quick Five-Step Social Plan.

Social Plan Part 1: Discover and Explore

The first part of the social media plan is to become familiar with the types of social media and various social media features. Based on the definition of social media given in this chapter, search and identify various social media channels. Go beyond the well-known networks such as Facebook, YouTube, and Twitter. After identifying several digital social channels, explore the features unique to each and use those features to determine social

	Helpful	Harmful
Internal	**S** Strengths	**W** Weaknesses
External	**O** Opportunities	**T** Threats

Figure A.1. SWOT Analysis Graphic Template

Source: "SWOT analysis," Wikipedia, last modified January 15, 2015, http://en.wiki pedia.org/wiki/SWOT_analysis.

Table A.1. Social Media Audit Template

Who	Where (Channel/Environment)	What (Type of Content/ Sentiment)	When (Date/Frequency)	Why (Purpose/KPI*)	Problem Opportunity 1 2 3 4 5
Company					
1.					
2.					
3.					
Consumer					
1.					
2.					
3.					
Competitor					
1.					
2.					
3.					

* KPI is key performance indicators.

media categories. In other words, what is the main activity on the channel? Why does it exist? Finally, provide examples of how marketers could take advantage of each channel. The best way to learn the most about a social media channel is to open an account and become a user. After exploration report the following:

1. Based on the definition of social media, list five different websites or apps that you feel are social media channels. Explain why each one was chosen.
2. Explore each channel and explain the features and capabilities of each.
3. Look at each channel's features, determine the main differences between each, and place the channels into categories such as photo sharing or news aggregation.
4. Explain three ways a marketer could use each channel for promotion.

Social Plan Part 2: Adding to the Noise

Is the organization adding to the clutter? In the earliest stages of a social media plan, the goal is to start getting a sense of the brand's image in the marketplace. Take an inventory of all marketing and advertising activities and messages. Then determine how pushy the brand's marketing communication has become. Is the brand heavily reliant on push marketing through traditional media? In social media, is the brand intrusive with one-way sales-focused posts, or are posts helpful and responsive? Make a list or spreadsheet of all consumer touch points in traditional, digital, and social media. Analyze the type of messages the company is promoting in each, and report the answers to the following questions:

1. Is the communication company-focused or consumer-focused?
2. Is the information useful, newsworthy, entertaining, or valuable?
3. Do consumers perceive the message as an unwanted interruption or a welcome message?
4. Take an inventory of all brand marketing and advertising activities and rate the "pushiness" of brand communication. Is the brand over-reliant on traditional media? Are they using social media as more of a one-way communication channel?

Social Plan Part 3: Quantifying Engagement

Ask and answer these questions: Is the brand integrating the consumer's voice into the organization? In what areas are consumers being integrated and engaged, and how much? In this part of the social media plan, visit all the active social media accounts for the brand, product, and/or service. Visit each account and scroll down the posts. Who is talking? Is it only the brand or are consumers responding? When consumers do respond, does the brand respond back? Is the brand fixing customer-support problems via social media? Has the brand ever considered or used consumer product or service ideas given in social media feedback? Conduct this research and then report your findings in these areas:

1. List all brand social media channels with account names and active brand participants.
2. Gauge the interaction by quantifying brand versus consumer posts.
3. Provide example responses in each category: customer support, product/service ideas, promotions, and appreciation.
4. Explain any evidence that the brand has acted on customer social media contributions such as improving the product or service or using brand content.
5. List possible social media channels where the brand's consumers are active but the brand is not.

Social Plan Part 4: Objectives, Target, Situation Analysis, and Audit

In this part of the social media plan, first identify quantified and time-bound business objectives and specifically define the target audience for listening and communication. Then gather a snapshot of the organization's industry, recent performance of the brand, existing marketing campaign, and all current social media talk and traditional marketing promotion for the product or service and its competitors. This part of the plan is about identifying where the business or organization wants to go and where it is currently. Cover these four areas in this report, following the process and tools outlined in this chapter:

1. Identify overall SMART business objectives.
2. Perform a situation analysis and develop a complete SWOT table.
3. Explain the current marketing campaign and identify key themes, images, and taglines.
4. Define a target audience with multiple bases of segmentation.
5. Perform a social media audit, report results, and describe insights gained.

Social Plan Part 5: Repair Plan and Big Idea

In this part of the social media plan, go back to the social media audit to quantify and analyze negative versus positive social media content. In addition, the tool Socialmention .com may help in quantifying overall social media sentiment toward the brand. If negative commentary is significant, specifically identify customer-service, product, operations, HR, or marketing-message problems that may be causing negative social media talk. Create an interdepartmental plan to fix the root cause of negative comments. Even if negative talk isn't significant, identify a plan to reduce the negative comments that are there. Next gather and conduct consumer research through various primary and secondary methods to discover a key actionable consumer insight that leads to a campaign big idea that is interesting and has legs. Report all research, findings, plans, and ideas in these areas:

1. Identify top brand social complaints and the root business-unit cause.
2. Devise an interdepartmental plan to fix issues and reduce negative talk.
3. Gather all research and uncover a key actionable consumer insight.
4. Create an interesting big idea that has legs across traditional and social media.

Social Plan Part 6: Integrate Traditional Marketing with Social Strategy

In this part of the social media plan, focus on integration of traditional marketing, advertising, PR, and digital marketing efforts with the new social media strategy. Collect and analyze information on all marketing efforts for the brand. What techniques are being used? What is the core message or promotion? Is there a common character, theme, or concept? Is there a brand or campaign tagline? Make note of current efforts and include what is being formed in the new social media plan, accounting for and explaining how current traditional efforts will be integrated into the new social effort. It may be found that a new traditional marketing, advertising, and PR effort or campaign is needed, and thus your plan should make those recommendations. Report all findings and ideas in these areas:

1. Identify all traditional brand marketing, PR, advertising, and digital efforts.
2. Explain the current promotion, concept, character, theme, and tagline.
3. List ways in which the current effort could be integrated with the new social media big idea.
4. If a new traditional marketing or advertising campaign and promotion are needed, explain what they should be.

Social Plan Part 7: Select Social Networks, Blog Platforms, and Forums

In this part of the social media plan, explore all the major social media networks. Research each, looking at the size and makeup of the users. Does the target audience match the main users of the network? What kind of content is popular? What is the culture of the network? Do these characteristics match brand, product, service, and big idea? Do the same exploration and comparison for blogs and forums. Could the brand benefit from a blog? Which platform would be best? What about a forum? Should the organization start its own, or participate in existing forums? Report all findings and ideas in these areas:

1. Identify the top social networks where the target audience is active.
2. For each social network, describe the main type of content and culture.
3. Find existing brand, product, or service blogs and forums. How could the brand participate?
4. Is there a need for a customer-support forum or other type of forum?

Social Plan Part 8: Choose Most Strategic Content Sharing

Explore and choose content-sharing channels that best fit your social media plan. Consider all the top social media sharing networks. Research each, looking at the number and makeup of the users to ensure a match with your target audience. Do the brand, product, or service and the big idea fit the type of content that is shared on the channel? How can the organization leverage the real-time, seasonal, and topical characteristics of microblogging? What type of content is ideal for sharing—text, photo, or video? Report all findings and ideas in these areas:

1. Identify microblogs where the target audience is active.
2. Describe the type of content that is shared and popular on each.
3. Find photo- and video-sharing networks that match the target audience.
4. Explain what content the brand could create.

Social Plan Part 9: Strategic Use of Location, Ratings, and Reviews

Take an in-depth look at geo-location channels and features in social networking sites. Also analyze ratings and review sites and features on social networks. How can these features benefit the brand and campaign? Where is the target audience? Are they checking in or looking up ratings and reviews about the products and services? Where are they doing it? What can the brand do to leverage these features and influence conversation and discovery? What type of content (text, photo, or video) is needed to best take advantage of these social services? Report all findings and ideas in these areas:

1. Identify geo-location channels or social networks with geo-location features where the target audience is participating.
2. Describe the type of activity and content that is popular on each.
3. Find the rating and review networks or retail websites where the target audience is most active. In what social networks may they also be discovering ratings and reviews?
4. Discover and explain how the organization can best leverage this information about the brand to help meet business objectives.

Social Plan Part 10: Buzz Building and Knowledge Sharing

People love to share knowledge. Look at the major social bookmarking and social-knowledge channels. What valuable information or partnerships can the brand form? What questions can the organization answer? How does knowledge-sharing fit with the social media insight and big idea? Which users of social-bookmarking and knowledge channels match most closely with the target audience? Also take an in-depth look at podcasts. Is there an opportunity to start a brand podcast or partner with an existing program? Is the target audience actively listening to podcasts and looking for the type of insight and information the brand can deliver? Report all findings and ideas in these areas:

1. Identify the major social-bookmarking and knowledge-sharing sites where the target audience is active.
2. Describe the type of activity and content that is popular on each, and list the type of content the brand could provide that matches the social media plan's big idea.
3. Find the top podcasts to which the target audience is listening, and on which platform they are most active.
4. List and explain possible new podcast shows the brand could create or current shows the brand could contribute to and sponsor.

Social Plan Part 11: Adding Crowdsourcing into a Campaign

Take the social media plan beyond marketing promotion and communication to other aspects of the Four Ps or Four Cs. What social intelligence does the organization need or could it benefit from? Are they launching a new product? Perhaps the brand could use insight into existing products or services for improvement. Or maybe the brand could use additional insight from consumers to create advertising or social media content. What specific project could create a crowdsourcing campaign? Report all thoughts, plans, and ideas in these areas:

1. Identify needs traditional research is currently serving at the organization, and list how social media research could support those efforts.
2. Does the brand have an ongoing social-media-monitoring system in place? What formal social research plan could be put in place?
3. List marketing projects, such as product design and advertising creation, currently done in-house.
4. Of the list above, identify the top projects that could benefit from crowdsourcing. Explain how and why.

Social Plan Part 12: Creating Branded Content and Motivating Brand Evangelists

Take the social media strategy, consumer insight, and big idea to the next level with branded content and brand evangelism. What content is the target audience looking for? What type of content do they tend to view and share? Develop ideas for educational as well as entertaining text, photo, and video content. Will the content be brand-generated or co-created? Where will it be distributed? Also, devise a strategy and policy to engage and reward brand evangelists. What information, products, promotional trips, or events can the organization offer the most loyal and outspoken fans? Set guidelines in terms of scale and scope for the evangelists and the reward program. Report all thoughts, plans, and ideas in these areas:

1. Identify the information and entertainment needs of the target audience. List the main types of content they view and share.
2. Explain the types of content the brand can create to match target audience interests. Plan content to be brand-generated, consumer-generated, or co-created.
3. Research and identify the organization's most active customers in social media.
4. Create a brand evangelist program to both engage and reward the brand advocates. Spell out specific policies, promotions, and events.

Social Plan Part 13: Creating Cross-Functional Social Care

If the organization does not have an active social care program, now is the time to plan it. First investigate and analyze the existing system that is in place. Is there a customer-service department? How do they currently find out about customer needs? What system are they using? Is customer service limited by delivery method or hours? Is the organization conducting social media monitoring? If so, who is doing it? Are other departments involved? Table A.2 describes a plan for a cross-functional social-care team. Report all thoughts, plans, and ideas in these areas:

1. Identify the current system. Explain what kind of social media monitoring is occurring. Is it 24/7 or intermittent? What systems are being used?
2. Identify the employees responsible for social media monitoring. What department are they from? Is the team cross-functional?
3. Plan a structure for a new cross-functional social-care team that can address all areas of social information efficiently and effectively. What systems are needed?
4. Plan the marketing responsibility in a cross-functional social-care team by explaining how marketing will provide social support. Also provide a briefing on the brand communication style and big idea for the social media plan.

Table A.2. Cross-Functional Social-Care Team Organization and Responsibilities

Department	Responsibility
Customer Service	Set up to be the main point of contact for service-related issues
Marketing	Promote social support and provide brand briefing on communication style
Corporate Communication/PR	Develop crisis and stakeholder communication plans
Legal	Define social media policies that govern agent responses
Human Resources	Define hiring profiles and set training standards for social agents

Source: Kim Keating and Dave Evans, "Benchmarking Social Media Customer Service: Uncovering Opportunities & Best Practices for Social Care," TELUS International, accessed February 20, 2015, http://www.telusinternational.com/social_care_study.

Social Plan Part 14: Compile the Parts and Sell the Story

For this final part of the plan, collect all other social plan parts, 1 through 13, that have been completed throughout the book. Pull these sections together into one cohesive social media marketing story. Strategically it is a plan to follow, but also a story to sell. Even though most leaders know social media is important and want to do something with it, most are still skeptical of social media methods. This plan will serve as a reference to follow, but also to show and present to organization decision-makers in order to get social media efforts approved and running.

Begin by pulling out the main sections from each part of the plan completed from chapter 1 to chapter 13. Compile the sections into a single report that tells the overall social media story, from research, target audience, and insight to big idea, selected social channels, and content. As you tell the social media plan story, remember to support and quantify everything with outside references and data to build a strong and convincing argument. Don't forget to define social media terms for full context and understanding. Most executives may not be familiar with social media terminology. Also, remember that a picture is worth a thousand words. Use screen grabs and charts and graphs when appropriate to provide a more complete and convincing vision of the proposed effort.

Finally, put the pieces together in an order that makes sense. Start with a big picture of the current situation, objectives, and background leading up to the brilliant-solution big idea and executions in the selected ideal social media channels. Explain why you chose these channels and help people see what the campaign will look like with example content posts. Show at least one "mock up" post per social media channel, visually set in screen grabs of the environment to make each post look as real as possible. Also provide example consumer response through comments and other interactions. While structure of the final plan document and presentation can vary, below is an example social media plan format and order to follow:

1. Provide an overview of the brand, product or service, and current marketing activities.
2. Identify the target audience and describe their social media use.
3. Identify overall business objectives and social media campaign objectives.
4. Include the social media audit results and describe the insights gained.
5. Present the overall social media strategy and big idea.
6. Provide the social media channels and rationale behind their selection.
7. Write and design example content for each social channel to bring the big idea to life.
8. Identify metrics by channel and objective to show how success will be measured.
9. Don't forget an overall introduction and conclusion or executive summary.

Measurement and ROI are important. Be sure to link SMART objectives with big idea content in each social channel and indicate what metrics will be measured. See table A.3 for an example chart that easily organizes and links social media plan objectives to social channels and metrics or key performance indicators (KPIs). Place social media campaign objectives across the top with objectives such as increasing awareness, increasing

Table A.3. Sample Social Media Marketing Campaign Metrics

	Increase Awareness	Increase Engagement	Improve Customer Service
Facebook			
Instagram			
YouTube			
LinkedIn			

engagement, or improving customer service. For more detail, these objectives can be quantified in the chart with the SMART objectives, such as "Increase awareness by 20 percent in six months." Next list the social media channels that have been selected down the left column. For each objective and corresponding social media channel, list the specific metric that will measure each objective.

For example, awareness could be measured with likes on Facebook and views on YouTube. To take this further, plug in current levels (of likes, views, etc.) and give the new totals that show what activity will meet objectives in each channel. Fill in as much or as little detail as needed, but this format should provide a simple way to sum up and visualize the entire social media effort.

Once the formal written report is complete, create a fifteen- to twenty-minute presentation to sell the plan in person to organization management and decision-makers. Keep slides simple, using them for visual support, and tell the audience the social media story. Show them how to see the forest for the trees to social media success.

Appendix B: Quick Five-Step Social Plan

Here is a simple, step-by-step approach to developing a complete, integrated social-media-marketing plan. This is a condensed version of the social plan parts within each chapter, plus important figures and tables. Complete these sections to develop a cross-disciplinary social media strategy for any brand, product, service, or organization. Work through each of these steps, 1 through 5, to build a comprehensive social media marketing plan to be presented, approved, and activated.

1. Define Current Business and Social Situation

For the first part of the social media plan, identify quantified and time-bound business objectives and specifically define the target audience for listening and communication:

- Identify overall SMART business objectives.
- Define a target audience with multiple bases of segmentation.

	Helpful	Harmful
Internal	**S** Strengths	**W** Weaknesses
External	**O** Opportunities	**T** Threats

Figure B.1. SWOT Analysis Graphic Template

Source: "SWOT analysis," Wikipedia, last modified January 15, 2015, http://en.wiki pedia.org/wiki/SWOT_analysis.

Table B.1. Social Media Audit Template

Who	Where (Channel/Environment)	What (Type of Content/ Sentiment)	When (Date/Frequency)	Why (Purpose/KPI*)	Problem Opportunity 1 2 3 4 5
Company					
1.					
2.					
3.					
Consumer					
1.					
2.					
3.					
Competitor					
1.					
2.					
3.					

* KPI is key performance indicators.

Gather a snapshot of the organization's industry, recent performance of the brand, and all current social media talk and traditional marketing promotion for the product or service and its competitors:

- Perform a situation analysis and a complete SWOT table.
- Perform a social media audit, report results, and describe insights gained.

2. Create a Big Idea and Plan Integration

If negative commentary was found to be significant, identify customer service, product, operations, HR, or marketing message problems that need to be fixed before moving forward with a social media plan.

Then gather and conduct consumer research through primary and secondary methods to discover a key actionable consumer insight that leads to a campaign big idea with legs:

- Gather all research and uncover a key actionable consumer insight.
- Create a big idea that has legs across traditional and social media.

Make note of current traditional marketing, advertising, PR, and digital marketing efforts and explain how current traditional efforts will be integrated into the new social effort:

- Explain the current promotion, concept, character, theme, and tagline.
- List how the current effort will be integrated with the new social media big idea.

3. Select Social Media Channels

Explore all the major social media channels. Research each for size and makeup of the users, content, and culture. Consider channels in the categories of social network, blog, forum, microblog, media sharing, geo-location, rating and review, social bookmarking, and social knowledge. Select the most appropriate channels for target audience, message, and big idea:

- Identify the top social channels where the target audience is active.
- For each social network, describe the type of content, culture, and how the big idea fits.

4. Integrate Non-Marketing Social Activity

Take the plan beyond marketing promotion and communication to other aspects of the Four Ps or Four Cs. What social intelligence does the organization need and what projects or functions could be performed by crowdsourcing?

- List how social media research could support research efforts.
- Identify projects or functions that could use crowdsourcing.

Identify educational and/or entertaining text, photo, and video content for content marketing sharing. Also, devise a strategy and policy to engage and reward brand evangelists:

- Explain the content the brand can create or co-create to match target audience interests.
- Create a brand-evangelist program to both engage and reward the brand advocates.

Analyze the current customer-care system and plan a structure for a cross-functional social-care team:

- Identify the current customer-service system and how social media is monitored.
- Plan a structure for a cross-functional social-care team to address all social information.

5. Finalize Social Media Plan

Collect information from other steps into one cohesive social-media-marketing strategy. Compile the sections together into a single report that tells the overall social media story from objectives to sample content.

Start with a big picture of the current situation, objectives, and background leading up to the brilliant-solution big idea and executions in the selected ideal social media channels. For measurement, link SMART objectives with metrics for content in each social channel to determine plan key performance indicators (KPIs).

Follow this example social media plan format:

1. Provide an overview of brand, product or service, and current marketing activities.
2. Identify target audience and describe their social media use.
3. Identify overall business objectives and social media campaign objectives.
4. Include the social media audit results and describe insights gained.
5. Present the overall social media strategy and big idea.
6. Provide the social media channels and rationale behind their selection.
7. Write/design example content for each social channel to bring the big idea to life.
8. Identify metrics by channel and objective to show how success will be measured.
9. Don't forget an overall introduction and conclusion or executive summary.

Table B.2. Sample Social Media Marketing Campaign Metrics

	Increase Awareness	Increase Engagement	Improve Customer Service
Facebook			
Instagram			
YouTube			
LinkedIn			

Once the formal written report is complete, create a presentation to sell the plan through in person to organization management and decision-makers.

Appendix C: Social Media Tools and Resources

Here is a list of social media tools and resources to get started learning, listening, analyzing, creating, organizing, scheduling, and measuring. Honestly, there are too many to list here, but this will get you started. Discover more and new resources as they are introduced by visiting www.postcontrolmarketing.com.

Social Media News and Insights

Chris Brogan: www.chrisbrogan.com/blog
Convince and Convert: www.convinceandconvert.com
FTC Disclosures: http://1.usa.gov/1eBRixc
Gartner Digital Marketing: blogs.gartner.com/digital-marketing
Grow: www.businessesgrow.com
Hubspot's Inbound Hub: blog.hubspot.com
Jeff Bullas: jeffbullas.com
Mashable Social Media: mashable.com/social-media
RazorSocial: www.razorsocial.com
Social Media Examiner: www.socialmediaexaminer.com
Social Media Explorer: www.socialmediaexplorer.com
Social Media Law Bulletin: www.socialmedialawbulletin.com
Social Media Marketing Magazine: www.smmmagazine.com
Social Media Today: socialmediatoday.com
Social Mouths: socialmouths.com/blog

Social Media Podcasts

Content Inc.: contentmarketinginstitute.com/content-inc-podcast
The Marketing Companion: marketingpodcasts.com/the-marketing-companion
Social Media Examiner: www.socialmediaexaminer.com/tag/podcast
Social Pros Podcast: socialpros.podbean.com
This Old Marketing: contentmarketinginstitute.com/pnr-with-this-old-marketing
   -podcast

Social Media Monitoring and Metrics

Addict-o-matic: addictomatic.com
Brandwatch: brandwatch.com
Cision: www.cision.com/us/social-software
Critical Mention: www.critical mention.com
Hootsuite: hootsuite.com
How Sociable: howsociable.com
Lithium: lithium.com
Meltwater Ice Rocket: www.icerocket.com
Nielsen Social: www.nielsensocial.com
Oracle Social Cloud: www.oracle.com/us/solutions/social
Radian6 (Salesforce): www.exacttarget.com/products/social-media-marketing/
    radian6
Row Feeder: rowfeeder.com
Simply Measured: simplymeasured.com
Social Mention: socialmention.com
Sysomos: www.sysomos.com
Trackur: www.trackur.com

Online Data Collection

Cyfe: www.cyfe.com
Google Analytics: www.google.com/analytics
Google Trends: www.google.com/trends
Keyhole: keyhole.com
Kiss Metrics: www.kissmetrics.com
Klout: klout.com
Kred: kred.com
Mention: en.mention.com
Omgili: omgili.com
Quantcast: quantcast.com
SEMrush: www.semrush.com
SharedCount: www.sharedcount.com
Social Bakers: www.socialbakers.com
Soovle: soovle.com
Talkwalker Alerts: www.talkwalker.com
Topsy: topsy.com
Tweetreach: tweetreach.com
Twitter Advanced Search: twitter.com/search-advanced
YouGovProfiles: yougov.co.uk/profiler#

Social Media Research

Affinio: www.affin.io
Forrester: www.forrester.com/social-media
Gallup: www.gallup.com
Global Web Index: www.globalwebindex.net
Kantar Media SRDS: srds.com
Nielsen Social Media Reports: www.nielsensocial.com
Pew Research Center: www.pewinternet.org
Roper Center: www.ropercenter.uconn.edu
Simmons: simmonsssurvey.com
Social Explorer: www.socialexplorer.com
Social Media Collective: socialmediacollective.org
Social Technographics Profile: www.empowered.forrester.com/tool_consumer.html
Statista: www.statista.com

Social Media Graphics Tools

Adobe Kuler: color.adobe.com/create.color-wheel
Canva: www.canva.com
Design Seeds: design-seeds.com
Easelly: www.easel.ly
Google Fonts: www.google.com/fonts
Over: madewithover.com
PicMonkey: picmonkey.com
Pictaculous: pictaculous.com
Piktochart: piktochart.com
Word Swag: www.wordswag.co

Social Content Scheduling and Automation

Buffer: bufferapp.com
Crowdbooster: crowdbooster.com
dlvr.it: dlvr.it
Edgar: meetedgar.com
HubSpot: hubspot.com
IFTTT: ifttt.com
Later Bro: laterbro.com
Post Planner: www.postplanner.com
Short Stack: www.shortstack.com
SocialOomph: www.socialoomph.com
Sprout Social: sproutsocial.com

TweetDeck: about.twitter.com/products/tweetdeck
Woodbox: woodbox.com
Zapier: zapier.com
Zendesk: www.zendesk.com

Trade Associations, Awards, Conferences

Brand Innovators: brand–innovators.com/events
Content Marketing World: www.contentmarketingworld.com
INBOUND: www.inbound.com
The Mashies: mashable.com/mashies
Online Media Marketing Awards: www.mediapost.com/ommaawards
The Shorty Awards: shortyawards.com
Social Media Marketing World: www.socialmediaexaminer.com/smmworld
Social Media Strategies Summit: socialmediastrategiessummit.com
Social Media Week: socialmediaweek.org
Summit: summit.adobe.com/na
SXSW: sxsw.com
SXSWedu: www.sxswedu.com
The Webby Awards: www.webbyawards.com
Word of Mouth Marketing Association: womma.org

Index

Note: Page references for figures are italicized.

About the Author

Keith A. Quesenberry is an assistant professor of marketing at Messiah College, where he teaches marketing, social media marketing, digital marketing, and advertising. He previously taught at Johns Hopkins University and Temple University, and teaches in the graduate Integrated Marketing Communications program at West Virginia University. Prior to teaching, he spent nearly twenty years in marketing and advertising as an associate creative director and copywriter at advertising agencies such as BBDO and Arnold Worldwide. His client experience spanned from startups to Fortune 500s such as Delta Airlines, Exxon Mobil, PNC Bank, and Hershey Foods.

His advertising campaigns have garnered prestigious awards such as the One Show, National ADDYs, and London International Awards, and have been featured in the trade publications *Ad Age*, *Adweek*, *Brandweek*, and *Lurzer's International Archive*. His social media campaigns have been recognized by the industry, including a PRSA (Public Relations Society of America) Bronze Anvil for word-of-mouth and an OMMA (Online Media, Marketing and Advertising) Award. He is also a contributing author to *MarketingProfs* and *Social Media Examiner*, where one of his articles was recognized as a Top 40 Content Marketing and Top 5 Visual Marketing article of 2014.

Professor Quesenberry has made appearances on MSNBC, and his research and expert opinion have been featured in publications such as the *Harvard Business Review*, the *New York Times*, *Entrepreneur* magazine, and *Forbes*. His research has been published in journals including the *Journal of Marketing Theory and Practice* and the *International Journal of Integrated Marketing Communication* and in *Ad Age* Research Reports. Follow him @Kquesen on Twitter or subscribe to his blog at www.postcontrolmarketing.com.